studies in jazz

Institute of Jazz Studies
Rutgers—The State University of New Jersey
General Editors: Dan Morgenstern and Edward Berger

1. BENNY CARTER: A Life in American Music, *by Morroe Berger, Edward Berger, and James Patrick, 2 vols., 1982*
2. ART TATUM: A Guide to His Recorded Music, *by Arnold Laubich and Ray Spencer, 1982*
3. ERROLL GARNER: The Most Happy Piano, *by James M. Doran, 1985*
4. JAMES P. JOHNSON: A Case of Mistaken Identity, *by Scott E. Brown;* Discography 1917–1950, *by Robert Hilbert, 1986*
5. PEE WEE ERWIN: This Horn for Hire, *as told to Warren W. Vaché Sr., 1987*
6. BENNY GOODMAN: Listen to His Legacy, *by D. Russell Connor, 1988*
7. ELLINGTONIA: The Recorded Music of Duke Ellington and His Sidemen, *by W. E. Timner, 1988; 4th ed., 1996*
8. THE GLENN MILLER ARMY AIR FORCE BAND: Sustineo Alas / I Sustain the Wings, *by Edward F. Polic;* Foreword *by George T. Simon, 1989*
9. SWING LEGACY, *by Chip Deffaa, 1989*
10. REMINISCING IN TEMPO: The Life and Times of a Jazz Hustler, *by Teddy Reig, with Edward Berger, 1990*
11. IN THE MAINSTREAM: 18 Portraits in Jazz, *by Chip Deffaa, 1992*
12. BUDDY DeFRANCO: A Biographical Portrait and Discography, *by John Kuehn and Arne Astrup, 1993*
13. PEE WEE SPEAKS: A Discography of Pee Wee Russell, *by Robert Hilbert, with David Niven, 1992*
14. SYLVESTER AHOLA: The Gloucester Gabriel, *by Dick Hill, 1993*
15. THE POLICE CARD DISCORD, *by Maxwell T. Cohen, 1993*
16. TRADITIONALISTS AND REVIVALISTS IN JAZZ, *by Chip Deffaa, 1993*
17. BASSICALLY SPEAKING: An Oral History of George Duvivier, *by Edward Berger;* Musical Analysis *by David Chevan, 1993*
18. TRAM: The Frank Trumbauer Story, *by Philip R. Evans and Larry F. Kiner, with William Trumbauer, 1994*
19. TOMMY DORSEY: On the Side, *by Robert L. Stockdale, 1995*
20. JOHN COLTRANE: A Discography and Musical Biography, *by Yasuhiro Fujioka, with Lewis Porter and Yoh-ichi Hamada, 1995*
21. RED HEAD: A Chronological Survey of "Red" Nichols and His Five Pennies, *by Stephen M. Stroff, 1996*
22. THE RED NICHOLS STORY: After Intermission 1942–1965, *by Philip R. Evans, Stanley Hester, Stephen Hester, and Linda Evans, 1997*
23. BENNY GOODMAN: Wrappin' It Up, *by D. Russell Connor, 1996*
24. CHARLIE PARKER AND THEMATIC IMPROVISATION, *by Henry Martin, 1996*
25. BACK BEATS AND RIM SHOTS: The Johnny Blowers Story, *by Warren W. Vaché Sr., 1997*
26. DUKE ELLINGTON: A Listener's Guide, *by Eddie Lambert, 1998*

27. SERGE CHALOFF: A Musical Biography and Discography, *by Vladimir Simosko, 1998*
28. HOT JAZZ: From Harlem to Storyville, *by David Griffiths, 1998*
29. ARTIE SHAW: A Musical Biography and Discography, *by Vladimir Simosko, 2000*
30. JIMMY DORSEY: A Study in Contrasts, *by Robert L. Stockdale, 1998*
31. STRIDE!: Fats, Jimmy, Lion, Lamb and All the Other Ticklers, *by John L. Fell and Terkild Vinding, 1999*
32. GIANT STRIDES: The Legacy of Dick Wellstood, *by Edward N. Meyer, 1999*
33. JAZZ GENTRY: Aristocrats of the Music World, *by Warren W. Vaché Sr., 1999*
34. THE UNSUNG SONGWRITERS: America's Masters of Melody, *by Warren W. Vaché Sr., 2000*
35. THE MUSICAL WORLD OF J. J. JOHNSON, *by Joshua Berrett and Louis G. Bourgois III, 1999*
36. THE LADIES WHO SING WITH THE BAND, *by Betty Bennett, 2000*
37. AN UNSUNG CAT: The Life and Music of Warne Marsh, *by Safford Chamberlain, 2000*
38. JAZZ IN NEW ORLEANS: The Postwar Years Through 1970, *by Charles Suhor, 2001*
39. THE YOUNG LOUIS ARMSTRONG ON RECORDS: A Critical Survey of the Early Recordings, 1923–1928, *by Edward Brooks, 2002*
40. BENNY CARTER: A Life in American Music, Second Edition, *by Morroe Berger, Edward Berger, and James Patrick, 2 vols., 2002*
41. CHORD CHANGES ON THE CHALKBOARD: How Public School Teachers Shaped Jazz and the Music of New Orleans, *by Al Kennedy,* Foreword *by Ellis Marsalis Jr., 2002*
42. CONTEMPORARY CAT: Terence Blanchard with Special Guests, *by Anthony Magro, 2002*
43. PAUL WHITEMAN: Pioneer in American Music, Volume I: 1890–1930, *by Don Rayno, 2003*
44. GOOD VIBES: A Life in Jazz, *by Terry Gibbs with Cary Ginell, 2003*
45. TOM TALBERT—HIS LIFE AND TIMES: Voices from a Vanished World of Jazz, *by Bruce Talbot, 2004*
46. SITTIN' IN WITH CHRIS GRIFFIN: A Reminiscence of Radio and Recording's Golden Years, *by Warren W. Vaché, 2005*
47. FIFTIES JAZZ TALK: An Oral Retrospective, *by Gordon Jack, 2004*
48. FLORENCE MILLS: Harlem Jazz Queen, *by Bill Egan, 2004*
49. SWING ERA SCRAPBOOK: The Teenage Diaries and Radio Logs of Bob Inman, 1936–1938, *by Ken Vail, 2005*
50. FATS WALLER ON THE AIR: The Radio Broadcasts and Discography, *by Stephen Taylor, 2/2006*
51. ALL OF ME: The Complete Discography of Louis Armstrong, *by Jos Willems, 4/2006*
52. MUSIC AND THE CREATIVE SPIRIT: Innovators in Jazz, Improvisation, and the Avant Garde, *by Lloyd Peterson, 8/2006*
53. THE STORY OF FAKE BOOKS: Bootlegging Songs to Musicians, *by Barry Kernfeld, 10/2006*

The *Annual Review of Jazz Studies* is published by Scarecrow Press and the Institute of Jazz Studies at Rutgers—The State University of New Jersey.

Manuscripts, editorial correspondence, and any comments or suggestions should be sent to:

The Editors, Annual Review of Jazz Studies
The Institute of Jazz Studies
Dana Library, Rutgers—The State University
185 University Avenue
Newark, NJ 07102

Publishers should send review copies of books to the same address, marked to the attention of the book review editor.

Authors preparing manuscripts for consideration should follow *The Chicago Manual of Style*, 15th edition. In particular: (1) manuscripts should be original word-processed copy; (2) except for foreign-language quotations, manuscripts must be in English; (3) all material must be neat and double-spaced, with adequate margins; (4) notes must be grouped together at the end of the manuscript, *not as footnotes* at page bottoms, following either of the two documentation styles in chapters 16 and 17 of *The Chicago Manual of Style,* 15th edition; (5) authors should append a two- or three-sentence biographical note; (6) each music example or complex table must be on a separate sheet in computer-generated, camera-ready form; authors should take into account that each example or table, and its caption, will have to fit within a page frame of 4 × 6 inches (10.5 × 16 cm.); (7) all materials should be submitted both in digital form and in hard copy, with the text in Microsoft Word; (8) if any music examples are transcribed from recordings, a cassette or CD of the recordings must be included to facilitate reading the paper and checking the accuracy of transcriptions (a recording is not necessary for printed music or examples composed by the author).

Authors alone are responsible for the contents of their articles and for obtaining permission for use of material under copyright protection.

ANNUAL REVIEW OF JAZZ STUDIES 13
2003

Edited by
Edward Berger
Henry Martin
Dan Morgenstern

Managing Editor
Evan Spring

Associate Editor
George Bassett

The Scarecrow Press, Inc.
Lanham, Maryland • Toronto • Oxford
and
The Institute of Jazz Studies
Rutgers—The State University of
New Jersey
2007

SCARECROW PRESS, INC.

Published in the United States of America
by Scarecrow Press, Inc.
A wholly owned subsidiary of
The Rowman & Littlefield Publishing Group, Inc.
4501 Forbes Boulevard, Suite 200, Lanham, Maryland 20706
www.scarecrowpress.com

PO Box 317
Oxford
OX2 9RU, UK

ISSN 0731-0641

ISBN-13: 978-0-8108-5890-9 (hardcover: alk. paper)
ISBN-13: 978-0-8108-5945-6 (pbk.: alk. paper)
ISBN-10: 0-8108-5890-8 (hardcover: alk. paper)
ISBN-10: 0-8108-5945-9 (pbk.: alk. paper)

∞™ The paper used in this publication meets the minimum requirements of American National Standard for Information Sciences—Permanence of Paper for Printed Library Materials, ANSI/NISO Z39.48-1992.
Manufactured in the United States of America.

CONTENTS

PREFACE

With this volume of *Annual Review of Jazz Studies*, several changes will be apparent to our readers. Most obvious is the change in format—the book is being issued in both hardcover and paperback, with an updated cover—which we hope will keep costs down while maintaining a high-quality publication. There have also been significant changes in our editorial team. As noted in the last issue, David Cayer, cofounder of *Journal of Jazz Studies* (*ARJS*'s predecessor) and the guiding light behind this publication for over three decades, has chosen to relinquish his editorial duties. We are pleased that he will continue to contribute to *ARJS* and to the *Studies in Jazz* series. We also noted the return of George Bassett, an experienced editor with musical training who worked on *Journal of Jazz Studies* many years ago. Evan Spring assumes the newly created position of managing editor. A graduate of the Master's Program in Jazz History and Research at Rutgers–Newark, Evan has already demonstrated his superb editing skills, organizational abilities, and dedication in coordinating and assembling this issue.

What has not changed is our commitment to provide a forum for the ever-expanding range and depth of jazz scholarship. The rise of jazz in the academy over the past two decades has produced a new generation of trained scholars who are examining the music and the culture that produced it from a variety of critical perspectives. Nowhere is this phenomenon more evident than in the tremendous increase in technical musicological analyses submitted over the past few years. Publications like *ARJS* are the only outlets for these important articles, which, because of length, degree of detail, and often the subject matter itself, would never see the light of day in the popular jazz press.

A case in point is Anders Svanoe's extensive study of the little-known but highly original saxophonist Sonny Red—a definitive tribute combining oral history, discography, and charts of every one of his recorded compositions. The other major articles in this issue demonstrate the diversity of approaches used by today's jazz scholars. Charles Hartman's contribution, while ostensibly analyzing a composition by Steve Swallow, ranges far beyond the discussion of a single piece or even song form in general. Matthew Santa offers a compelling new perspective on John Coltrane's compositional approach, a topic discussed in previous issues. In her examination of Miles Davis's classic "Walkin'," Alona Sagee applies a different methodology: tracking the evolution of an artist through successive recordings of the same piece.

In the works is something of a departure for *ARJS*: an issue devoted entirely to pianist-arranger-composer Mary Lou Williams. The Institute of Jazz Studies became the repository of the massive Mary Lou Williams Collection in 1999. Annie Kuebler, the archivist who processed the collection with the help of an NEH grant, will serve as guest editor. The issue will contain photographs and memorabilia from the collection, papers delivered at a Mary Lou Williams conference held at IJS in 2002, and interviews conducted especially for this volume.

"WRONG TOGETHER": STRUCTURES, NORMS, AND STANDARDS

Charles O. Hartman

Every apprentice jazz musician learns most of *The Real Book*: the unofficial (and long illegal) bible of standard tunes and their standard chord progressions, at once the common language of the profession and the catalog of its rites of passage. In 1994 Steve Swallow released an album slyly titled *Real Book*, with a cover that duplicates the look of the famous fake book right down to the ring left by a careless drink.[1] The 10 tunes in Swallow's collection have melodies and chord progressions that obliquely recall jazz standards, while each one turns some aspect of standard-ness on its head.

The ballad called "Wrong Together" (figure 1) is as quietly subversive as anything on the album. There is already something odd about a tune that will resolve in the key of F whose first melody note is F♯, but the mystery runs deeper than tonality. Like many of Swallow's compositions, it has an asymmetrical structure without sounding irregular or arbitrary. A player who is used to four- and eight-measure phrases, like those that make up most of the standards in the other *Real Book*, may have a strangely hard time remembering—and improvising on—the chord progression of this 17-bar tune. Like some other essential, quirky compositions ("Blue in Green," "Peace"), "Wrong Together" defies our habit of thinking in powers-of-two units: 4, 8, 16, 32 beats and measures per phrase, section, and chorus.[2]

The tradition of foursquare symmetry is so deeply rooted that it makes sense to ask (as, in another culture, we might not) *why* Swallow's tune is 17 measures long. Something, we feel, must be missing or added. Understanding how the structure works would help us comprehend the tune in ways useful for good listening and coherent performance. In "All the Things You Are," the normal 32 measures are extended to 36, but a little study of the lead sheet quickly shows where the "extra" four bars intrude: measures 30 through 33 delay the expected resolution from 29 to 34. Take out those four bars, and the tune would have a conventional shape. But "Wrong Together" is not simply a 16-bar tune with a measure inserted somewhere. Making sense of its progression requires looking much further into its details.

Analyzing a tune's structure is recognizing similarities.[3] When we say that a standard tune like "Alone Together" (maybe one source of Swallow's title) has an AABA structure, we mean that the sections labeled A are all "alike." But the similarities do not always amount to exact repetitions. In "All the Things You Are," not only does the last strain have the four-measure extension, but the second A strain shifts into a different key. We still recognize it as "the same," because the

Figure 1: "Wrong Together," from liner notes to Steve Swallow's *Real Book,* Xtra WaTT 7, 1994

progression following Cm in measure 9 is the same as the progression following Fm in measure 1. What we recognize as repetition is not identical chords, but identical relations from one chord to the next.

So when we wonder how "Wrong Together" works, it is natural to begin by looking for repeated sections. Right away, we notice that harmonically measure 2 repeats measure 1, raised a minor third. We notice it especially easily because the melody repeats almost as exactly as the chords, shown in figure 2. But this one-measure unit, though it recurs several times in the tune and serves as a kind of signature for it, is too small to give us a handle on the larger structure.

Figure 2: Measures 1–2

Partly because we so readily recognize power-of-two units, we are likely to hear measures 1–4 as a unified phrase. We notice with satisfaction, then, that measure 5 is the beginning of a highly similar phrase, transposed up a minor third (just as, *within* the first phrase, measure 2 transposes measure 1). This near repetition keeps working for two and a half bars. In measure 7, tracking the corresponding earlier progression from Fmaj7 to B♭7 in measure 3, we expect the A♭ to be followed by a D♭7. Instead, the A♭ drops to G7, a shift down a minor second instead of a fifth. Still, this divergence might be less severe than it seems. The difference between the expected resolution and the actual one is a tritone, a common interval of chord substitution in modern jazz; the G7 we get might be standing in for the D♭7 we anticipated. Indeed, the chords following the G7 end in the same place as the expected sequence would have ended:

expected: Gm C7 | B♭m7 E♭7 | A♭ D♭7 | C7 F7
actual: Gm C7 | B♭m7 E♭7 | A♭ G7 | Cm F7

This analysis looks promising, on paper. We appear to have uncovered a structure in which the harmony of the first four bars is repeated (shifted up a minor third) in the next four, with one minor harmonic variation.

Yet leaving aside how the pattern looks, we don't actually *hear* the tune as following this structure. Rather, we hear something different starting somewhere in the middle of the second four bars, around measure 7. Our ear for structure is being pulled two ways at once. One reason is traceable to the melody. The long note in measure 4 clearly completes a phrase, and we expect long notes to do that. But the next long note (the high E♭ held over an A♭ chord) arrives not in measure 8, but in measure 7; and the next after that comes just two bars later, in measure 9. Since phrase terminations are implied in measures 7 and 9 rather than in measure 8, the break we might have heard at the end of eight bars, if the four-bar phrases were working the way we are used to, is obscured by the phrase structure that the melody insists on. We are more likely to hear measures 8–9 as a separate two-bar phrase, as shown in figure 3.

The four measures 12–15, on the other hand, *do* recapitulate measures 1–4 perfectly, even in the same key, and in melody as well as harmony. This is the most obvious large pattern in the tune. When we arrive at measure 12, we hear a return to the beginning. It feels very much like coming to the midpoint (bar 17) in an ABAB standard—the second most common structure of jazz tunes, as in "My Romance" or "Out of Nowhere." So perhaps the real structural question is how we got to this recapitulation point in measure 12 from the cadence in measure 4. This seven-bar stretch looks like the culprit in the tune's weird shape.

To hear how this transition occurs, we must back off a step and listen again to the smallest units of harmonic progression. Throughout the tune, of all the successive pairs of chords (first chord to second, second chord to third, and so on),

Figure 3: Measures 7–9

a large majority—25 out of 34 pairs—follow standard V–I relationships, such as Em to A7 in the first measure, or C7 to F from the second measure into the third. Every exception to this common pattern, aside from the final turnaround, is a shift down a second: either major (three of them) or minor (the other five). The five descending minor-second progressions all initiate minor cadences, either VI–V–i or III–ii–V–i. (This is strictly true only if the last chord in measure 11 is—plausibly—respelled as B7♭5 rather than F9♯11.) The three major-second progressions (going into measures 2, 6, and 13) all step down from a dominant to a minor chord: A7 to Gm, for instance. This is a much more abrupt shift, more unsettled tonally. It stands out as the most striking gesture in the tune's harmony, and also in melody, which follows the same pattern in every case. We might think of this progression down a major second as a compressed version of a normal II7–(V)–i cadence, as shown in figure 4.

Of course the full, uncompressed ii–V–I cadence occurs very frequently throughout "Wrong Together," resolving at the beginnings of measures 3, 5, 7, 9, 11, 14, and 17. (In just one of these seven cases, measure 5, the cadence is in minor, ii–V–i, though F major is well enough established that we hear the progression as iii–[V7 of ii]–ii.) The first five of these cadences are packed very closely together, as in such ii–V–I-based tunes as "Joy Spring" or "Giant Steps." Each of these three-chord cadences is separated from the next by a single transitional chord—always a dominant seventh, though it may resolve down a fifth, a major second, or a minor second.

These are still very small structural units. Casting about for larger patterns, we may notice the *sequence* of these ii–V–I sequences. They resolve on F, G, A♭, B♭, and C—as though, within the tune's overall F-major tonality, the cadences outlined an F-minor scale. Perhaps this covert minor quality helps explain the elegiac tone of the composition (and one aspect of its title). This is intriguing, but it still does not seem to explain the tune's overall structure.

Figure 4: Measures 1–2 with interpolated D7 chord in parentheses

The last two of the ii–V–I cadences both resolve on the tonic F major, and both are preceded by three chords rather than the single chord separating all the earlier cadences. This lengthening of cadential rhythm helps slow the tune toward its end. The change also marks off measures 12–17 as a separate section. This same part of the tune, as we saw earlier, is distinguished also by the harmonic and melodic recapitulation that begins in measure 12.

Here is a paradox: we identify these measures as a separate section both because of their difference from the rest of the tune (the more widely spaced cadences), and because of their similarity (as a melodic and harmonic recapitulation). That is the way with musical patterns: sameness in difference and variation within continuity hone, between them, the edge of our attention.

The paradox makes us rethink the comparison noted earlier between this ending section (measures 12–17) and the beginning of the tune. Now we can see that what misled us, back at the beginning, was the tempting similarity between measures 5–8 and measures 1–4 (the familiar four-bar units). In our search for structural understanding, it turns out that we can do better by treating not the beginning of the tune but its ending as the "seed" phrase from which the whole structure develops:

Em A7 | Gm C7 | F B♭7 | Am7 D7 | Gm C7 | F   (mm. 12–17)

This sequence resolves the tune neatly at its end, of course, like the final part of any conventional chord progression. But in this case, we can also see the ending sequence as the basis for the beginning of the tune. From this angle, the variation is the beginning rather than the end: measures 1–6 alter the sequence at a single crucial point that does not seem crucial until we look back at it from measures 12–17:

Em A7 | Gm C7 | F B♭7 | Am7 D7 | Gm C7 |B♭m . . .   (mm. 1–6)

The last chord shown here (B♭m in measure 6) now emerges clearly as a deceptive cadence. It resembles the startling C dominant chord in the fourth measure of the second movement of Beethoven's Fifth Symphony—a dramatic moment that Peter Schickele parodies, and honors, by having the incompetent P. D. Q. Bach replace the melody's startling and dynamic E♮ with a bland, terminal A♭ over tonic A♭ major.

What is important about the newly discovered role of measure 6 is that it revises how we hear the tune by contradicting our first impression of the opening sequence. At first we understood the sequence [Gm C7 | B♭m], in measures 5–6, as a predictable transposed repetition of the [Em A7 | Gm] at the beginning. But once we have worked backward from the last section of the tune, we understand how the composer has undermined the conventional four-bar phrases he appeared to be giving us at the start. In retrospect, almost all the dividing points in the structure shift, and at last we are ready to account for the asymmetry that made the middle part of the tune so hard to grasp.

The overall structure of "Wrong Together" is actually ABA. The three strains are essentially each six measures long, but the pattern is fully spelled out only in the third, final section. (Most tunes seem to work the other way: an original opening strain, the others variations on it. In Swallow's tune, everything refers back from the end, not onward from the beginning.) Meanwhile, the first A strain is cut short by the B♭m in measure 6, so it's five measures long rather than six:

Em A7 | Gm C7 | F B♭7 | A7 D7 | Gm C7 | (B♭m instead of F)

The B strain is a full six bars long, but contrasts with the A strains before and after. It turns out to have a neatly symmetrical internal structure: three repetitions of a two-measure cadential pattern, each first resolving on a major-seventh chord (stepping upward through the parallel-minor scale, A♭, B♭, C), each then falling a half-step down to a dominant chord:

B♭m E♭7 | A♭Maj7 G7 (mm. 6–7)
Cm F7 | B♭Maj7 A7 (mm. 8–9)
Dm G7 | CMaj7 B7 (mm. 10–11)

Once we see it, this pattern defines the B section of the tune quite sharply.

From the outset, the difficulty was to perceive this B-strain pattern. What obscured it from view was the deceptive four-bar segment that seemed to begin in measure 5, just one bar before the real B strain begins. At first we hear measure 6 as the second bar in a four-bar phrase; therefore we miss hearing it as the beginning of the six-bar middle section of the tune. "Wrong Together" invokes our 2-4-8-16 expectations exactly in order to subvert them. Here is the tune's opening chord sequence as we hear it first, and then as we understand it later:

heard: Em A7 Gm C7 F B♭7 A7 D7 | Gm C7 B♭m E♭7 A♭? . . .
analyzed: Em A7 Gm C7 F B♭7 A7 D7 | Gm C7 | B♭m E♭7 A♭ G7 | Cm F7 B♭ A7 | Dm G7 C B7 Em A7 Gm C7 F B♭7 A7 D7 | Gm C7 F . . .

Now we have the basic phrase of the tune: the mildly polytonal but lyrically cogent six-measure pattern that ends it. And now we can hear the beginning as a curtailed version of the same thing, and measures 6–11 as a contrasting B strain built from simple two-bar units. Once we hear this structure, we can know where we stand all through it, chorus after chorus. To maintain that knowledge, only at one moment—in measure 5—do we need to listen carefully for the six-measure phrase about to start, rather than to the four-measure phrase that will never resolve itself. "Wrong Together" is not a 16-bar tune plus one, but an 18-bar (6-bar times three) structure condensed by a one-measure overlap between the first and second phrases.

One more symmetry in the harmonic structure is worth pointing out. Gm9 chords occur four times in the chorus of "Wrong Together." The first two occurrences are three measures apart, as are the last two; the two pairs are separated by eight measures. In each pair, the Gm is approached first obliquely from A7, then more decisively from D7. The same melody note (A, the ninth of the chord) accompanies all four; the only variation is that in the last case (measure 16) the A is held over as a suspension from the preceding chord, so that the harmonic tension of A over Gm is reduced as the tune settles down to its resolution. These very similar Gm9 moments, though as noted before they are too brief to tell us much about the underlying structure, help to make the whole tune *feel* coherent even before we understand it.

A more important point is that the relation between melody and harmony is worth studying throughout this tune. As in many of Swallow's compositions, the melody seems to follow from the chord progression rather than the other way around, as though the main function of melody were to outline the harmonies. (An extreme example of this method is "Ladies in Mercedes" from the *Duets* CD by Swallow and Carla Bley, covered on Gary Burton's CD *Generations*.) In "Wrong Together" what gives the melody its lyrical strength, despite this apparently functional role, is an obsessively recurring pair of harmonic tensions: the ninth over a minor chord, and the sharp eleventh over a dominant. (The one is poignant, the other more dynamic.) The first four notes of the tune display this basic pattern, and almost all of the melody can be heard as ringing changes on it. The only important exceptions are the long notes that end phrases, each of which rests stably on the fifth of its chord. So the melody repeatedly moves forward through the minor-ninth and sharp-eleventh dissonances, and then pauses on perfect fifths, which sound almost more static than tonics.

The beauty of the performance of "Wrong Together" on *Real Book*, it is worth adding, might prevent even careful listeners from noticing the tune's rigorous, witty logic. (Surely no reader will fall into the trap of believing that understanding the logic damages the beauty of the tune or the performance.) Mulgrew Miller's elegant, unaccompanied opening piano solo decorates, more than states, the melody; Tom Harrell's lyrical flugelhorn arrives at a clear exposition only at the end of the track—just as the basic chorus itself comes clearest at its end. In between, Swallow's own spare, precise bass solo cuts across the melody at sharp angles, emphasizing its dissonant possibilities and commenting on its relation to the harmony. Listening to these players at work while at the same time comprehending how the structure of "Wrong Together" supports their inventions can only increase our appreciation for both.

* * *

Once my fascination with Steve Swallow's tune had led me as far as the understanding of it outlined here, I offered my analysis to the composer himself. He seemed to appreciate its perspective, and nothing in his response (e-mail,

August 1, 2004) gravely undermined what I have said so far. He did, however, suggest an alternative version of the tune's structure, and considering this has led me to some broader speculations. Swallow said this:

> You're right that it's not a sixteen bar tune with an extra bar, more an eighteen bar tune with a "one-measure overlap between the first and second phrases." We differ in this: I have tended to see the eighth bar, not the sixth, as the beginning of the B section. I suspect this is the result of my placing greater emphasis on melodic analysis, where you have focused on the piece's harmonic structure.

This distinction of emphases seems plausible: I have given reasons for identifying the sixth bar as the covert beginning of a new harmonic section, but what makes it covert is that the melody arrives just one bar later at a long, apparently phrase-ending note and a bar after that begins a new sequence (bars 8 and 9 are repeated, with a shift, in bars 10 and 11).

The distinction between a melodic partition of the tune and a harmonic one recalls a phenomenon in the different world of lyric poetry. Melody and harmony are both coherent systems in which the tune's events (notes, intervals, chords) participate. I use the word "system" loosely—an even vaguer word like "pattern" would do almost as well—to call attention to the fact that while both are made up of the same elements, melody pursues its own logic while the harmonic progression pursues its separate one. In a poem, those different kinds of systems might be formal units like rhymed stanzas on the one hand and sentences on the other, composed of the same words, but organizing or articulating the words in two ways that may be at odds with each other.

A clear example occurs early in W. B. Yeats's "No Second Troy." The poem's form is three quatrains rhymed *abab*. The poem begins:

> Why should I blame her that she filled my days
> With misery, or that she would of late
> Have taught to ignorant men most violent ways,
> Or hurled the little streets upon the great

—a quatrain in which the two rhyme sounds ("days / ways," "late / great") are unusually bound to each other by the shared vowel, which emphasizes the closed, complete feel of the quatrain. (The same happens in the second quatrain: "desire / fire," "mind / kind.") The opening sentence could, as the form urges us to feel, end with that fourth line. Instead, it continues through the fifth:

> Had they but courage equal to desire?

As we read this fifth line, we are aware, on some level, of finishing one unit (the question) at the same time that we are beginning another (the second stanza). We are feeling both the pause of completion and the pull of a new outset. The whole poem is doubled in this way: the three four-line stanzas cut across sentences of five, five, one, and one lines. Furthermore, the sentences are all questions, and like the poem they compose, they all have two edges. "What could have made her peaceful," the poet asks, and if we hear a calm, rhetorical question that wants an obvious answer ("Nothing") without much thought, we also hear a turbulent, even anguished interrogation of the past and the damage it continues to do him. "Was there another Troy for her to burn?" Of course not, as the title affirms; yet burning has occurred and apparently still occurs. This division in the poem's speech, which we can dramatize as an internal struggle between the speaker and emotions he strives to master as they threaten to master him, is present even in the break after the first line: "Why should I blame her that she filled my days" is one kind of question, one stance toward past experience; "With misery" transforms it into quite another, without exactly canceling the first line's effort toward serenity. On a still smaller scale, the meter of the poem is ambiguous at key points, the start of each question: "what could she have done, being what she is" shifts its tone as we shift stress between the first word and the second. The printed text is silent about this choice, and presumably we can't choose both ways in a single reading (aloud, at least), but we can also hardly avoid going back, as the speaker goes back, to review what we have experienced from another angle.

These effects, typical of the language of poems, have effects on us that are still more uncanny for our hardly being consciously aware of them. In the same way, I would argue, the double articulation of Swallow's tune by melody and harmony creates a tension within our hearing that helps account for the tune's otherwise mysterious power.

In Swallow's note responding to my analysis, he suggests not one but three alternative structures. On the bandstand, he recounts, he answered a quick question from drummer Adam Nussbaum with the brief code, "seven, four, six." He adds:

> Another possible perspective: Hiding in there is a symmetrical AABA tune, but instead of 32 bars it's a reworking of a 4-4-4-4 structure, 4-3-4-6. In that analysis once again the eighth bar is the overlap bar, serving as both the resolution of the preceding three bars and the commencement of the four-bar B section. . . . The last section is six instead of four bars for the same reason the last section of "All the Things You Are" is extended. I see it as a kind of periodic sentence.

Among all four alternatives, there is striking agreement on one point: the tune's 17 bars fall into two groups, the first 11 (divided one way or another) as against the last 6.

I have sometimes proposed a Law of Lyric Structure: that poems always fall into two parts. (It's self-fulfilling, of course; if someone offers three parts for a poem, I can always argue that one of the dividing points is less important than the other.) This observation directs our attention to the placement of the turning point between the parts. The Law concerns what I want to call "structure" as distinct from "form": it claims that whatever the patterns of stanzas, rhymes, and so on—which may be common to many poems—each individual poem's unique statement turns on a single, primary reversal. (One kind of student poem fails because it has no second act; for anything to seem to happen in a poem, at least two things have to happen.) Yet between form and structure one connection arises, if we explain the bizarre longevity of the sonnet (seven centuries haven't killed it off) on the ground that its *formal* division into eight and six lines encourages and emphasizes a *structure* whose proportions are satisfying.

Those same proportions—something offset more or less sharply from 1:1—show up in "Freytag's Pyramid," the traditional diagram of a narrative plot with its climactic peak skewed toward the end. (A plot skewed the other way produces the experience we call "anticlimactic.") Poems have structures rather than narratives (even if they contain narratives), but the same considerations of shape or trajectory apply. Entirely symmetrical poems are rare; Robert Herrick's "Upon Julia's Clothes" adopts that unusually stable configuration precisely because it is peculiarly a poem of erotic appreciation more than of desire. Steve Swallow's tune, by any analysis, conforms to the satisfying, usual principle: its 11:6 structure is more skewed than the sonnet's 8:6, but in the same neighborhood. (Do all these values converge on the Golden Section, so prized in the visual arts?)

Two counterexamples to this norm among lyric poems help throw it into clearer relief. William Blake's "A Poison Tree" begins with a neat, moralistic stanza that would not feel out of place in a school primer:

> I was angry with my friend,
> I told my wrath, my wrath did end.
> I was angry with my foe,
> I told it not, my wrath did grow.

Blake, though, seeing that the very neatness undermines the moral truth the lines state, lets the second half of the stanza "grow" into a monstrous fable about planting wrath as an "apple" that the "foe" will see and covet and eat, with the triumphant, horrifying conclusion,

> In the morning glad I see
> My foe outstretched beneath the tree.

(The illustration in Blake's engraving of the poem makes the stakes clear: the poisoned foe's posture on the ground is a crucifixion.) The sharpest division in this poem, the point on which the most turns, balances the two-line story of anger with a friend against the karmic toil worked out by the last 14 lines. (The fourth line, the end of the first stanza, feels like a turning point only until we go on to the second stanza and find ourselves already locked into the direction wrath has set.) We feel no anticlimax because the long latter story has its own well-proportioned internal plot; but the larger moral point of "A Poison Tree" lies precisely in the grotesque disproportion between the two dramas it recounts. In that sense the poem's effect depends on our awareness of how, and why, it departs from the norm.

Elizabeth Bishop's "Insomnia" starts, innocuously enough, with a night wanderer noticing "the moon in the bureau mirror" and admiringly observing about the moon that

> By the Universe deserted,
> *She*'d tell it to go to hell.

The italics comment ruefully on the speaker's own contrasting passivity. She winds herself up to a kind of turn—at the expected point, in the 11th of 18 lines—with the would-be jaunty self-command "So wrap up care in a cobweb . . ." But the poem's final lines about the mirror's "world inverted"

> where the heavens are shallow as the sea
> is now deep, and you love me.

abruptly change everything. No "you" has appeared previously; an apparently trivial case of "insomnia" suddenly acquires a cause. The last four words stand across the poem's deepest chasm from the whole rest of it. Why the inordinate delay, when any poet half as technically impeccable as Bishop knows better than to introduce such a pronoun, and such a dramatic situation, at the last moment? Because the poem's speaker has been fighting off the last words' realization, and its attendant grief, all along. Her own drama, in other words, is played out in the delay itself, and appears in the poem's structure as a severe disparity between parts, opposite to Blake's, but just as dependent on a reader's sense that norms have been violated.

Precisely as violations, these two examples underscore the satisfaction we derive from the norm in most poems, and in most jazz tunes. It may be possible to find tunes as far from the average as Blake's and Bishop's poems. "Giant Steps" is at its most harmonically frantic in the first six measures, and the remaining 10 settle into a steadier rhythm of ii–V–I cadences. J. J. Johnson's "Lament" builds toward a climax whose delay to the 27th of 32 bars simply makes it all the more climactic. But any 12-bar blues (even a reworking like "Blue Train") reaches its peak in the harmonic shift located exactly two-thirds of the way through; and a large majority of tunes, like "Wrong Together," take a similar general shape.

In any time-based art—it is easy to find parallel examples in film and choreography—the import of what we experience at each moment depends on our sense of where we are within the elapsed time of the whole. A camera shot 80 minutes into a Quentin Tarantino film feels very different from the same shot, if we can imagine such a thing, 80 minutes into a film by Akira Kurosawa that we know will go on for three hours. It is through overwhelming, continuous extension in time that Gavin Bryars's *Jesus' Blood Never Failed Me Yet* freights all its succeeding moments with meaning that exceeds their poignancy. We might be in the vicinity of certain highly abstract principles common to this whole family of arts. In that larger context, the message of "Wrong Together" is twofold: the pleasures of a classical overall shape, coupled with a strangeness of structural detail that gives our time-experience an entrancing and alerting texture.

NOTES

1. For readers not familiar with jazz musicians' practice, it might be useful to define "fake book" as a collection of abbreviated notations that show only the melody and chord sequence of a composition, presenting in a compact form the materials on which jazz improvisers usually base their work.
2. Just how strange is this asymmetry? This question becomes difficult as one tries to move beyond intuitive answers. A copy of *The Real Book* contains 428 tunes, of which roughly 117 (27.3%) have structures that approximate an AABA pattern, such as "Don't Get Around Much Any More" or "Impressions"; 105 (24.5%) have approximately ABAB structures, such as "My Romance"; and about 44 (10.3%) are straightforward blues. Another few dozen are obvious variants like AAB and some condensed 16-bar forms. These standard structures account for about 70% of the book. The precision of these counts, however, is deceptive. Variations abound: "A Night in Tunisia" is AABA but with a recurring "interlude"; "Footprints" is a blues, but in 24 bars of 3/4 time; though "Once I Loved" feels unmistakably like other ABAB tunes, its first half is 16 bars long while the second is 28; and so on. It is easy to imagine disagreements about the classification of tunes that might alter these percentages significantly; some uncertainty haunts even the definition and identification of A and B strains.

   Furthermore, though *The Real Book* has come to occupy the position of a compilation of standards—in the sense that players who have not worked together before expect each other to know most of its tunes—it does not seem to have been constructed with exactly that purpose. Rather, the collection constitutes an argument in favor of certain trends new in the 1970s; neither Michael Gibbs's "Feelings and Things" nor Frank Zappa's "Peaches en Regalia" turns up in the set lists of pickup jazz groups. The proportion of unusual structures, then, may be higher than in some hypothetical "normal" collection of standards, and a tune like "Wrong Together" may be more extraordinary than the figures given here indicate.
3. Elsewhere (as in the opening chapter of *Jazz Text: Voice and Improvisation in Poetry, Jazz, and Song* [Princeton, 1991]) I have, like many other critics, discussed the structures of jazz solos. My subject here requires a different kind of analysis, focusing on the work of the jazz composer, a composer of frameworks for improvisation, rather than that of the improviser.

NONATONIC PROGRESSIONS IN THE MUSIC OF JOHN COLTRANE

Matthew Santa

John Coltrane's album *Giant Steps*, released in 1960, introduced a new kind of composition to the list of jazz standards, and thus made a mark on the history of jazz. This new kind of composition was exemplified by the album's title track, with its striking harmonic progression; this progression and similar progressions elsewhere in Coltrane's music will be the focus here.[1] These progressions will be discussed as paths through systems that alternate between dominant seventh chords and major triads and emphasize parsimonious voice leading, at least in an abstract sense. I call such systems *nonatonic systems*, because they have 9 of the 12 pitch classes in a chromatic division of the octave, and those pitch classes divide the octave as evenly as possible (e.g., [C,C♯,D,E,F,F♯,G♯,A,B♭]); such a collection is often called a nonatonic collection. One should note that the complement of the nonatonic collection is the augmented triad, meaning that the pitch classes missing from any given nonatonic collection form an augmented triad (e.g., [C,C♯,D,E,F,F♯,G♯,A,B♭] joined with [E♭,G,B] would form a chromatic scale). In the language of pitch-class set theory, the nonatonic collection is referred to as (01245689T), with *T* representing the integer *10* and all of the integers representing semitones from a referential pitch class.[2] I have recently used nonatonic systems to explain similar harmonic progressions in the music of nineteenth-century composers.[3] This chapter will focus on aspects of voice leading in the nonatonic system and how they are reflected in a group of Coltrane's compositions: "Giant Steps," "Countdown," and "26-2."

Example 1 illustrates a nonatonic system. Example 1a provides a graphic representation of the nonatonic system; each Δ in Example 1 designates a major triad, while each "7" designates a dominant seventh chord. In clockwise motions from chord to chord in the nonatonic system, each dominant seventh chord resolves to its own tonic, and each tonic moves to the dominant seventh chord whose root is a minor third above. The incomplete dominant seventh chord is used in the nonatonic system in order to keep the cardinality of each group within the system the same: three notes per chord. The incomplete dominant seventh that omits the fifth is commonly found because not all four notes of the dominant seventh chord are necessary in order for that harmony to carry both its key-defining tritone and its bass note, which plays such an important part in establishing its function.

Example 1b shows the smoothest possible three-voice realization of the nonatonic cycle beginning on CΔ. (I will use the word "cycle" throughout to refer exclusively to a chain of clockwise or counterclockwise moves through a system.) In the three-voice realization, the voice leading between adjacent chords in the nonatonic system

a) A nonatonic system

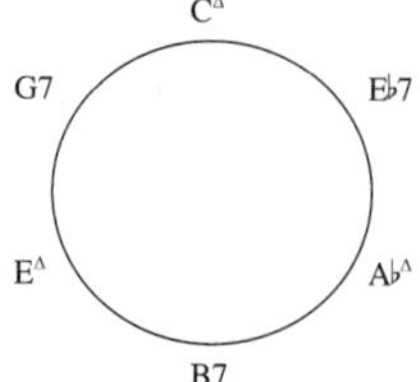

N.B.: "Δ" indicates a major triad; "7" indicates a major-minor 7th chord

b) A three-voice realization of the nonatonic cycle beginning on C

N.B.: The PVLS between any two chords in the nonatonic cycle is 0.

c) A four-voice realization of the nonatonic cycle beginning on C

[B C D♭ E♭ E F G A♭ A] = pitch-class content of this cycle's three-voice realization

[D F♯ B♭] = remaining pitch classes added by fourth voice

Example 1: A nonatonic system and its realization as a cycle in three and four voices

results in two voices moving by semitone in contrary motion, while the third voice retains a common tone, as is shown in Example 1b. What is particularly striking about the nonatonic cycle is that it reveals to us the duplicity of the voice-leading pattern connecting major triads and their respective dominant seventh chords: the same voice-leading pattern that takes a major triad to its own dominant seventh chord (a counterclockwise move in the cycle) may *also* take it to a dominant seventh chord whose root is a minor third above the root of that triad (a clockwise move). Conversely, the same voice-leading pattern that takes a dominant seventh chord to its tonic (a clockwise move) may *also* take it to a major triad whose root is a minor third below the root of that seventh chord (a counterclockwise move).

Example 1c is divided into an upper staff that shows the three-voice realization of the nonatonic cycle beginning on CΔ, and a lower staff that adds a fourth voice to the realization; the added fourth voice completes each dominant seventh chord by providing the 5th of the chord. The added voice moves by step through a whole-tone scale and is thus relatively smooth, though by no means as smooth as the three-voice realization. It is also worth noting that the addition of the fourth voice provides the three pitch classes missing in the three-voice realization of the cycle, thereby completing the aggregate and challenging the cycle's nonatonic labeling; the pitch-class content of the nonatonic cycle's three-voice realization in Example 1b is [B,C,D♭,E♭,E,F,G,A♭,A], while the fourth voice adds B♭, F♯, and D, the fifths of the E♭7, B7, and G7 chords, respectively. However, because the fourth voice is not essential to the voice leading of the cycle, I will still refer to the cycle as nonatonic, even when it is realized in four voices.

In order to observe one significant feature of nonatonic systems, it is necessary to define a consistent way of measuring the degree of parsimony for each voice leading, taking into account *parsimonious voice leading sums*, abbreviated "PVLS."[4] The approach taken here is outlined in Example 2. First, I define the PVLS function as follows: given chord X, composed of pitches x1, x2, . . . x*n*, and chord Y, equal in cardinality to chord X and composed of pitches y1, y2, . . . y*n*, and a parsimonious voice leading between them that maps x1 onto y1, x2 onto y2, . . . x*n* onto y*n*, let int1 be the ordered pitch interval from x1 to y1, let int2 be the ordered pitch interval from x2 to y2, . . . , let int*n* be the ordered pitch interval from x*n* to y*n*, and let PVLS (X, Y) be a function that returns the absolute value of the sum total of int1, int2, . . . int*n* (Example 2a). In this chapter, I will consider only the smoothest possible voice leading between two chords, though this function could be used in other contexts.

a) Definition for Parsimonious Voice-Leading Sum (PVLS)

The total amount of voice-leading motion expended in one direction, measured in semitones. One could also state it mathematically as:

PVLS (X, Y) = | int1 + int 2 + … int*n* |

where int1, int2, etc. are the motions connecting chords X and Y.

N.B.: This definition could be applied to all chord types, but only the smoothest possible voice leading between major triads and major-minor seventh chords will be considered here.

b) Two examples of the PVLS function

Mapping of C$^{\Delta}$ onto A♭$^{\Delta}$:

int 1 = 0 (C onto C), int 2 = -1 (E onto E♭), int 3 = +1 (G onto A♭)

PVLS (C$^{\Delta}$, A♭$^{\Delta}$) = | 0 + -1 + 1 | = 0

Mapping of C$^{\Delta}$ onto B7:

int 1 = -1 (C onto B), int 2 = -1 (E onto D♯), int 3 = +2 (G onto A)

PVLS (C$^{\Delta}$, B7) = | -1 + -1 + 2 | = 0

Example 2: Parsimonious voice-leading sums

Please compare Example 1b and Example 2b. As one may observe, the PVLS of a movement between *any* two chords in the nonatonic system is 0. Adjacent chords in the system have already been discussed in the context of the cycle shown as Example 1b. However, consider nonatonic progressions that move clockwise or counterclockwise through the system, but skip one chord, such as CΔ to A♭Δ. The absolute value of the sum of ordered pitch intervals—0 (C onto C), –1 (E onto E♭), and +1 (G onto A♭)—is still 0. And consider nonatonic progressions that skip two chords, such as CΔ onto B7. The absolute value of the sum of ordered pitch intervals, –1 (C onto B), –1 (E onto D♯), and +2 (G onto A), is also 0. Because of its PVLS consistency, the nonatonic system communicates the same feeling of seamlessness that one experiences when listening to Cohn's hexatonic system. Example 3 shows the four transpositions of the nonatonic system. Following Cohn, these transpositions are labeled as Northern, Southern, Eastern, and Western for heuristic purposes.

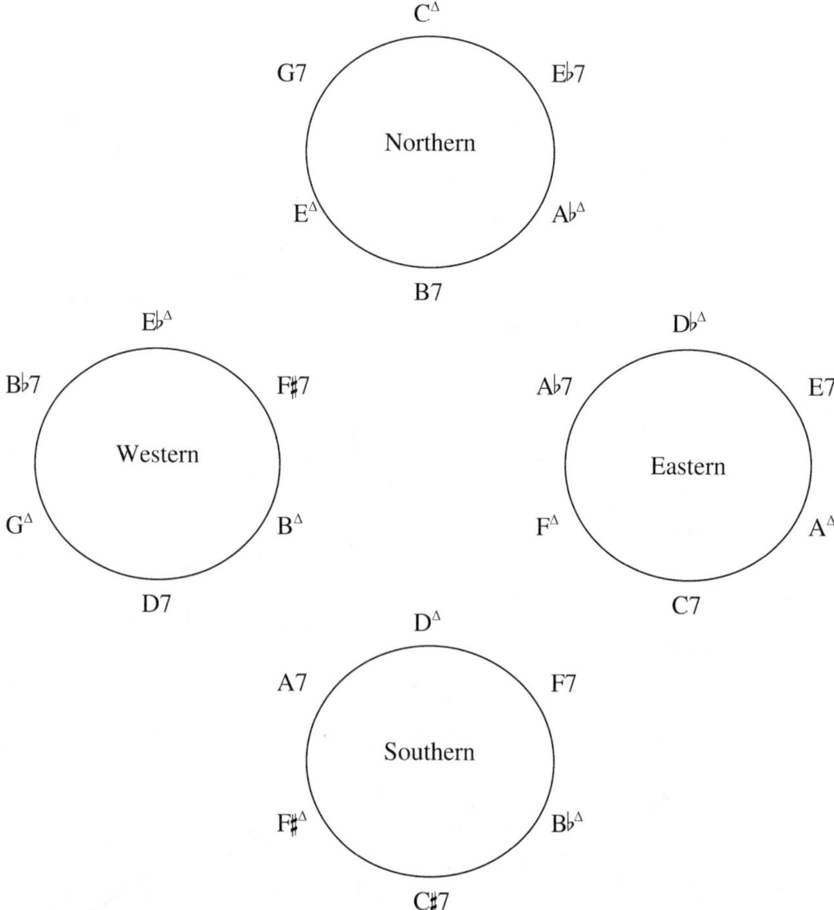

Example 3: The four nonatonic systems

The four transpositions taken together comprise all 12 major triads and their respective dominants.

Example 4 provides an analysis of the chord changes in "Giant Steps." The tune opens with five of the six chords from the Western nonatonic system, presented as five clockwise motions through the system (cf. Examples 3 and 4). In the next measure (m. 4), the music becomes slightly more grounded in G major as a II–V–I progression unfolds in that key. The minor chord built on scale degree 2 cannot be explained as part of the nonatonic cycle but is clearly part of a descending fifth progression in G. However, starting with the D7, m. 4 begins another run through the Western nonatonic system, and this time all six chords of the cycle are presented in their clockwise ordering. In the remainder of "Giant Steps," each tonicized key area in the Western system is prolonged by the addition of a II chord, as in m. 4. It should be noted that while the chords given in this particular lead sheet do not have extensions, it is common practice for jazz musicians to add extensions to suit their own taste and style. While such common extensions might thicken the voicings of the chords, they would most probably not obscure the sense of smooth voice leading that the underlying nonatonic cycle lends to the harmonic progression.

Example 5 provides an analysis of the chord changes in Coltrane's composition "Countdown." In "Countdown," minor seventh chords in mm. 1, 5, 9, and 13 and

m. 1
Western system -------------------------------------( )------------
B$^{\Delta}$ D7 | G$^{\Delta}$ B♭7 | E♭$^{\Delta}$ | A- D7 |

m. 5
--( )------------
G$^{\Delta}$ B♭7 | E♭$^{\Delta}$ F♯7 | B$^{\Delta}$ | F- B♭7 |

m. 9
----------------( )--------------------------------( )------------
E♭$^{\Delta}$ | A- D7 | G$^{\Delta}$ | C♯- F♯7 |

m. 13
----------------( )--------------------------------( )------------
B$^{\Delta}$ | F- B♭7 | E♭$^{\Delta}$ | C♯- F♯7 ||

As published in Aebersold (1983), 3.

$^{\Delta}$ = major triad (Aebersold recommends adding major 7th and 9th)
- = minor triad (Aebersold recommends adding minor 7th and major 9th)
7 = dominant seventh chord (Aebersold recommends adding major 9th)
For a list of suggested chord extensions, see Aebersold, Ibid., 31.

Example 4: Chord changes to Coltrane's "Giant Steps"

major sevenths added to all tonicized chords embellish what are otherwise straightforward presentations of nonatonic cycles. In mm. 1–4, all six chords of the Southern system are presented in their clockwise ordering; in mm. 5–8, all six chords of the Northern system are presented in their clockwise ordering; and in mm. 9–16, all six chords of the Southern system are again presented in their clockwise ordering, with an additional repetition of V7–I in B♭ major. Each of the minor chords functions as a chromatic lower neighbor chord to the dominant seventh chord it precedes. Jazz musicians frequently embellish a functional harmony by preceding it with a nonfunctional chromatic neighbor chord either above or below it, and then moving to the functional harmony; this well-known tradition is often called "side-slipping."

Example 6 provides an analysis of the chord changes in Coltrane's composition "26-2." In this tune minor chords that prolong key areas again embellish what are otherwise straightforward presentations of nonatonic cycles. In mm. 1–3, all six chords of the Eastern system occur in their clockwise ordering. In mm. 4–6, five of the six chords of the Southern system are presented in their clockwise ordering, and the root of the expected sixth chord of the system is shared by the next chord, though the quality of that chord is not major, but minor (this deviation is highlighted in the example with an exclamation point). The following two measures, which present II–V progressions in the keys of C and F, respectively, end the first A section of this 32-bar AABA song form. The B section can also be tied to the nonatonic system, though minor chords that prolong key areas obscure its presence. Nevertheless, four chords from the Southern system are presented in their clockwise ordering in mm. 18–20 (A7–D–F7–B♭), and four chords from the Eastern system are presented out of order in mm. 22–25

m. 1				
	Southern system--			
E-	F7 I B♭$^{\Delta}$	D♭7 I G♭$^{\Delta}$	A7 I D$^{\Delta}$	I
m. 5				
	Northern system--			
D-	E♭7 I A♭$^{\Delta}$	B7 I E$^{\Delta}$	G7 I C$^{\Delta}$	I
m. 9				
	Southern system--			
C-	D♭7 I G♭$^{\Delta}$	A7 I D$^{\Delta}$	F7 I B♭$^{\Delta}$	I
m. 13				
E-	I F7	I B♭$^{\Delta}$	I E♭7^{+4}	II

As published in Aebersold, Ibid., 10.

Example 5: Chord changes to Coltrane's "Countdown"

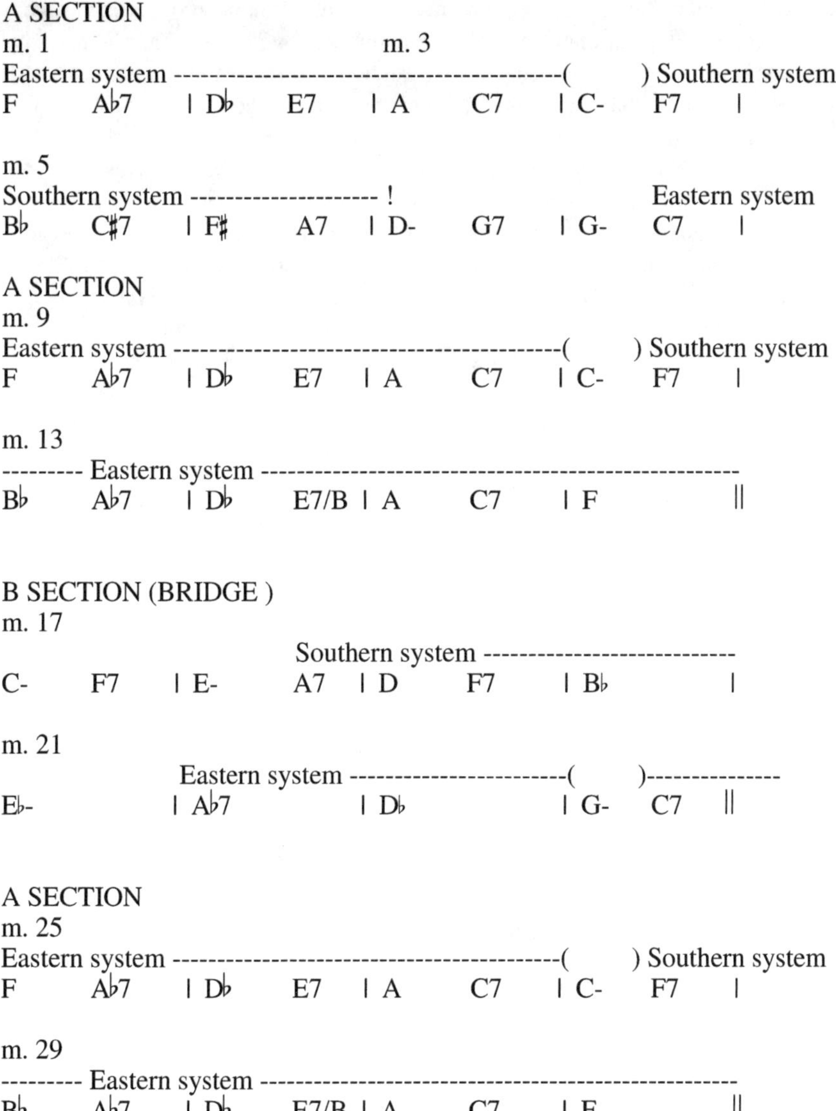

A SECTION
m. 1 m. 3
Eastern system --( ) Southern system
F A♭7 | D♭ E7 | A C7 | C- F7 |

m. 5
Southern system -------------------- ! Eastern system
B♭ C♯7 | F♯ A7 | D- G7 | G- C7 |

A SECTION
m. 9
Eastern system --( ) Southern system
F A♭7 | D♭ E7 | A C7 | C- F7 |

m. 13
--------- Eastern system --
B♭ A♭7 | D♭ E7/B | A C7 | F ||

B SECTION (BRIDGE)
m. 17
Southern system ---------------------------
C- F7 | E- A7 | D F7 | B♭ |

m. 21
Eastern system ----------------------( )--------------
E♭- | A♭7 | D♭ | G- C7 ||

A SECTION
m. 25
Eastern system --( ) Southern system
F A♭7 | D♭ E7 | A C7 | C- F7 |

m. 29
--------- Eastern system --
B♭ A♭7 | D♭ E7/B | A C7 | F ||

As published in Aebersold, Ibid., 4.

Example 6: Chord changes to Coltrane's "26-2"

(A♭7–D♭–C7–F), the last of which also serves to kick off the nonatonic cycle in the third and final A section.

Performances of and improvisations on "Giant Steps" and the other Coltrane compositions discussed here will not necessarily reflect this smooth voice leading. The melodies of these tunes do not at all and have been intentionally omitted thus far to avoid distracting the reader from my focus: the harmonic progression as it exists in an abstract form that exemplifies parsimonious voice leading. The underlying parsimonious voice leading of the progression, regardless of the extent to which it is realized on the musical surface, affects the sound of those pieces in which it is found. This is not to say that the abstract form has nothing to do with the musical surface; indeed, the tradition of improvising from guide-tone lines is widely known, and the guide-tone line is nothing more than a path that moves by step or by common tone through the harmonic progression of a given composition. Example 7 provides some nonatonic-inspired possibilities for improvisation on "Giant Steps" to illustrate this point. The "improvised" line given as Example 7a is rhythmically reduced in Example 7b to highlight its relationship to a parsimonious nonatonic cycle: one semitonal move in each motion from chord to chord (D♯–D, C–B, B–B♭, A♭–G), and two common-tone retentions, D and B♭. Similarly, the "improvised" line given as Example 7c is reduced in Example 7d to highlight its relationship to a parsimonious nonatonic cycle: the whole-tone line that is harmonized with diatonically

Example 7: Nonatonic-inspired possibilities for improvisation on "Giant Steps"

planing triads is the same "fourth voice" found in the parsimonious four-voice realization of the nonatonic cycle. Finally, the "improvised" line given as Example 7e is reduced in Example 7f to highlight its relationship to a parsimonious nonatonic cycle: it combines two semitonal moves (D♯–D and B–B♭) with two common-tone retentions (F♯ and D) and the whole-tone line shown above.

One striking feature of the tune to "Giant Steps" is that the total pitch-class content of the melody forms the Southern Nonatonic Collection (the pitch classes forming the harmonies of the Southern Nonatonic System). Example 8a provides the melody to "Giant Steps," while Example 8b provides the Southern Nonatonic Collection for comparison. The odds of a random sampling of 25 pitch classes adhering solely to a single nonatonic collection are less than 3%, a fact that suggests this correspondence is significant. (The missing pitch classes—C, E, and A♭—are not absent because of a lack of harmonic opportunity, either; each is the seventh of a dominant seventh chord that occurs at least three times in the composition.) However, a comparison of Examples 1, 4, and 8 will reveal that none of the melodic motions in "Giant Steps" corresponds to a parsimonious realization of the nonatonic cycles found therein. Neither "Countdown" nor "26-2" has a melody drawn from a single nonatonic collection.

There is at least one example of the nonatonic system in jazz outside of Coltrane's music: the bridge to "Have You Met Miss Jones?" by Richard Rodgers and Lorenz Hart. Example 9 provides an analysis of the chord changes from the bridge, which treats the listener to a quick run through the Southern nonatonic system.

In many ways the harmonic language of jazz resembles models of nineteenth-century Romantic harmony, and the nonatonic system reinforces this idea by providing the analyst with many specific examples from the literature. Example 10a provides mm. 11–17 from Franz Liszt's song "Das Veilchen." The harmonic progression in mm. 1–12 can be grasped easily enough with a conventional Roman-numeral analysis, but the progression of tonicized major triads in mm. 12–17, E♭–G–B, suggests that the octave here is partitioned into major thirds. Because each of these major triads is tonicized by its dominant, this passage

a) "Giant Steps" melody

b) Southern Nonatonic Collection (the pitch classes forming the harmonies of the Southern Nonatonic System)

Example 8: "Giant Steps" melody compared to the Southern Nonatonic Collection

m. 9
Southern system ( )----------------------( )----------
$B\flat^{\Delta}$ | $A\flat$- $D\flat7$ | $G\flat^{\Delta}$ | E- A7 |

m. 13
------------------ ( )----------------------( )----------
D^{Δ} | $A\flat$- $D\flat7$ | $G\flat^{\Delta}$ | G- C7 |

Example 9: Chord changes to the bridge of the Rodgers and Hart tune "Have You Met Miss Jones?"

yields a complete statement of the Western nonatonic system. Though the ordering of the harmonies does not result in a smooth clockwise or counterclockwise progression through that system, the maximally close voice leading is identical to that of the system; between any two adjacent chords in this passage, two voices move in contrary motion by semitone and one voice holds a common tone. And whereas the song as a whole relies more heavily on traditional fundamental-bass progressions, the nonatonic passage given here is stated three times and thus accounts for 21 of the song's 67 measures. Example 10b shows the extent to which the maximally close voice leading of the nonatonic system is realized in pitch space on the surface of the music. This graph is reductive in that it shows only those voice-leading moves that match the pattern of the nonatonic system, and the rhythmic character of the passage has been reduced to its note-against-note contrapuntal frame. In this graph the dotted lines between chords reflect common tones that are registrally displaced, while the solid lines reflect octave displacements of what might have been realized as a stepwise voice-leading motion. The bass note in parentheses is not literally present in the music, but is nevertheless implied by the musical context.

This chapter has demonstrated that nonatonic systems are useful in understanding the harmonic progressions found in Coltrane's compositions "Giant Steps," "Countdown," and "26-2." It has also shown instances of the nonatonic system in works that predate these Coltrane compositions, both within the world of jazz and outside of it. Its focus has been on the smoothest possible voice leading of the nonatonic cycle and how this voice leading is reflected in Coltrane's compositions before their realizations in performance; it makes no claim that performances of and improvisations on "Giant Steps" and the other Coltrane compositions discussed will reflect this smooth voice leading. However, it does claim that the underlying parsimonious voice leading of the progression affects the sound of those pieces and that careful study of such underlying voice-leading patterns might be helpful to those jazz performers who use guide-tone lines to structure their improvisations or more generally to those who are sensitive to such parsimonious relations.

a) Music

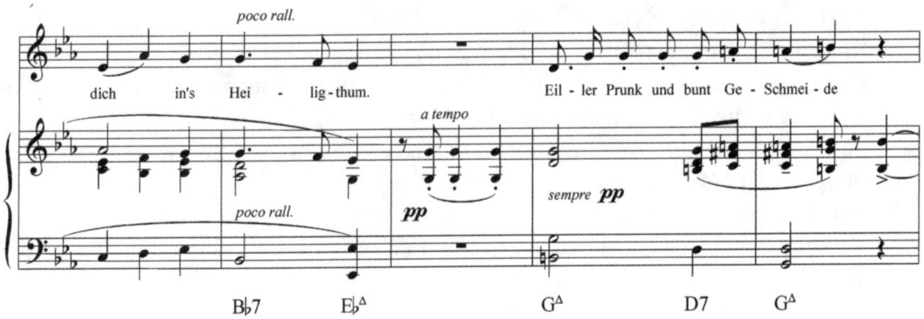

b) Voice-leading graph of path through Western nonatonic system in mm. 12-17

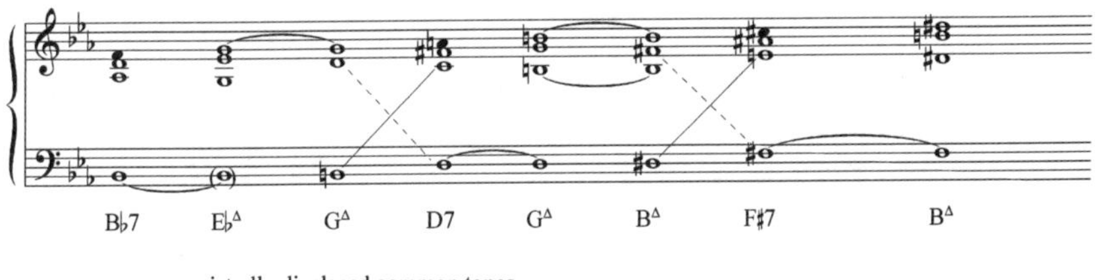

- - - - - - = registrally displaced common tones
——— = registrally displaced stepwise voice leading

Example 10: Liszt, "Das Veilchen," mm. 11–17

NOTES

I would like to thank David Smyth, Guy Capuzzo, and Henry Martin for their thoughtful comments and suggestions on earlier versions of this chapter.

1. For earlier studies of these harmonic progressions, see David Demsey, "Chromatic Third Relations in the Music of John Coltrane," *Annual Review of Jazz Studies* 5

(1991), 145–80, and Masaya Yamaguchi, "A Creative Approach to Multi-Tonic Changes: Beyond Coltrane's Harmonic Formula," *Annual Review of Jazz Studies* 12 (2002), 147–67. The current chapter differs from those cited in that it takes a Neo-Riemannian tack, exploring the abstract parsimonious voice leading of the progressions. Also, Lewis Porter has linked the origin of these harmonic progressions in Coltrane's music to Nicolas Slonimsky's *Thesaurus of Scales and Melodic Patterns*. See Porter, *John Coltrane: His Life and Music* (Ann Arbor: University of Michigan Press, 1997, 149–50).

2. For those readers unfamiliar with pitch-class set theory, pitch classes are families of pitches related by octave equivalence and enharmonic equivalence, and are represented by the integers 0 through 11 (e.g., C = 0, C♯, / D♭ = 1, D = 2, etc.). Throughout this chapter the letter *T* will be used to represent the integer *10* whenever it is part of a string of integers (just as the letter *E* could have been used to represent the integer *11* if necessary). The set class (01245689T) represents [C,C♯,D,E,F,F♯,G♯,A,B♭] as well as any transposition of that collection, or any group of pitches enharmonically equivalent to it or its transpositions.
3. Matthew Santa, "Nonatonic Systems and the Parsimonious Interpretation of Dominant-Tonic Progressions," *Theory and Practice* 28 (2003), 1–28. My nonatonic system is a variant of Cohn's hexatonic system. See Richard Cohn, "Maximally Smooth Cycles, Hexatonic Systems, and the Analysis of Late-Romantic Triadic Progressions," *Music Analysis* 15, no. 1 (1996), 9–40.
4. The PVLS function defined here is a variant of Richard Cohn's *directed voice leading sum* ("DVLS") function. See Richard Cohn, "Square Dances with Cubes," *Journal of Music Theory* 42, no. 2 (1998), 283–96. The PVLS function is equivalent in most respects to Cohn's DVLS function, except that Cohn defines the DVLS function with respect to triads, whereas in this article, the PVLS is generalized to include all chord types, though only major triads and dominant seventh chords are considered here.

BIBLIOGRAPHY

Aebersold, Jamey. *Play-A-Long*, vol. 28, *John Coltrane*. New Albany, IN: Jamey Aebersold Jazz, Inc., 1983.

Anson-Cartwright, Mark. "Chord as Motive: The Augmented Triad Matrix in Wagner's *Siegfried Idyll*." *Music Analysis* 15, no. 1 (1996), 57–71.

Childs, Adrian. "Moving beyond Neo-Riemannian Triads: Exploring a Transformational Model of Seventh Chords." *Journal of Music Theory* 42, no. 2 (1998), 181–93.

Clampitt, David. "Alternative Interpretations of Some Measures from *Parsifal*." *Journal of Music Theory* 42, no. 2 (1998), 321–34.

Cohn, Richard. "Maximally Smooth Cycles, Hexatonic Systems, and the Analysis of Late-Romantic Triadic Progressions." *Music Analysis* 15, no. 1 (1996), 9–40.

———. "Neo-Riemannian Operations, Parsimonious Trichords, and Their *Tonnetz* Representations." *Journal of Music Theory* 41, no. 1 (1997), 1–66.

———. "Square Dances with Cubes." *Journal of Music Theory* 42, no. 2 (1998), 283–96.

———. "Introduction to Neo-Riemannian Theory: A Survey and a Historical Perspective." *Journal of Music Theory* 42, no. 2 (1998), 167–80.

———. "As Wonderful as Star Clusters: Instruments for Gazing at Tonality in Schubert." *Nineteenth-Century Music* 22, no. 3 (1999), 213–32.

Demsey, David. "Chromatic Third Relations in the Music of John Coltrane." *Annual Review of Jazz Studies* 5 (1991), 145–80.

Douthett, Jack, and Peter Steinbach. "Parsimonious Graphs: A Study in Parsimony, Contextual Transformations, and Modes of Limited Transposition." *Journal of Music Theory* 42, no. 2 (1998), 241–63.

Fraim, John. *Spirit Catcher: The Life and Art of John Coltrane*. West Liberty, OH: Great House, 1996.

Gollin, Edward. "Some Aspects of Three-Dimensional *Tonnetze*." *Journal of Music Theory* 42, no. 2 (1998), 195–206.

Hook, Julian. "Cross-Type Transformations, GIS Homomorphisms, and Generalized Transposition and Inversion." Paper presented at the Indiana University Graduate Theory Association Symposium, February 25, 2000.

Hyer, Brian. "Tonal Intuitions in *Tristan und Isolde*." Ph.D. diss., Yale University, 1989.

———. "Reimag(in)ing Riemann." *Journal of Music Theory* 39, no. 1 (1995), 101–38.

Jost, Ekkehard. "Spontaneitat und Klischee in der Jazzimprovisation, dargestellt an John Coltranes Giant Steps." In *Kongress-Bericht Berlin* (1974), 457–60.

Kelly, Michael. "Harmonic Formulae and Other Compositional Devices Found in the Music of John Coltrane before 1961." M.A. thesis, State University of New York at Buffalo, 1987.

Kopp, David. "A Chromatic System of Tonal Transformations." Paper presented at the annual meeting of the Society for Music Theory, October 31, 1996.

Lewin, David. "Some Ideas about Voice-Leading between Pcsets." *Journal of Music Theory* 42, no. 1 (1998), 15–72.

Porter, Lewis. *John Coltrane: His Life and Music.* Ann Arbor: University of Michigan Press, 1997.

Santa, Matthew. "Nonatonic Systems and the Parsimonious Interpretation of Dominant-Tonic Progressions." *Theory and Practice* 28 (2003), 1–28.

Yamaguchi, Masaya. "A Creative Approach to Multi-Tonic Changes: Beyond Coltrane's Harmonic Formula," *Annual Review of Jazz Studies* 12 (2002), 147–67.

MILES DAVIS'S IMPROVISED SOLOS IN RECORDINGS OF "WALKIN'": 1954–67

Alona Sagee

"Walkin'," a 12-bar blues composed by Richard Carpenter, was, according to Jack Chambers, played *nightly* by Miles Davis and his group from April 1954, the time he first recorded it, into the mid-1960s.[1] Since Davis performed "Walkin'" virtually hundreds of times, it is an appropriate model for illustrating the transmutations of his improvisational style during a crucial and revolutionary period in his career. Twenty-four Davis performances of "Walkin'," recorded from 1954 to 1967, have been issued commercially.[2] In this same span of time, Davis formed various quintets and sextets with leading exponents of jazz, collaborated repeatedly with composer Gil Evans, and recorded the immensely influential *Kind of Blue*.

"WALKIN'": 1954, 1956, 1958

The introduction and theme statement of "Walkin'," as played in all of Davis's performances (sometimes with slight alterations), appear in Example 1.[3] The first recorded version of "Walkin'" by the Miles Davis sextet was made on April 29, 1954.[4] Davis's solo, as transcribed by Ian Carr,[5] appears in Example 2. Davis's style here is a continuation of bebop language and phrasing with a mainly vertical approach to the chord changes—at times outlining the harmonies, and at other times merely suggesting them through note choices. Despite the existence of a modal conception in blues improvisation since before the 1920s—the term *modal conception* referring to a horizontal-scalar approach to the choice of pitches played or sung over a vertically conceived accompaniment of slow-moving harmonies while resisting their vertical pull—any modally conceived phrasing in Davis's solo is sparse and unobtrusive. During the entire solo, Davis remains within the confines of the tonal framework of the blues, without any dramatic effort to extricate himself.

Before abandoning this initial recording of "Walkin'," we should note this imaginative and thought-provoking interpretation by John Szwed:

> Miles took seven improvised choruses on "Walkin'," with a poise and self-control that were new to his playing and to jazz. The listener can hear him waiting calmly for ideas before he plays and working those silences into the fabric of his solo. The effect is one of hearing him think, with the audible thought process itself becoming part of the music.[6]

Example 1: "Walkin'": Introduction and theme statement

The second version of "Walkin'," recorded live at the Blue Note in Philadelphia on December 8, 1956, by the Miles Davis quintet,[7] is somewhat faster than the 1954 version. Although Davis's solos (three choruses at the beginning and two at the end) are entirely new from a melodic and rhythmic standpoint, the boppish syntax of the phrasing and the vertical approach to the harmony have not changed much from the recording made over two and a half years earlier.

The last recording of "Walkin'" by the Davis band before the appearance of *Kind of Blue* (March–April 1959) was made during a radio broadcast from New York's Café Bohemia on May 17, 1958.[8] Although the language of his eight-chorus solo is still derived from bebop, Davis sounds somewhat less confined by tonality, and also freer rhythmically than in the 1954 and 1956 recordings. Presumably Davis's increased flexibility was encouraged by the presence of pianist Bill Evans, who had joined the band about five weeks earlier to replace Red Garland.[9] Also, on April 2, 1958, shortly before Evans joined the band, Davis had recorded "Milestones" (originally titled "Miles" on the Columbia LP *Milestones*). "Milestones" was composed by Davis as a basis for modal improvisation[10] and

Example 2: "Walkin'": Miles Davis's solo

has been described by Ekkehard Jost as the "first step on the road to *modal playing*."[11] In his autobiography Davis recounts:

> This was the first record where I started to really write in the modal form and on "Milestones," the title track, I really used that form. . . . The challenge here, when you work in the modal way, is to see how inventive you can become melodically. It's not like when you base stuff on chords, and you know at the end of the thirty-two bars that the chords have run out and there's nothing to do but repeat what you've done with variations. I was moving away from that and into more melodic ways of doing things. And in the modal way I saw all kinds of possibilities.[12]

In other words, "Milestones" may be viewed as the first stage in the crystallization of the modal jazz style, which played an important part in freeing the improviser from the harmonic constraints of bebop.

KIND OF BLUE AND ITS AFTERMATH

Before we proceed to the next recording of "Walkin'," recorded live in Stockholm on March 22, 1960, a brief characterization and evaluation of *Kind of Blue*, recorded the previous year, is essential.

The *Kind of Blue* recordings represent the crystallization of a new musical dialect—modal jazz—and serve as models for much of the modal jazz of the 1960s. The five pieces composed by Davis for *Kind of Blue*[13] use modes (instead of chords) as the harmonic underpinning for creating melodic lines.[14] This strategy focuses the improviser's attention on horizontal (melodic) thinking, as opposed to the vertical (chordal) thinking of the bebop-oriented improviser, who runs up and down the rapidly changing chords. The desire to create an uninterrupted melodic line, free of harmonic constraints, led to this scalar-horizontal approach of modal jazz. Another trait of these pieces is their slow harmonic rhythm; each harmony remains unchanged for as long as two, four, eight, or more bars before a fresh chord brings a new harmonic atmosphere. In this way, the volatile harmonies of bebop, in which chords customarily change once or twice in a bar, are replaced by static, slow-moving harmonies, a basic feature of modal jazz. These slow-moving chordal successions result in an almost complete abandonment of functional harmony, which is controlled by a diatonic hierarchy, in which one chord leads inevitably to the next until the final resolution is reached. The nonfunctional harmonies in modal jazz themes do not exert a demanding pull toward a particular chordal resolution, thereby progressing more freely.

The years 1958 to 1960 witnessed additional explorations of the modal idiom by Davis in collaboration with Gil Evans. These explorations include several passages from the album *Porgy and Bess*,[15] recorded in 1958, after *Milestones* and foreshadowing *Kind of Blue*. Similar trends are found in *Sketches of Spain*,[16] recorded in November 1959 (after *Kind of Blue*) and March 1960.

In *Kind of Blue*, Davis is featured in the double role of composer and virtuoso improviser. It seems indeed strange that, despite the great success and popularity of these historic recordings, Davis made no effort to compose new pieces that could serve as a basis for modal jazz improvisation until 1965. Nevertheless, it must not be imagined that from 1959 to 1965 Davis abandoned modal jazz in all of its aspects. On the contrary, he adhered, in the main, to the principles laid down in *Kind of Blue*, the chief difference being in the *compositions* he chose for improvisatory treatment: old and new popular songs and instrumental pieces (some by Davis himself) prevalent among jazz musicians, i.e., standards. The material Davis used for his recordings after *Kind of Blue* was similar to what he used from 1948 to 1959, but the *treatment* of the material changed. In this way, *Kind of Blue* can be understood as a momentary thunderbolt that entered deep into the psyche of its composer, Miles Davis, and the artists who played with him, together with the musicians and music lovers who enjoyed this inspired performance. The increased freedom of the modal approach of *Kind of Blue*—in form, duration of chords, tonality, melody, and rhythm—were carried over to Davis's recordings in succeeding years.

"WALKIN'": MARCH 1960

A transcription by this writer of Davis's solo on the "Walkin'" recorded in Stockholm on March 22, 1960,[17] appears in Example 3. After the usual introduction and theme statement played by the entire ensemble, Davis embarks on a lengthy solo of 13 choruses, a large portion of which stems from a linear-horizontal conception. In the first three choruses Davis's somewhat bare accompaniment consists of bass and drums alone, without piano. In bars 1–4 of the first chorus, the repeated A♭s of the trumpet create the effect of a high-registered pedal point, which tends to obscure the blues harmonies underlining those bars. For the remainder of the first chorus and all of the second, the harmonies are hinted at by Davis's choice of notes, abetted by the bass line.[18] In the third chorus (with its upbeat), Davis seems to stray from the original key (F), improvising in G for the first four measures, thus forming a superimposition of G on F, with the bass remaining in F—as evidenced by the transcription of Chambers's bass line in Example 4. In measures 5 and 6 of the third chorus, Davis returns to the repeated A♭s with which he started the first chorus. These repeated A♭s do not outline the B♭7 chord of these measures in the vertical bebop manner of arpeggiation, and can instead be regarded as a unifying motive. They are followed in the next two bars by a phrase that is a close variant of the phrase that followed the repeated A♭s at the beginning of the first chorus. Especially because of this parallel between the first and third choruses, it may be concluded that the first half of the third chorus is chiefly horizontal whereas the second half is mainly vertical.

Example 3: "Walkin'": Miles Davis's solo. *Continued on next page.*

Transcribed by Alona Sagee

Example 3, continued

Example 4: "Walkin'": Excerpt from the bass part (sounding as written)

In the last quarter of the third chorus, pianist Wynton Kelly finally joins forces with the rhythm section by giving sporadic responses to the trumpet's clipped phrases. For a little more than half of the fourth chorus, Davis's main preoccupation is toying with the major and minor thirds above the tonic (as King Oliver did back in 1923 in "Dippermouth Blues"[19]). The minimalistic short phrases separated by long silences lead to an abrupt outburst in the form of an upward, rapidly executed, two-octave-long, unidentifiable scale, whose highest tone falls a half step at the end. This fourth chorus is the product of a freely used horizontal improvisatory concept. After the trumpet's "eruption" the piano responds, and from the fifth chorus onward the piano's presence is fully felt. At the beginning of the fifth chorus Davis returns to the thirds he toyed around with in the fourth chorus, and he echoes them an octave and a fifth higher than before. From this point on the improvised line winds its way down, using the tones of an F Dorian mode with a flatted fifth added for a bluesy flavor. In the last four bars of the fifth chorus the line becomes less horizontal, but as soon as the sixth chorus is reached, Davis plays a series of phrases that not only blur the barlines (especially in the first seven measures) but also lead a melodic-harmonic independent existence of their own. Wynton Kelly senses the tonal and rhythmic instability of Davis's line, and he too deviates from the conventional blues changes. In the seventh chorus Davis reestablishes the original key but remains with the modal-horizontal conception, except that now he ties himself down to one particular scale: the F pentatonic minor with an added flatted fifth (termed by many the *blues scale*). The eighth chorus starts with a reversion to less horizontal tendencies, but in its last four bars the horizontal concept returns with notes of longer duration, reminiscent of the long-held tones in chorus 6.

Chorus 9 consists of three four-bar phrases, with the effect of a thrice-stated riff. Each phrase is built from one relatively long note, preceded by two or more short ascending notes, and followed by one or two comparatively short notes. This riff is a variation of the phrase articulated twice in the second half of chorus 8, forming a continuity of melodic invention. In addition, the three long notes in chorus 9 are all A♭s, recalling the repeated A♭s at the start of chorus 1 and the fifth and sixth bars of chorus 3. In chorus 10, the first six bars of the trumpet line originate in a horizontal approach that scarcely reflects the background harmonies played by the bass and piano. However, in the seventh bar the improvisation draws closer to its harmonic support, and thirds play a more prominent role in the melodic line. Chorus 11 reverts to the minimalistic-horizontal style of choruses 4 and 6, with only a bare harmonic hint here and there. In chorus 12 Davis exploits the tones of the key of A♭ minor. As in chorus 9, and to a lesser extent in chorus 6, he builds chorus 12 from three similar four-bar phrases. The third phrase exhibits some similarities in rhythm and contour with the first two phrases and at the same time develops and completes the first two phrases. This form is analogous to the traditional vocalized blues pattern, where the first phrase is repeated with a small variation in the second set of four bars, concluding with a completing or contrasting third phrase in the last four bars. These motivic similarities from various choruses are a unifying element in Davis's entire solo.

Chorus 13 is a general return to the phrasing and atmosphere of chorus 1, reinforced by the fact that Wynton Kelly has dropped out again. Even the ubiquitously quoted phrase from "If I Love Again" (first appearing in the last bar of chorus 1 and the first bar of chorus 2) is not neglected.[20] Davis rounds off his creative spree by playing another four bars after the end of chorus 13, consisting of one long note preceded by two ascending shorter notes and followed by two shorter notes.

The above analysis demonstrates that by the time of the Stockholm concerts in March 1960, Davis's solo improvisations at times reflected their harmonic underpinnings with a high degree of fidelity and at other times practically ignored them (with all the intermediate stages well represented). His guiding principle for the invention of independent musical ideas seemed to lie in the direction of a linear-horizontal approach but could also extend back in the opposite direction, even to include quotes of vertically based tonal phrases from familiar music.

"WALKIN'": LESS AND LESS RESTRAINT

Davis recorded "Walkin'" twice on October 13, 1960, in two separate concerts at the Konserthuset in Stockholm.[21] The tempo in the earlier concert (♩ = 290) was substantially faster than the March 22 version (♩ = 172), and the later concert (♩ = 308) was even faster. Similarly, Davis's first solo is less restrained than the March 22 performance, especially in the last six of its 18 choruses; the later solo, 22 choruses in length, is even more daringly free, right from the start. Sometimes, in both concerts, he freely makes excursions into remote tonal areas, while his accompanists strive to follow him, or he invents independent phrases that seem to have little rhythmic or melodic connection with what he has previously played, while the harmonic accompaniment remains stubbornly within the framework of a blues in F. In both October 13 versions, as in the March 22 performance, the piano remains tacit until the fifth chorus, when Wynton Kelly joins the proceedings.

The first two choruses of Davis's "Walkin'" solo in the later concert of October 13 (see Example 5) illustrate the freedom with which he improvised at this stage of his development after *Kind of Blue*. The phrases that make up the first 10 measures of the solo are built from the following four tones: F, A♭, B♭, and B♮. These initial horizontally contrived phrases outline no conventional harmonies whatsoever but arouse in the listener a train of thought and musical association linked to the blues. B♮ achieves special prominence in these 10 measures because of its longer durations and its placement on accented beats. This pattern of emphasis includes the B♮ played on the eighth note before the half rest in the third measure; in swing phrasing, this note is accented. Another B♮ accentuated by Davis comes on the last quarter note of the tenth measure. Throughout these 10 measures, B♮ functions as a *central pitch*. The central pitch becomes the focal point toward which the subordinate tones of a phrase or group of phrases are attracted. Central pitches (which may be also viewed as melodic pedal points) are symptomatic of a linear-horizontal concept of improvising. The improviser, ab-

Transcribed by Alona Sagee

Example 5: "Walkin'": First two choruses of Miles Davis's solo

sorbed in weaving phrases around a central pitch, becomes less conscious of the harmonies of the piece, although he does not forget them.

After the 10 measures just described, there begins a long phrase consisting wholly of eighth notes, stretching without a break from the second half of measure 11 in the first chorus through the third quarter of measure 9 in the second chorus. At first this elongated phrase seems to be enveloped in an aura of rising and falling half tones. On closer scrutiny, it is found that the entire phrase contains 46 minor seconds, 23 major seconds, 7 minor thirds, and 3 major thirds. David Liebman, in his book *A Chromatic Approach to Jazz Harmony and Melody,*[22] devotes a chapter to interval categories of melodic improvisation and characterizes phrases built from major and minor seconds and thirds as follows:

> When placed together consecutively in a line, they exhibit certain strong tendencies; sinuous shape, smooth texture, a seemingly endless and hypnotic contour which resists cadential resolution, singability and the ability to expressively play these intervals easily.[23]

The phrase in Example 2d on page 59 of Liebman's book has characteristics similar to Davis's elongated phrase. Both phrases are examples of what Liebman terms "non-tonal chromaticism," explained by him as follows:

> Non-tonal chromaticism refers to melodic lines and harmonies that have no discernible key or root orientation. Melodic shapes are determined by intervallic choices. It may be possible to hear a temporary tonal center due to certain circumstances such as melodic leading tone activity; the convergence of two or more melodic lines; or some type of harmonic reinforcement accompanying the line. But by and large, non-tonal chromaticism is keyless.[24]

According to Liebman, devising improvised melodies from certain interval categories is an essential technique for producing nontonal, chromatic sound qualities, independent of harmonic sources. Davis's intervallic improvisation in the long phrase described above thus gives the impression of a nontonal chromatic sound. This impression is bolstered by the fast tempo, as well as the absence of piano accompaniment from these choruses, which diminishes the clear tonal references of the blues, intimated here by the bass alone.

Nontonal chromaticism gave jazz musicians in the 1960s a device for adding color and variety to improvisation and gave listeners an opportunity to accustom themselves to higher levels of dissonance. Here Liebman expands on nontonal chromaticism:

> This is truly what can be called *free* music. In this case, *free* means free of tonal references. Concepts of densities, relative speeds, coloristic effects and overall sound groups, in a sense, replace the conventional understandings of what is meant by melody, harmony and rhythm. In the 1960s, free music was widely explored by many musicians, each with a different slant to the general style, usually based on the rhythmic concept and instrumentation.[25]

Although Davis had expressed skepticism and even contempt for the free jazz played by Ornette Coleman, Don Cherry, and Cecil Taylor,[26] by the time of the October 1960 Stockholm concerts he apparently experienced "weak moments" in which he played free phrases such as the 10½-measure nontonal phrase just analyzed.

"WALKIN'" WITH THE NEW RHYTHM SECTION

In April 1961, six months after the October Stockholm concerts, the quintet recorded "Walkin'" at the Blackhawk club in San Francisco.[27] The melodic patterns in Davis's 19-chorus solo are by and large reminiscent of those heard in his October 1960 performances. Here it would seem Davis is making an elegant résumé of vocabulary patterns that characterized his improvisational language at this stage.[28]

After the Carnegie Hall concert of May 19, 1961,[29] no known Davis recordings of "Walkin'" exist until July 1963 in Antibes. In the interim Davis was largely unsatisfied with the personnel in his band,[30] and it is reasonable to assume that his improvisational phraseology in any performances of "Walkin'" continued in the same vein as in the April 1961 recording. In the early part of 1963, significant changes in the quintet's personnel had a marked influence on its leader. The new rhythm section—Tony Williams on drums, Herbie Hancock on piano, and Ron Carter on bass—aroused Davis from a relatively unfruitful four-year period, during which he composed no original music with the same promise as "Milestones" or *Kind of Blue*. The recording of "Walkin'" from the jazz festival at Antibes, France, on July 27, 1963,[31] spotlights the adventurousness of the young players. The confident spirit and enthusiasm of Tony Williams, the youngest member of the group, propelled the entire ensemble to new plateaus of invention and virtuosity. In fact, it was Williams who coaxed Davis to reintroduce "Milestones" (absent from the band's books since its recording in 1958) to the quintet's performing repertoire.[32]

In the Antibes recording of "Walkin'," Davis's 16-chorus solo is not readily identifiable as blues even to the most inveterate listener, and it requires an extraordinarily concentrated effort to count the bars and keep one's bearings. Melodically and rhythmically his phrases have scarcely any connection to a blues harmonic framework, as evidenced in Example 6, a transcription of the third and fifth choruses. If up to the beginning of the 1960s Davis's approach was an intermingling of vertically and horizontally conceived patterns or phrases—with a gradual proportional growth of the horizontal ones—by July 1963 the horizontal concept was by far the dominant one.

Though freshly stimulated and liberated, Davis can still be identified by certain "trademarks," which took shape mainly after *Kind of Blue* and are closely affiliated with the horizontal approach. From 1963 on, these trademarks—including the sound of his horn, patterns heard in earlier solos, sections of nontonal chromaticism, phrases that begin and end in unexpected places, glissandi, and indeterminate pitches—are heard more frequently, boldly permeating his solos with pervasive freedom.

Example 6: "Walkin'": Third and fifth choruses of Miles Davis's solo

In 1964, Davis's live recorded performances of "Walkin'"[33] adhere to his recordings of the previous two years, but with a still freer approach and a more emphatic disregard for the restrictions of conventional jazz. When Wayne Shorter became Davis's regular saxophonist in September 1964, the quintet made another step in the direction of free jazz. Although Davis spoke disparagingly about free jazz and its practitioners, his solos on "Walkin'" in 1963 and 1964 come closer to free jazz than he would care to admit.

LIVE AT THE PLUGGED NICKEL: STREAM-OF-CONSCIOUSNESS PLAYING

The "breakthrough" in which the quintet's concepts were fully realized was eventually reached in the *Live at the Plugged Nickel* recordings of December 1965.[34] The freedom of the solos and accompaniment in these recordings has been likened to an unhampered stream of consciousness.[35] These words of Wayne Shorter, as reported by Todd Coolman in 1995, help illuminate this venture into stream-of-consciousness playing:

> We knew that everyone was taking a lot of chances. We were chance taking anyway but we were taking some *real* chances now. I would hear Herbie and myself at certain junctures, struggling with something. Miles would be grappling with something and when we finished, it was like he came out of the boxing ring but something

> refreshing was going on. The "arrival" [of the quintet's concepts] started to happen at the Plugged Nickel and we couldn't stop that arrival and everybody was celebrating individually in their own way.[36]

The *E.S.P.* album, recorded in January 1965 and consisting entirely of originals by the quintet members,[37] laid some of the groundwork for the burst of freedom at the Plugged Nickel performances 11 months later. Davis's sidemen (Shorter, Carter, Hancock, and Williams), by dint of their ages and musical backgrounds, were all closer to the avant-garde than Davis, their leader.[38] Bearing this in mind, we may describe the pieces in *E.S.P.* as fulfilling a double function. On the one hand, they reflect the avant-garde leanings of the new quintet and prophesy the unrestrained freedom of the *Plugged Nickel* performances.[39] On the other hand, they serve as a continuation and renewal of the horizontal modality that had its prototype in "Milestones" and *Kind of Blue*.

In his original pieces for *E.S.P.*, Shorter demonstrated a desire he shared with Davis to depart from typical standards as a basis for jazz improvisation. Here is Shorter, again quoted by Coolman:

> We started getting out of the chord structure thing or Tin Pan Alley, or whatever [Davis] called standards, and he heard some of the stuff that I was writing and then he started recording them and he wouldn't change *anything* because Miles was known for changing a lot of people's stuff. He would say later on, like in his book, 'There was no need to change anything on that.' He took a fancy to the way it was pointing. The music was pointing somewhere and he "got it." I think it got him more on track from where they were taking off from on *Kind of Blue*.[40]

As early as "Milestones" and *Kind of Blue,* Davis's compositions—with features such as oscillating movement of chords, absence of functional harmony, parallelism of chords,[41] quartal harmony, and ambiguous tonality—were designed to avoid the typical sound of the Tin Pan Alley genre, and to provide a foundation for a freer and fresher modernistic approach with an "unencumbered free-flowing sound."[42] The musical features of *Kind of Blue* serve as connecting threads, developing and evolving until reaching their ultimate intensification in *E.S.P.* and the Plugged Nickel recordings.

"WALKIN'" AT THE PLUGGED NICKEL

Two versions of "Walkin'" appear in the CD set *Miles Davis: The Complete Live at the Plugged Nickel 1965*; the first recorded December 22, 1965, and the second the following night. In both of his solos, Davis does not strictly adhere to the original 12-bar blues form from a rhythmic or harmonic standpoint. Alterations of the formal structure during Davis's solos occur by spontaneous agreement of the quintet members taking cues from each other. Davis plays in an unrestrained manner, without having to conform to any particular progression, since the quintet members do not follow the blues or any other preconceived harmonies.[43] Hancock's minimalistic comping during the first two choruses of Davis's solos does not disclose any functional harmonic blues progressions. Later, when his fill-ins intensify, Hancock's accompaniment is still estranged from standard blues harmonies. Davis is treading on the borderline between traditional jazz and free jazz, peering over that borderline to see what he can snatch from the free side before scurrying back to the border.

Because of the breakneck tempo (♩ = 308 the first night and ♩ = 336 the second night) and the disregard for the original harmonic changes, the only recognizable feature of "Walkin'" is the 12-bar length of its chorus—and even that cannot always be depended upon. The downbeat of a new chorus is usually marked by a signal such as a cymbal crash, a "plink" on the piano, or Davis starting a phrase, especially on the second night. In the first 10 choruses, thanks to Davis's phrasing, the units of 12 bars are distinguishable, though not readily. During the 11th and 12th choruses, however, long asymmetric stretches of nontonal chromaticism obscure the steady beat, as well as the initial beat of the 12th chorus. In the last four bars of the 12th chorus, a pause in Davis's solo shifts the focus to Williams, who plays a drum passage extending a measure and a half past the point where the 12th chorus is supposed to have ended. One can retroactively confirm the spot where the delayed 13th chorus begins after hearing Davis play the pitch F^1 (2:07)[44] on the downbeat of the 14th chorus. This F^1 is just one of many eighth notes constituting an unbroken chromatic passage, but its precise location appears to intentionally denote the beginning of the 14th chorus. Players at this level are flexible and adaptable enough to "swallow up" that extra beat and a half without losing their bearings. The location of the downbeat of the 15th chorus is not completely clear. Davis pauses for approximately eight measures, from the fifth bar to the last beat of the 14th chorus, instead of the first of the 15th, thus appearing to lose a beat—not an unlikely mishap at this dizzying tempo. Nevertheless, everything seems to fall into place in the 15th chorus. After the start of the 16th chorus (2:23) the formal structure is altered by the group's stream of consciousness, and an atmospheric change is felt as they enter into half time (2:34).[45] During this passage, which lasts over a minute (2:34–3:42), Davis plays uncomplicated, relatively tonal phrases, and the entire quintet creates a "bluesy" tinge of hard bop and soul as the mood calms down. After the tempo returns to its former pace (3:42), Davis's solo continues and the 12-bar units can once again be followed for at least the next four choruses (until 4:20). After this point Davis's solo provides no cues to follow and has no real direction or form, dissolving at its end into a kind of "fade out."

Although "Walkin'" is originally a blues in F, Davis by now no longer relied on the tonality of F major and the functional harmonic blues progression, as he had in his first recording of "Walkin'," in 1954. From 1963 onward, his improvisations on "Walkin'" used F as the basic tone, open to any type of scale or mode. Davis's Plugged Nickel solos consist mostly of nontonal chromatic passages and free-jazz-influenced textures, intermittently returning to the more tonal patterns of his vocabulary. The table in Example 7 charts the occurrences of nontonal and tonal improvised phrases in Davis's second "Walkin'" solo at the Plugged Nickel.

1. START

Chorus	Beginning of 12-bar Units	Tonal	Non-Tonal
1	0:15	0:15	
		↓	
		0:18	0:18
			↓
2	0:23		↓
3	0:32		↓
			↓
4	0:40	0:40	0:40
		↓	
		0:47	0:47
5	0:49		↓
6	0:58		↓
			↓
7	1:06	1:06	1:06
		↓	
		1:10	1:10
			↓
8	1:15	1:15	1:15

2. CONTINUATION

Chorus	Beginning of 12-bar Units	Tonal	Non-Tonal
8	1:15	1:15	1:15
		↓	
9	1:23	↓	
10	1:32	↓	
		1:34	1:34
			↓
11	1:40		↓
12	1:49		↓
			↓
13	1:58 "late" 6 beats	1:58	1:58
		↓	
		2:03	2:03
14	2:07		↓
			↓
15	2:15 "early" 1 beat	2:15	2:15
		↓	
		2:20	2:20
16	2:23		↓
			↓
		2:30	2:30

Example 7: "Walkin'": Tonal and nontonal passages in Miles Davis's solo. *Continued on next page.*

Chorus	Beginning of 12-bar Units	Tonal	Non-Tonal
		2:30 ↓	2:30
		2:46	2:46 ↓
		2:51 ↓	2:51
		3:00	3:00 ↓
		3:07 ↓	3:07
		3:36	3:36

Chorus	Beginning of 12-bar Units	Tonal	Non-Tonal
		3:36	3:36 ↓
	3:46	3:46 ↓	3:46
		3:50	3:50 ↓
	3:55		
	4:03		
	4:12	4:12 ↓	4:12
		4:20	4:20 ↓
			4:39

Example 7, *continued*

The table has four columns. The first column has the numbers of the choruses through the 16th chorus. After the 16th the numbers do not appear, because of the vagueness of the 12-bar units described above. The second column has the CD time markings for the beginning of each 12-bar unit of the solo. The third and fourth columns graphically represent the amounts of time (including rests) occupied by Davis's tonal and nontonal passages.

"WALKIN'": THE LAST RECORDING

After the Plugged Nickel engagement, nearly two years elapsed before Davis's next and final recording of "Walkin'," at a Paris concert on November 6, 1967.[46] If the 1965 recordings still retained some faintly recognizable links to tradition, the 1967 recording, whose breathless tempo matches the second Plugged Nickel version, put the finishing touches on the demolition of those links. Davis's short solo (under one and a half minutes) consists exclusively of nontonal chromatic passages, leaving no gaps for his former intermittent returns to a tonal center. If occasionally one hears a nontonal phrase containing a briefly sounded F, this event hardly serves to establish a tonal center. In the first part of the solo, one can detect hints offered by the drums, piano, or trumpet marking the downbeats of 12-bar segments. Later on these hints become more vague, and the formal outline loses its distinctness. The solos of Williams, Hancock, and Shorter, who follow Davis, do not conform to any preconceived melodic, rhythmic, or harmonic plan whatsoever and are actually movements of a collectively composed musical work reflecting the group's stream of consciousness.

To complement Davis's unrelenting nontonal chromaticism in this final 1967 version of "Walkin'," Hancock's piano fill-ins (as in the Plugged Nickel recordings) lose all resemblance to the jazz-blues voicings he used to back Davis in previous versions. Hancock fragmentarily interjects sonorities with unresolved dissonant qualities, such as a biting minor second (F and F♯ sounded together at the beginning of Davis's solo, and a trill from these two notes toward the end of the solo) and harmonies built by combining a perfect fourth, a minor second, and another perfect fourth (D♯–G♯–A–D), moving the whole construction up two semitones and then back down in parallel motion (at 1:03). These types of sonorities, while detached from traditional tertially built chords, have vague tonal tendencies, and their artistic effect is of a succession of colors, each with an autonomous quality. Their rhythmic placement follows the player's momentary, instinctive reactions to the circumstances. Hancock treats the listener to a rare assortment of original and piquant resonances that complement Davis's nontonal playing to perfection.

This 24th and ultimate recording of "Walkin'" marks the first time in which, during portions of Shorter's and Hancock's solos, the improvisers are left alone to play a free interlude of significant length, without having to adjust to any musical presence besides their own consciousness and imagination. The recapitulation of the theme at the end of the recording is played at a considerably slower tempo (♩ = 268) than the beginning, another indication of the increased performing freedom achieved by Miles Davis and his coplayers with their modal approach.

NOTES

1. Jack Chambers, *Milestones 2: The Music and Times of Miles Davis to 1960* (Toronto: University of Toronto Press, 1985), 62–63.

2. See Tom Lord, *The Jazz Discography,* CD-ROM (West Vancouver, BC, Canada: Lord Music Reference, 2004). Not all 24 versions of "Walkin'" are discussed in this article.
3. All the music examples are in concert key. Example 1 is based on the version in *The Real Book*, 5th ed., editor(s) not listed, facts of publication not given [199?].
4. *Walkin',* Prestige PRCD-7076-2. Includes besides Davis: Horace Silver, J. J. Johnson (listed as Jay Jay Johnson on the 1954 LP), Percy Heath, Lucky Thompson, and Kenny Clarke.
5. Ian Carr, *Miles Davis: A Biography* (New York: Morrow and Co., 1982), appendix A.
6. John Szwed, *So What: The Life of Miles Davis* (London: Arrow, 2003), 113–14.
7. *Miles Davis, The Legendary Masters Unissued or Rare, 1956–59*, Rare CD09. Includes besides Davis: John Coltrane, Red Garland, Paul Chambers, and Philly Joe Jones.
8. *Miles Davis All Stars, Live in 1958—59,* Jazz Band EBCD 2101-2. Includes besides Davis: John Coltrane, Bill Evans, Paul Chambers, and Philly Joe Jones.
9. Bill Evans had a large share in shaping modal jazz concepts in this period.
10. "Milestones" is characterized by slow, static harmonic rhythm and by the exploitation of modes instead of chords as a support for melodic creation.
11. Ekkehard Jost, *Free Jazz* (New York: Da Capo Press, 1981), 18.
12. Miles Davis, *Miles: The Autobiography,* with Quincy Troupe (New York: Simon and Schuster, 1989), 225.
13. It has been fairly well established that Bill Evans wrote "Blue in Green" (from *Kind of Blue*) even though Davis took the composer credit.
14. Ekkehard Jost states in *Free Jazz* (New York: Da Capo Press, 1981), 21, the following: "In March and April 1959, about a year after *Milestones*, the second LP representative of the early phase of modal playing was recorded, *Kind of Blue*. . . . The exemplary modal pieces are *So What* and *Flamenco Sketches*. But even *All Blues* and *Freddie Freeloader*—although on the 12-bar blues pattern—bear the stamp of modal playing too; there are no harmonic accessories like substitute chords, secondary dominants, etc., but only the unadorned blues pattern of three four-bar sequences."
15. Columbia CK 40647. "Summertime," "It Ain't Necessarily So," and "I Loves You Porgy" all contain sections in which Gil Evans replaces the original Gershwin harmonizations with ostinati and modally orientated, slowly changing (even static) chords.
16. Columbia CK 40578. A lengthy drone in "Saeta," which creates an effect of static harmony, and also the two oscillating chords in the accompaniment of "Solea," above which Davis plays a modal improvisation, are cases in point.
17. *Miles Davis in Stockholm 1960 Complete,* Dragon DRCD 228. Includes besides Davis: John Coltrane, Wynton Kelly, Paul Chambers, and Jimmy Cobb.
18. In the first half of the second chorus (including the half-measure upbeat) Davis plays some short, unconnected, hackneyed bits of popular tunes, "tongue in cheek" fashion. See David Baker, *The Jazz Styles of Miles Davis* (Miami, FL: Studio 224, 1980), 15, for the quotes in Miles Davis's improvisations.
19. Two recordings from 1923 of this piece by Oliver are in the LP (first) and CD (second) editions of the *Smithsonian Collection of Classic Jazz*. See Frank Tirro, *Jazz, a History*, 2nd ed. (New York: Norton, 1993), 86, for a transcription and a discussion of Oliver's solo from the LP edition, Smithsonian P6 11891.
20. See the last two notes in bar 10 and the first three notes in bar 11 of chorus 13, and also the two upbeat notes and the first three notes of chorus 2.

21. See Tom Lord, *Jazz Discography* (West Vancouver: Lord Music Reference, c. 1992–present), vol. 5. Includes besides Davis: Sonny Stitt, Wynton Kelly, Paul Chambers, and Jimmy Cobb.
22. David Liebman, *A Chromatic Approach to Jazz Harmony and Melody* (Rottenburg, Germany: Advance Music, 1991).
23. Ibid., 58.
24. Ibid., 30.
25. Ibid., 30.
26. Jack Chambers, *Milestones 2: The Music and Times of Miles Davis to 1960* (Toronto: University of Toronto Press, 1985), 5, 18–24.
27. *Miles Davis: In Person Friday and Saturday Nights at the Blackhawk, Complete*, Sony 14-472608-10. Includes besides Davis: Hank Mobley, Wynton Kelly, Paul Chambers, and Jimmy Cobb.
28. See Paul F. Berliner on the subject of figures, patterns, and phrases in *Thinking in Jazz: The Infinite Art of Improvisation* (Chicago: University of Chicago Press, 1994), 229.
29. "Walkin'" appears on *Live Miles: More Music from the Legendary Carnegie Hall Concert*, Columbia CK 40609.
30. See Jack Chambers, *Milestones 2: The Music and Times of Miles Davis to 1960* (Toronto: University of Toronto Press, 1985), 35–50.
31. *Miles Davis in Europe*, Sony SRCS 9303.
32. See Jack Chambers, *Milestones 2: The Music and Times of Miles Davis to 1960* (Toronto: University of Toronto Press, 1985), 56. This return to "Milestones" verifies Todd Coolman's observation in "The Miles Davis Quintet of the Mid-1960s: Synthesis of Improvisational and Compositional Elements" (Ph.D. diss., New York University, 1997), 5: "Kind of Blue seems to have been the earliest indication of the direction that Davis would pursue in the mid-1960s with his second great quintet."
33. Such as in *Miles Davis: The Complete Concert, 1964*, Columbia/Legacy C2K 48821; *Miles in Tokyo*, Sony SRCS 9112; and *Miles Davis in Berlin*, Sony SRCS 9304.
34. *Live at the Plugged Nickel* was drawn from three sets played on December 22, 1965, and four sets played the following night at the Plugged Nickel in Chicago. "Walkin'" was played both nights. All seven sets were recorded live by CBS Records, but the complete recordings were not released in the United States until 1995, as part of an 8-CD set, *Miles Davis: The Complete Live at the Plugged Nickel, 1965*, Columbia CXK 66955/67095.
35. See Todd Coolman, "The Miles Davis Quintet of the Mid-1960s" (Ph.D. diss., New York University, 1997), 19–20.
36. Ibid., 19.
37. Columbia/Legacy CK 46863. The titles of the pieces are "E.S.P." and "Iris" (composed by Shorter), "R.J," "Eighty One," and "Mood" (composed by Carter); "Little One" (composed by Hancock); and "Agitation" (composed by Davis).
38. See Jack Chambers, *Milestones 2: The Music and Times of Miles Davis to 1960* (Toronto: University of Toronto Press, 1985), 70–71.
39. The album *E.S.P.* was recorded in January 1965, and *Live at the Plugged Nickel* was recorded in December 1965. There were no intervening recording sessions to dull the impression of the *E.S.P.* pieces before the Plugged Nickel engagement began.

40. Todd Coolman, "The Miles Davis Quintet of the Mid-1960s" (Ph.D. diss., New York University, 1997), 24.
41. One outcome of nonfunctional harmony in modal jazz is the phenomenon of parallelism, in which one chord proceeds to the next with all its tones moving in tandem. This type of motion is found, for example, in the parallel chords played by the piano and winds in the modally based pieces "Milestones" (from *Milestones*) and "So What" (from *Kind of Blue*).
42. Mark Gridley, *Jazz Styles: History and Analysis*, 3rd ed. (Englewood Cliffs, NJ: Prentice Hall, 1988), 304.
43. See Henry Martin, "The Nature of Recomposition: Miles Davis and 'Stella by Starlight,'" *Annual Review of Jazz Studies* 9, 77–92. Martin shows that Davis's four-chorus "Stella by Starlight" solo, played just before "Walkin'" on the same set discussed here (first set on December 23, 1965, at the Plugged Nickel), features an evolving group-improvisatory technique, moving over the course of the solo from paraphrase to variation to recomposition. The extremely loose melodic, harmonic, and rhythmic treatment of the original tune, especially in Davis's last chorus, is similarly evident in "Walkin'."
44. The time markings that appear in parentheses from here onward are CD markings.
45. The tempo in this section is not exactly half time but a little slower (♩=160).
46. *The Paris Concert*, Suisa JZCD 341.

BLUESVILLE: THE JOURNEY OF SONNY RED

Anders Svanoe

The first time I heard Sonny Red on record, I wondered, "Who is this guy?" Luckily for me, I had stumbled on Curtis Fuller's *New Trombone*, which started my 12-year (and counting) crusade for Sonny Red (a.k.a. Sylvester Kyner). That record really caught my attention, since I had never before heard that much trombone and alto saxophone pairing on the front line. But there was something almost suspicious in how these two masterful musicians blended and embellished every note together as if they were one. It seemed they knew each other well. Almost too well. Red's organic sound on the alto saxophone was a perfect match for Curtis Fuller. I couldn't explain why I liked it so much, other than to say it was captivating, heartfelt, and *real*. Imperfectly perfect, if you can say that.

In the following weeks I looked for additional record dates that featured Sonny Red but found very few sessions available on CD. Not even *Out of the Blue*, perhaps his finest effort, was available in the U.S. Now Red's albums are finally resurfacing on CD and are beginning to attract positive attention. When these albums first came out in the late 1950s and early 1960s, they were sadly overlooked. This was a common problem for bebop alto players recording in the 1950s: there were just too many other great alto players recording a similar type of music, and Red's style somehow got lost in the mix. Had he recorded the same music 10 or 20 years later, would the reviews have been different?

Down Beat reviews of Red's early work on Blue Note, Savoy, and Jazzland usually got caught up in comparisons with Charlie Parker or Sonny Stitt, instead of assessing Red on his own merits. Pete Welding writes in his review of *Out of the Blue*, "Red merely uses Parker's mannerisms in his playing without having integrated them into an overall organic conception. . . . It's as if his sole criterion in the employment of Parker phrases in his improvising is that such and such a phrase fits over this particular chord, this line of Bird's over this chordal sequence. . . . At times, however, he gets a sound amazingly like Parker's, much closer, in fact, than Stitt has ever been able to get."[1]

Other *Down Beat* reviews from this period compared Red with Parker more favorably, and hinted at Red's promise as an alto saxophonist. John A. Tynan wrote in his review of Tommy Flanagan's *Jazz . . . It's Magic!* that "[Red] is revealed as a strongly assertive Bird-follower whose forceful, if not particularly independent, solos are carried on a tone not so tortured as some of his better known contemporaries."[2] In the review of Curtis Fuller's *New Trombone*, Don Gold wrote: "Kyner is a Bird-calling shouter, with fierce drive and emotional strength."[3]

Not until the late 1960s, after the ranks of Bird disciples had thinned, did Red garner favorable notice from the jazz critics. In his 1968 *Down Beat* review of Donald Byrd's *Blackjack*, Harvey Pekar wrote: "Charlie Parker obviously had a strong influence on Kyner, but it's also clear that he has developed his own style. His playing is at once gutty and plaintive. . . . His work is full of fresh and attractive melodic ideas, and well paced. He's an admirable musician—a jazzman whose playing is strong, imaginative and tasteful."[4] Finally a record reviewer was giving Sonny Red credit for being his own man. A recent entry on Sonny Red in the *Virgin Encyclopedia of Jazz* sums up how a musician such as Red should be viewed today: "A vigorous soloist with an inventive flair, Kyner's recordings suggest that his reputation deserves reevaluation."[5]

Sonny Red was a jazz survivor. Despite the extreme hardships he faced, Red still produced one of the most distinctive sounds I've heard on the alto saxophone. And to these ears, his saxophone sound is brought most sharply into focus through his ballad performances. Ira Gitler best sums up my feelings for Sonny Red in his liner notes to *The Mode*: "But then whatever Sonny Red does is authentic, for this is no jive cat out there looking for a gimmick. He has a flair for picking good old and new tunes which have not been overdone; his modal moments are thoughtfully taken; and when he plays the blues, as on 'Ko-kee,' he illustrates the statement that says, 'Jazz is not only a music but a way of life.'"

ORAL HISTORY

The interviews for this oral history are listed below. All the interviews were conducted by phone, with three exceptions, for which the interview location is noted. The interviewees are grouped according to where they were primarily in contact with Sonny Red. James "Beans" Richardson and Johnnie Garry, though they were very helpful, are not directly quoted in the oral history. Family members are indicated by their relationship with Red. The musicians are listed with their primary instrument. The Red quotations come from a lecture he gave on September 9, 1978, as part of a series at the University of Connecticut called *Black Experience in the Arts*. The Donald Byrd segments come from a 2003 letter to Nicole Kyner.

Detroit
Malvin McCray (saxophonist), 9/6/00 and 1/30/01
James "Beans" Richardson (bassist), 12/9/01, Detroit
Charles Boles (pianist), 6/19/02
Claude Black (pianist), 9/20/05

Detroit and New York
Yusef Lateef (saxophonist), 3/1/98 and 6/26/02
Barry Harris (pianist), 3/24/98

Curtis Fuller (trombonist), 10/20/99, Daleville Hotel, New York
Kiane Zawadi (Bernard McKinney) (euphoniumist), 11/15/99
Tommy Flanagan (pianist), 11/20/99
Phil Lasley (saxophonist), 5/21/00 and 5/23/00
Frank Gant (drummer), 6/20/02
Frank Foster (saxophonist), 7/11/02
Charles McPherson (saxophonist), 7/17/02
Louis Hayes (drummer), 9/4/02

New York
Jimmy Heath (saxophonist), 5/21/98
Art Zimmerman (record producer and owner, Zim Records), 3/8/99
Dave Bailey (drummer, Jazzmobile director), 3/24/99
Talib Kibwe (saxophonist), 9/2/99
Johnnie Garry (Jazzmobile historian), 4/6/99
James Spaulding (saxophonist), 10/20/99, Jazz Standard, New York
Orrin Keepnews (record producer and cofounder, Riverside Records), 2/16/00
Cedar Walton (pianist), 7/3/02

Family: Detroit and New York
Nicole Kyner (daughter), 1/10/02
James Kiner (brother), 6/12/02 and 6/16/02
Roberta Marie Leach (sister), 6/16/02
Elena Knox (ex-wife), 6/18/02
Jaffiria Leach-Orr (niece), 4/15/03
Sheila Kiner (niece), 9/14/05

Dodge City: From the Mississippi Delta to Detroit, 1932–57

Sylvester Kyner, later known as Sonny Red, was born December 17, 1932, in Belzoni, Mississippi, to Lottie Lee McAfee-Kiner (1909–89) and Jeff Kiner (?–1937). Sylvester had four siblings—Ira Lee (1928–85), Roberta Marie (1929–), Rodell (1930–2003), and James (1934–2004)—but he was the only family member whose last name was spelled with a "y," as verified on his birth certificate. The first four years of his life were spent with his family in Humphreys County, Mississippi. In the spring of 1936, lack of educational opportunities and poor living conditions compelled Lottie and her five children to board a Greyhound bus and flee north to Detroit, Michigan, where they moved in with Lottie's sister Ira Lee Cox-Frederick (1902–89) at 8630 Beaubien. Jeff Kiner followed his wife and family shortly afterward, getting a job with the Levine Waste Paper Company, but he died a few months later at the age of 29. According to Red's ex-wife, Elena Knox, Red believed that the cause of his father's death was pneumonia resulting from poor working conditions on the docks. At some point in the late 1930s, the family moved to 9198 Goodwin. Once settled in Detroit, the Kiner family still found life challenging. Working several jobs while taking care of five children was very difficult for Lottie Lee McAfee-Kiner, but with hard work and extreme determination, she was able to successfully raise her family.

Sonny Red

I'm from the rural Mississippi. Like Congo Square in New Orleans and Mississippi is coming right up from the Delta, so to speak. We had all the street singers, the guitar players, and minstrel shows. I got music from the street, which is how most composers get it from. I moved to Detroit when I was four.

Roberta Marie Leach

We lived by a river, out in the country, when we lived in Mississippi, right across from Louisiana. I remember we had to take a boat to get to school, where there were crocodiles, snakes, and crayfish. But my dad loved to hunt, he was a hunter, and he would take people out hunting. And my mother said, "Look, I got to get

Figure 1: Sonny Red as a young boy. (Courtesy Roberta Marie Leach)

out of here!" At that time, we didn't even have any friends to play with. So we moved to Detroit in the spring of 1936. I remember that trip because I was holding Sylvester's hand while we crossed the street in Cincinnati. We had never seen a streetcar before, and we were almost killed. Oh, I'm glad we left.

Jeff Kiner came to Detroit about a month after my mother, and he got a job with the Levine Waste Paper Company. He was a couple of years older than my mother. We didn't know a lot about him. We didn't even know the kin people on his side. Anyway, he died of pneumonia.

My mother had asthma. My father would bring her washing and ironing, and when we came to Detroit, my mother worked for a Mr. and Mrs. Gibson in Grosse Pointe. They were artists, I know. My mother did her personal ironing and my aunt, Ira Lee Cox-Frederick, did the cooking.

James Kiner

All five of us were born in Mississippi. I was probably three when we came to Detroit. That was in 1936. I have few recollections of those days except the things that were told to me by my sister or my mother. We came to Detroit by Greyhound bus. It was a pretty rough trip with five kids, you know?

Nicole Kyner

My grandmother, my nana Lottie Lee, pretty much ran away from her husband, Jeff Kiner. She realized that her kids weren't going to get educated down in Mississippi. She'd only had an eighth-grade education. Lottie saved up enough pennies—she kept them in a flour sack—to move up with her sister, who lived up in Detroit. So, she got her kids on a bus and went as far north as they could go, which was Detroit, because she knew somebody. It was just a flight sort of thing. I always thought that was such a brave thing to do, to just get up and leave.

As I said, my nana left for Detroit without her husband. But he came back up to Detroit, especially when he heard, somehow heard, that she had a house. Lottie was doing well in Detroit because she was a domestic, a house cleaner. But there was some to-do about Jeff coming up since everything was going so well. There wasn't a lot of talk about Jeff Kiner.

James Kiner

[Sonny and I] had a neat relationship. As kids we used to fight all the time, because I couldn't fight with my older brothers! Sylvester was only about a year and some months older than me. But later on, and especially when I came into the service, we got along pretty well. I could talk to him about things, serious things, and he seemed to listen a lot.

I remember living on Goodwin; that's where we spent most of our time as kids. This would have been in the late 1930s or early 1940s. I have the most memories from Goodwin. Curtis Fuller used to live over us on Goodwin. I think he was a foster child for a while. He lived with Oscar and Ella Johnson, who lived over us

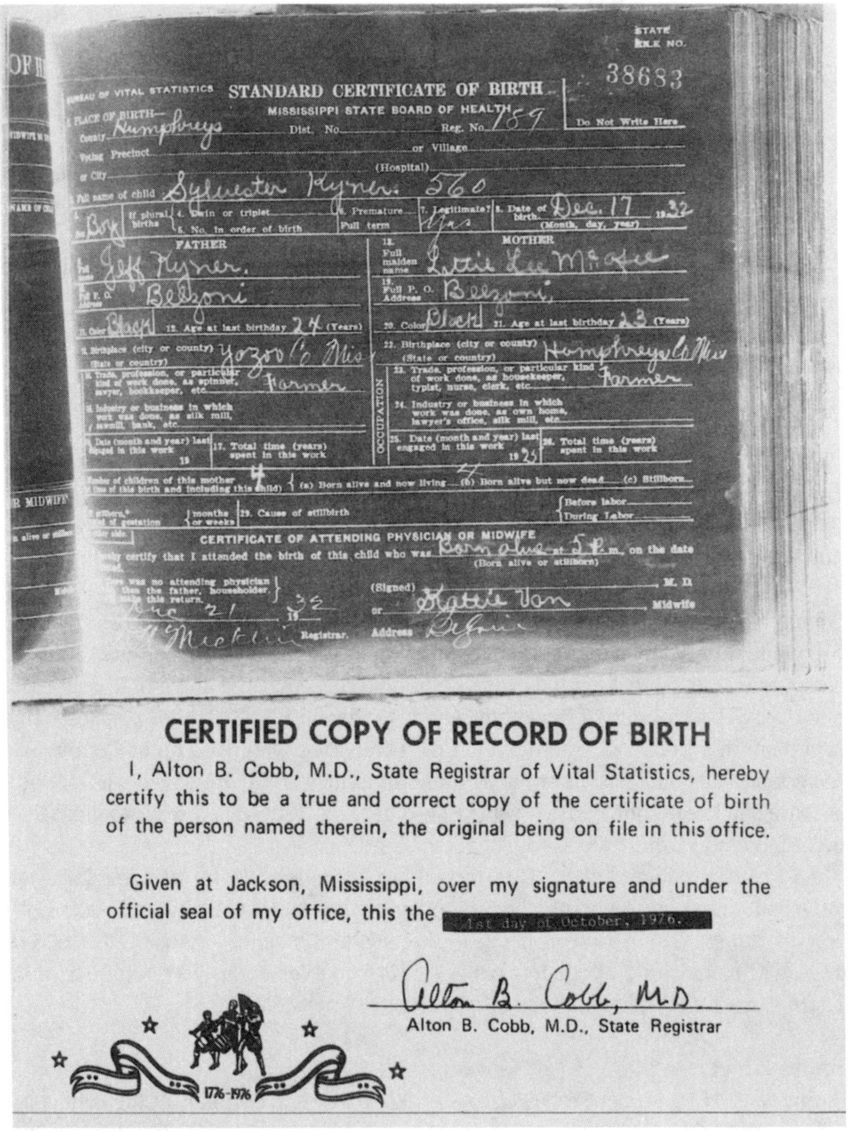

BUREAU OF VITAL STATISTICS STANDARD CERTIFICATE OF BIRTH

MISSISSIPPI STATE BOARD OF HEALTH

STATE FILE NO. 38683

Do Not Write Here

1. PLACE OF BIRTH— County Humphreys Dist. No. Reg. No. 789

Voting Precinct or Village

or City (Hospital)

2. Full name of child Sylvester Kyner. 560

3. Sex Boy | If plural births 4. Twin or triplet 5. No. in order of birth | 6. Premature Full term | 7. Legitimate? Yes | 8. Date of birth Dec. 17 1932 (Month, day, year)

FATHER

9. Full name Jeff Kyner.

10. Full P. O. Address Belzoni

11. Color Black 12. Age at last birthday 24 (Years)

Birthplace (city or county) (State or country) Yazoo Co Miss

Trade, profession, or particular kind of work done, as spinner, sawyer, bookkeeper, etc. Farmer

Industry or business in which work was done, as silk mill, sawmill, bank, etc.

Date (month and year) last engaged in this work 19 | 17. Total time (years) spent in this work

MOTHER

12. Full maiden name Lettie Lee McAfee

13. Full P. O. Address Belzoni

20. Color Black 21. Age at last birthday 23 (Years)

22. Birthplace (city or county) (State or country) Humphreys Co Miss

23. Trade, profession, or particular kind of work done, as housekeeper, typist, nurse, clerk, etc. Farmer

24. Industry or business in which work was done, as own home, lawyer's office, silk mill, etc.

25. Date (month and year) last engaged in this work 1925 | 26. Total time (years) spent in this work

OCCUPATION

Number of children of this mother at time of this birth and including this child) 4 (a) Born alive and now living (b) Born alive but now dead 2 (c) Stillborn

If stillborn, period of gestation months or weeks | 29. Cause of stillbirth | Before labor / During labor

CERTIFICATE OF ATTENDING PHYSICIAN OR MIDWIFE

I hereby certify that I attended the birth of this child who was Born alive at 5 P.m. on the date above stated. (Born alive or stillborn)

(Signed) M. D. or Hattie Van Midwife

Address Belzoni

Filed Dec 21 1932

McKee Registrar.

CERTIFIED COPY OF RECORD OF BIRTH

I, Alton B. Cobb, M.D., State Registrar of Vital Statistics, hereby certify this to be a true and correct copy of the certificate of birth of the person named therein, the original being on file in this office.

Given at Jackson, Mississippi, over my signature and under the official seal of my office, this the 1st day of October, 1976.

Alton B. Cobb, M.D.

Alton B. Cobb, M.D., State Registrar

1776-1976

Figure 2: Sonny Red's birth certificate.

for most of our young lives, when we were kids. I used to look out for them when my mother did day work. That's how I knew Curtis Fuller. In 1949 we moved up to 233 Leicester where my sister was pregnant with her daughter.

Curtis Fuller

I first met Sonny Red when we were kids in Detroit. We were about the same age. When my sister would come to the orphanage on Sundays to visit me, she would take me back to the old neighborhood. Sonny used to meet me in the backyard with his rust-colored knickers to play marbles. We'd be goofing around and he'd poke me in the eye or something. I always thought he was a bad little tough kid. Those freckles he had, that little look on his face, like he was a mean guy. I was afraid of him, you know? But we had this thing going on. As I grew up, and later on in life, we crossed paths again. We were always around each other. That's how I knew Sonny Red.

Frank Gant
I remember meeting Red when I was 9 or 10 years old, and I had a numbers route—I was picking up numbers. I was on the street around the corner from my house, and here's Red doing some hustling! I didn't know what he was doing, but he was hustling some kind of way. I ran into him and said, "Red, how you doing, man?" because I knew him from the neighborhood and his brothers.

Claude Black
Sonny had kind of a dry humor. He was funny. When he was young, he was the jitterbug. He used to walk with his finger pointed down to the ground. He was the jitterbug man. [*Laughs.*] Sonny came from this kind of wild neighborhood. Goodwin was a rough street; I remember that because I walked him halfway home one day.

James Kiner
Mr. [Elbon] Boals was our stepfather, my mother's longtime boyfriend. He was around when we lived on Goodwin, so before 1949. He died in 1958, I believe. They had a common-law marriage, because back in those years if people stayed together for a length of time—I don't know the exact length, maybe seven years—then they had a common-law marriage in Michigan. This law ended in 1957. I can remember that since I took some law classes.

Sheila Kiner
Mr. Boals was my granddad, as far as I knew. He would take us to the baseball games, and to the Easter parade, every Easter, he and my grandmother. It was really nice having him around. I think he was *the greatest*. It's hard coming into a family of mostly boys and being accepted by the boys. My dad [Ira Kiner, Red's brother] even liked him, and he didn't like anybody.

Elena Knox
After Jeff Kiner passed, Lottie married Mr. Boals, who I never met because he died before I knew Sonny. Mr. Boals was somebody Sonny really cared about. I don't remember him saying anything negative about the years that Mr. Boals was their stepfather. I mean Mr. Boals took on this whole gang of kids, you know? Mr. Boals stayed with his mother [Lottie] until he died. Nana was a strong, well-loved—I mean, just adored—person, who everybody gathered around. She was the glue that kept it all together. She was wonderful to me and was just as splendid as she could be.

Jaffiria Leach-Orr

I knew I was named after my grandfather Jeff, but I never made the connection that Mr. Boals was not Jeff. Mr. Boals for all purposes for me, was my grandfather, but I called him "Mr. Boals." I'm not calling him "granddaddy," I'm calling him "Mr. Boals." He was a wonderful grandfather, kind of quiet and reserved, always had a big smile, and he was an excellent cook. A lot of activity happened in the kitchen; it was a big kitchen where everyone sat at the kitchen table, did homework, and had meals. It was the center, where we all came together.

James Kiner

My mother did just about all that she could to keep the family afloat. She did day work, she worked in the factory a couple of years during the war, and she worked in one of the black nightclubs in the city, Lee's Sensation. She just about did it all—scrubbing floors, washing dishes. Ira, my oldest brother, always stayed in trouble. My mother spent a lot of her resources on him. I remember one time she worked three jobs just to keep him out of jail. He was getting into gang fights at that time. To tell you the truth, he was the oldest, but he was like the baby of the family. I think when my dad died, Ira was impacted the hardest. He would have been eight years old. He would have known my dad, you know?

Nicole Kyner

Everyone was close to Nana. She was the queen bee. I think they all knew how much they owed her, because she had done so much for them. The kids always had a place to come home to. My uncle James lived with her until he was 45 or so, and so did Marie for many years. I mean, everybody stayed there. Even my cousin Jaffiria, Marie's daughter, lived there. Nana was an extraordinarily gracious, generous, and quiet woman. She was a tremendous person.

Sylvester attended Sherrard Elementary School, beginning in 1938, and then Hutchins Middle School from 1944 to spring 1947. Music was common in the Kiner household. In 1949 the Kiners moved to 233 Leicester Court, near Goodwin.

Roberta Marie Leach

Oh, Sylvester loved music! I took piano lessons and started on the C melody sax in high school, and Sylvester picked it up from there. There's about six years' difference between the two of us.

Malvin McCray

Sonny grew up in a musical family. His mother had a piano in the house. She was a very nice and beautiful lady. Sonny had a beautiful family.

Claude Black

Detroit was such a stage for the music. The atmosphere was so beautiful at the time. You know, our parents were into the music. Our parents would come and

Figure 3: Roberta Marie Leach in the 1970s. (Courtesy Roberta Marie Leach)

hang out at the Royal Blue to hear King Porter and people like that. Sonny and all of us used to listen to all of those people.

James Kiner

How Sylvester got into the type of music he got into, I couldn't tell you, but I can tell you this: We had an older brother, Ira, who was out there during the so-called jitterbug days. The first jazz records that we had in the house were brought there by him. Like, Count Basie would have been one of the guys that he would have brought in, but there were others. It wasn't a lot of music but was probably good enough for it to have an effect on everybody.

Sylvester started playing at a very young age. He was probably in junior high, or maybe before that, as a matter of fact. My mother bought him a horn. Now we're talking about a very poor family. She found the bucks to buy the horn. I can recall her making him practice his C melody saxophone with a metronome, so she stuck with him on that. As a kid, Sylvester had a good soprano voice, when he used to sing in school. Early school, like K–6, and they used him on the stage singing in his soprano voice. Like "Ave Maria," which now, thinking of him, it's kinda funny. But he did have a good little voice then.

Curtis Fuller

Sonny played very good piano. I don't know where he got the training, but I'm certain it wasn't all by ear. You don't hear all that! Red came from a musical environment, like another musical family in town, the McKinneys: Bernard McKinney, Ray McKinney and Harold McKinney. All those players, they came to be the best, you know?

Elena Knox

The house that Sonny grew up in on Leicester Court was just darling. I remember visiting it, and it was immaculately kept. It was a little old-fashioned house, a single-family dwelling, and it was attached to another house that shared a common wall. Marie lived there, with Nana, his mom, Marie's daughter Jaffiria,

Figure 4: 233 Leicester Court, one of Red's early homes in Detroit. (Courtesy David Clements)

Sonny when he was there, and sometimes Rodell. His mother's sister, Auntie, lived next door.

Jaffiria Leach-Orr

As soon as you walk in the house there was a room, that used to be a dining room, but they changed it to a den or family room with a piano, stereo, china cabinet, a beautiful marble table, a couch, and olive green carpet. My grandmother always had shades of turquoise that would pick up that olive green; it was really a very pretty house. In the basement we had a Ping-Pong table and a dartboard. The upright piano was down in the basement; that's where the jam sessions were when I was a little kid. I used to be afraid of those old coal furnaces, booming in the background, so my mother and grandmother got a spinet piano in either 1963 or 1964—I still have it. They put the spinet upstairs, so I would be more comfortable practicing up there. But the upright piano stayed downstairs in the basement.

It's difficult to determine the source of Sylvester Kyner's nickname, "Sonny Red," but opinions point to "Sonny" as a common nickname for a boy growing up in the 1930s and 1940s and "Red" as a reference to Sylvester's natural red hair. For an industrial arts shop project in high school, he used a router to etch the name "Sonny Red" into a finished board. Professionally his name would continually be in flux. On his 1957 Savoy recording, he is identified as "Sonny Redd." On a Paul Quinichette recording from the same year, he becomes "Red Kyner." On a Curtis Fuller recording from the same year, liner note writer Robert Levin refers to him as "Sonny Red Kyner." Ira Gitler's liner notes refer to him as "Sylvester Kyner Junior." For the Blue Note and Jazzland dates, he is once again "Sonny Red." The Blue Note session charts submitted to the Library of Congress in his handwriting are signed "Sylvester Kyner." His Social Security application uses the original family spelling, "Sylvester Kiner." The charts in his sketchbook from the 1970s are signed "Sonny Redd," except for one entry with the single "d." The 1978 Jazzcraft date with Howard McGhee, the benefit concert flyer from December 1979, and a 1981 letter from the National Endowment for the Arts all use "Sonny Redd."

Nicole Kyner

I think his family started calling him Sonny, and the "Red" came from his hair. He had reddish hair. It was kind of henna red, but it was natural.

Charles McPherson

We used to call Sonny Red "Red." Physically, he was red. He had freckles and he had reddish hair, so I'm sure that had about 90 percent to do with everything.

Frank Gant

Well, he was red, his color, not really *red* hair, but he was light skinned and had freckles.

James Kiner
I remember people always called Sylvester "Sonny Red" when we lived on Goodwin. He was a young guy, probably 12 years old, or even a little younger, when he got the nickname. I don't know how it got started, but maybe in black culture we called guys Sonny. Probably Sonny Stitt had the same type of situation. Very few people that I can recall called my brother Sylvester. Within the family we did—I certainly did. My family, my mother and my sister, would have called him Sylvester. It's not a great name, you know, 'cause you think about Sylvester the cat.

Donald Byrd
He disliked being called Sylvester.

Jimmy Heath
Sonny didn't like to be called Sylvester. We got in a fight over this once!

Barry Harris
I always called Sonny "Sonny Red." I never called him Sylvester Kyner. He didn't like that.

Orrin Keepnews
The whole thing that nobody could quite understand about his name, and nickname, and such was very confusing. I'm one of the people that had to deal with his legal name on contracts and such. He apparently never did a name change or anything; he was Sylvester Kyner, and it was kind of hard to tell how he was using "Sonny Red." First of all, it was as if it was one name, almost. He didn't appreciate "Sonny Red Kyner." He basically was self-described as "Sonny Red," as if that was all the name that he had. Didn't make any secret of his name, but I mean, in terms of use, it was that kind of thing that was all obviously perfectly clear to him, and obviously not perfectly clear to other people.

Elena Knox
Sonny referred to himself as "the baby boy" in a joking way, you know? He had that little boy look until he was up in his 30s.

In the early- to mid-1940s, Sonny Red took his first saxophone lessons from William Gardner on the C melody saxophone, which Red would eventually trade in for an alto saxophone. From the fall of 1947 to 1952, Red attended Detroit's Northern High School, dropping out temporarily for the 1950–51 school year. During those years he formed close musical associations with Curtis Fuller, Kiane Zawadi, Donald Byrd, Barry Harris, Paul Chambers, and Tommy Flanagan. Some of these relationships were formed in the concert band, led by Orville Lawrence. Lawrence exposed his students to many different types of music and encouraged them to try other instruments. Red also met and played with other teenagers in Detroit during informal jam/practice sessions at the homes of Barry Harris and Joe Brazil.

Roberta Marie Leach

We lived on Goodwin when William Gardner taught my brother saxophone. I gave Sylvester his first saxophone, a C melody saxophone. We got it from the pawnshop, and of course later on he traded it in for an alto.

James Kiner

My sister had music in school, and so did Sylvester. Plus, Sylvester studied with a good friend of the family that also played. His name was William Gardner, who lived probably a block away from us on the same street. He was just some guy who played alto for a while. He wound up being a drug addict in the end, and I know that this was during the 1940s. It didn't last long because of the drugs.

Sylvester practiced quite often at home. Sometimes he'd go in the backyard and practice in the summer, because it was too warm in the house. Both Curtis Fuller and Sylvester were into music. I think Curtis was playing trombone at that time. Probably another guy my brother hung out with would have been Paul Chambers. He went to Northern for a while. I remember that 'cause Paul and I had a fight one time and I cut his finger. Now I look back and think, "Oh my God!" We were good friends and we were all hanging out. It's just one of those things that happens, I guess. And, there was a guy named Claire Roquemore too. But he wasn't around long, because he died. He was into drugs, very early.

Donald Byrd

[*From a 2003 letter to Red's daughter Nicole Kyner—Ed.*] Let me begin by saying I think of your father very often. He was one of my closest friends. We met at an Intermediate school named Hutchins in Detroit, Michigan in 1945. We had many of the same classes. We were in the concert band and the jazz orchestra. We played for the dances given at the school. This was the beginning of our long and continuous association musically and personally.

Sonny Red

I studied with a cat named Mr. Lawrence. He was the bandmaster. I always used to think he didn't know what was happening, but I used to hear the waltzes. Strauss, Tchaikovsky, and Maurice Ravel—all the masters. But it stuck with me, you know? I heard Charlie Parker, Dizzy [Gillespie], Coleman Hawkins, and Lester Young, and I knew that *they* heard the masters also. There's only one place to get music from—that's a master. I had the pleasure of playing with them all.

Figure 5: Northern High School. (Courtesy Anders Svanoe)

Elena Knox

The band teacher at Northern was well loved by Sonny and the other fellas that were in the band. Mr. Lawrence was thought of with great fondness. He also gave them instruments when they had none.

Sonny Red

I went to school with Tommy Flanagan, the great piano player with Ella [Fitzgerald]. He was a schoolmate. I used to look over his shoulder all the time and watch him play. He was gifted then. He was perfect. He was mature. At 17 or 18, Tommy Flanagan was the same way, a beautiful musician.

Tommy Flanagan

I went to Northern High School with Sonny Red. I got to meet all those guys because I was playing clarinet in the band. We jammed together in the auditorium classes, usually at the end of them. We had a very loose music teacher named Orville Lawrence. We did play a few overtures and he also gave us opportunities to fool around with the other instruments. That was just a way for me to get out of another class and play in the band for a couple of hours in the auditorium. There was always a piano in that auditorium. I played clarinet through high school and then I quit right afterwards, you know, after the piano took over. It took over me early. The main thing was we had a teacher that was so loose he didn't take up that much time with us. He sat at the desk and mostly was writing, band arrangements for something. I think he played with some group. Anyway, when it came time to grade us, he used to have us sit out in the auditorium and he used to throw our report cards to us, he'd fling it out like a frisbee: "Flanagan," *vroom,* "Kyner," *vroom*—you know? Stoney Nightingale [*spelling unknown—Ed.*], the tenor player, he was in high school with us, too.

Phil Lasley
Sonny came up on the north end of Detroit with a hell of a tenor saxophone player, Stoney Nightingale. They were from the same neighborhood and started out together. Malvin McCray is a part of that group. They were all older than I am.

Charles Boles
I first met Sonny Red when he had those knickers, you know. He and I were very good friends. That was sometime in the '40s. We went to grade school and high school together. We both went to Northern. Later on, we played together as teenagers. We played for mostly teenage gigs, high school–type things. And we used to go up to Barry Harris's house and play. That was the training ground, going to Barry Harris's house every day. In those days it was Barry Harris, Paul Chambers, and Claude Black. But Sonny and I played around Detroit, a few little gigs, and then he left for New York.

I was in the band in high school. I played bells, because I couldn't get into the band as a piano player. That band was a hell of a band. The first year there was Paul Chambers—he was just starting to play bass—and Sonny Red on alto. Tommy Flanagan was not in that band because he had graduated already. So we're talking sometime around 1948 or 1949. But Tommy came up there every day and sat in on the little jam session.

James Kiner
Sylvester quit high school for a while and went back. He was very smart, very good in school. But he had an attitude. The attitude-type thing was for we black kids, you know, dealing with the world at that time. We'd fight teachers most of the time, and you just develop these attitudes about it. Looking back it might have been silly, but at that time, it was appropriate. But my brother, he was pretty good at everything that he attempted to do. He was gifted at music.

Sylvester graduated high school in 1952. That was a conscious decision on his part when he was 16, 17: to go back to school and stick with music, because he didn't want to be hanging out gambling, running around, and smoking recreational drugs. Maybe he had seen somebody go down that way? I don't know. But he had to make a real decision that he wouldn't drop out of school. I talked to him about that. I never understood how easily he was able to do it. Maybe it wasn't easy to make that decision. But he made it, and it worked out for him. My mother, she had one son going down that lane. Ira, my oldest brother, was involved in gambling, crooked gambling, which is the way life goes, I guess. Actually, Sylvester was very good at that! Sylvester had excellent hands. He was excellent at pool. He could have been a pool shark. Good dice shooter. Good with cards. All of that kind of stuff he learned from my oldest brother, Ira. That was the going thing at the north end of town at that time. Everybody wanted to be a pool shark, everybody wanted to be slick, and Sylvester somehow got away from that. He made that decision at about 16, that this wasn't what he wanted to do.

Roberta Marie Leach
Sylvester dropped out of high school for one year. He dropped out because he didn't agree with everything, you know, the rules. The principal wanted to give him a scholarship to go to law school, because he said Sylvester was such a strong, argumentative-type person. The assistant principal, Mr. Holt, came and talked to my mother, and Sylvester went back to school the next year, and he graduated.

Frank Foster
I remember a story about Sonny Red that doesn't even involve music. We were going down the street in Detroit one day in 1950, and the police frequently stopped young blacks on the street if they looked suspicious. And Sonny Red and I must have looked suspicious this day. I don't know why, because we weren't up to anything. The cops stopped us and padded us down. I had a jackknife in my possession, with a three-inch blade. They didn't find any drugs on us, or anything else. So the cop asked me, "Do you want this knife?" and I said, "Yes, I want it!" Then he proceeded to break the blade against a stone fence, and he handed it back to me.

Roberta Marie Leach
Sylvester had a paper route and worked for R. L. Polk & Company, which was some type of business. He also worked at one of the Dodge plants, but he would always go to sleep in the elevators, and other employees would protect him saying, "We don't know where he is." But after some time, they fired him.

Nicole Kyner
My dad was very bright in high school, and at this point he was really focused on music. This continued to be his focus for the rest of his life, without question.

After graduating from high school in 1952, Sonny Red performed in many of the best jazz clubs in Detroit. He frequently gigged and sat in at Klein's Show Bar, the Crystal Show Bar, the Twenty Grand, the World Stage, the Rouge Lounge, the Blue Bird Inn, and the Mirror Ballroom. Red also participated in frequent jam sessions at the West End Hotel, a popular after-hours spot for musicians. Besides working steadily with Barry Harris, Red had a few opportunities to sit in with Charlie Parker, Miles Davis, Yusef Lateef, and Sonny Stitt. Other early gigs included trombonist Frank Rosolino's combo in April–May 1954 at Klein's Show Bar, three days with Billie Holiday sometime during 1954, and Art Blakey's Jazz

Figure 6: 1952 Northern High School graduation picture. (Courtesy Nicole Kyner)

Messengers during the fall of 1954 in Philadelphia. Red continued to work on and off with the Jazz Messengers through the summer of 1955.

Sonny Red
In 1949 we had a band with the great Barry Harris, the piano player and teacher. I stayed with his band until 1953. In 1954, I worked with Billie Holiday while she was in Detroit for three days. It was three of the most beautiful days I've ever

spent in music. She would sing and would give me so much to strive for, like trying to captivate that style of hers, you know, emulate that sound. I always like to believe that the voice is the first instrument, other than Mother Nature, then the horn. I always strived to make the horn sound like the voice. That's an art form. So, you have to be listening for the sound, later for the horn itself. Only to sing through the horn and make the people feel it—that's what it's all about. I've spent my life trying to do this.

Barry Harris
I started a group with Claire Roquemore on trumpet and Sonny Red on alto in the late 1940s. Sonny was the hippest cat of the three of us! He used to practice all the time. Red used to love to play pool. In fact, he played more pool than saxophone.

Kiane Zawadi
Sonny and I came up with Barry Harris's septet sometime in the early to mid-1950s. We had Claire Roquemore on trumpet, Tate Houston on baritone sax, Sonny on alto, and Barry Harris on piano. After Claire Roquemore left the band, we had a guy named Teeter Ford on trumpet. That band played a few gigs around and rehearsed Barry's music. Barry is my mentor and probably was Sonny Red's too. We used to hang out together. Red used to play pool. We would talk about general things like girls and stuff like that. Yeah, he had a lot of fun.

Frank Gant
I remember seeing Red, he was swinging, in Barry Harris's band. Playing bebop. William [Teeter] Ford was also in the band, on trumpet. I loved to play with Teeter! They were playing at the Craftsmen's Club, or one of the ballroom clubs. I went up to Red and said, "Red, man, listen to you, how did you get that good? You got to be an inspiration for me." I said, "If you can do it, I know I can do it."

James Kiner
Sylvester and Barry Harris were good friends, but they argued all the time. Musical type differences. What you're playing, what I'm playing. They were still excellent friends, though.

Charles Boles
Sonny Red could be confrontational at times. But Barry Harris knew how to cool him out. Barry Harris could be confrontational too. Those guys argued all the time over the music. It was always over the music, the approach to the music. Barry was everybody's mentor, so everybody followed what he said. He had a system, and he still teaches that system. Sonny Red and Charles McPherson were Barry's students. All the musicians that came through that era were probably Barry's students.

Charles McPherson

Sonny Red would be a couple of years older than me. So when we were coming up in Detroit, when I first started playing and getting interested in jazz, Red was already playing really well. I remember hearing of him, and the first time I saw him was at some dance at the Ferry Center, a hall that people would rent out to give dances and dinners, or whatever. This was around 1953. Someone said, "There's Sonny Red." He was playing alto and sounded very much like Charlie Parker. And I was very much into Charlie Parker, especially then, and here was this young guy able to actually come somewhere near that.

I don't know how formally Sonny studied with Barry. Now, I studied with Barry. I studied in the real sense of the word. I'm over at his house every day for three or four hours, really taking instruction and learning. Sonny Red was closer to Barry's age, and I don't know if the teacher-pupil was in place as much as [with,] say, me. But I'm sure [that] by osmosis, or some kind of way, there was learning going on. And Barry was definitely more knowledgeable than Sonny Red, especially at that time. Barry was a real good piano player, and a little older as well.

Kiane Zawadi

Charlie Parker was playing a Monday matinee at the Crystal Lounge. I remember Bird let Sonny and I play a tune while he took a break. While Bird was sitting in the audience, he was grinning at us. At that time, we knew that he wasn't displeased with our playing. We were so in awe of him.

Tommy Flanagan

Bird came to the Mirror Ballroom one day to play. At that time, Barry [Harris] and Sonny Red were old enough to sit in with Bird. I was always afraid to do that, but I did a couple of times. Bird had a quintet; he would do this just maybe once every couple of years, because he had a son in Detroit. Red got to be kinda close with Sonny Stitt when he was in Detroit. They both liked to play a lot, like all those horn players, like Coltrane never stopped playing. Red also had a close association with Donald Byrd. They're about the same age.

I was playing with Billy Mitchell's band at the Blue Bird Inn when Miles was in residence there for about two or three months [*probably late 1953 to early 1954—Ed.*]. The band was Thad Jones, Billy Mitchell, Elvin Jones and James Richardson. Several young guys used to come by to sit in, and Sonny Red was one of them, along with a trumpet player, Claire Roquemore.

Curtis Fuller

Miles came to Detroit to live. He was there and Sonny Red was standing in with him. Miles met a girl and moved there. Her name was Jean Spencer [*spelling unconfirmed—Ed.*]. She was the daughter of a guy in a dance and singing group. That group was very popular at that time, and Mr. Spencer was the young bright guy in the band. His daughter and Miles took up. She was singing—she had a very good voice. But Sonny was with them, you know, in that crowd. Sonny went and met him [Miles] when Bird came to Detroit, and he fooled around in Detroit for a while. Wardell Gray was in Detroit, and Yusef [Lateef] was a big figure around Detroit. And Sonny was in with all those guys.

Frank Gant

When Miles was over on the West Side, there was a club called the Blue Bird Inn. Now, that was the real test of being accepted in Detroit. You had to do the Blue Bird. And once you did that, you're cool. You would be ready to move on out, if necessary. I played the Blue Bird with Yusef [Lateef] and Barry [Harris].

I remember seeing Red a few times down at Joe Brazil's. I first started to play drums by going down to Joe Brazil's. The way I got there was Doug Watkins, the bass player, pulled me over there since Doug and I went to the same high school. Anyway, he was telling me to go sit in, and I told him that I wasn't ready yet. But he told me to come on by there anyway. So I went there and sat in with Barry on piano, Joe Brazil [on alto saxophone], Donald Byrd [on trumpet], and Doug Watkins on bass. They played a tempo, extremely fast, and somehow or another I kept that tempo, and that's what opened the door for me. They said that the next time they were going to give me a call, and they did.

Tommy Flanagan

Joe Brazil was important on the scene and a good friend of Coltrane's. That was perfect for Trane. This was a place, just free to him, to play as long as he wanted to.

Kiane Zawadi

I remember one session that we did at Joe Brazil's place. We did a lot of jam sessions down there. Sonny was there and sometimes Barry. Ko-Ko [Kenneth "Cokie" Winfrey], the tenor player, used to live down at Joe's place, so he'd always be there for the sessions. That was around 1955 or 1956. I lived right down the street, so I was there a lot.

Tommy Flanagan

Frank Foster was instrumental in influencing Red to open up to more chord progressions.

Actually, Sonny learned that just by playing. That's how he picked it up.

James Kiner

There was somebody else that my brother played with, Frank Foster. Frank used to come by the house and they'd go over stuff together. They did a lot of practicing and writing. I don't know where Frank came from, but he might have been doing something over at Wayne State.

Frank Foster

When I went to Detroit, I met Sonny Red. He was one of the first people I met. Sonny Red and I were good friends, but every now and then something would happen where he would stop speaking to me for a few weeks. I don't know why he would stop speaking to me, but after a few weeks and after he'd gotten over what it was he was pissed off about, he'd start speaking to me again. Sonny Red knew the basics, but I was giving him some deeper information, some frills. Sonny and I used to get together and talk about the music and go to the jam sessions. We also played a couple gigs together at Klein's [Show Bar], where we got paid, but we mostly played jam sessions. Red played a little tenor when I knew him in Detroit, but he mostly played alto. I heard a recording where he was playing flute [in the 1970s], but I never heard or witnessed him playing any flute live. We never hung out while he lived in New York.

Curtis Fuller

My first night back from the service [*probably 1954–55—Ed.*] was at the Music Hall with Sonny Stitt, and Sonny Red was there at the concert. After the concert, we all went over to Rouge Lounge and jammed. Sonny Red and Sonny Stitt went after it. At this time, Sonny Red was one of the guys who was really into playing bebop. I always liked and admired him because of that. I mean he was Charlie Parker personified. Sonny Red was right in there. All the guys around town drew on each other musically. There was Lamonte Hamilton and [Kenneth] "Cokie" Winfrey. All those guys were like Charlie Parker's disciples.

Red's best friend at that time was Bernard McKinney, who is Kiane Zawadi. He was a trombone player, but now he's playing mostly euphonium. They had their own band.

Kiane Zawadi

Red once invited me to come up and work with Blakey in Philly. He said, "Come by there if you can get up here from Detroit and make this matinee," so I came up and played a matinee with him. After that he wasn't involved [with Blakey].

Curtis Fuller

Well I took Frank Rosolino's place at the Bowl-O-Drome. It was his group at the Bowl-O-Drome. It was a bowling alley with a jazz room. Sonny Red was playing with him at that time.

James Kiner

There were a couple of times where they did sort of a non–bar-type gig. We called it the World Stage. My brother played there. I remember he played there with a vibes player, a local guy. It was a nice setting for people. The audience sat in sort of a C formation with the rows set up, what you call arena-type seats.

Tommy Flanagan
Red played at the World Stage theater. All the musicians were there, because there was no age limit. It was just an open theater.

Phil Lasley
I first met Sonny Red when he was playing with Abe Woodley at the West End in Detroit. As a kid, I used to go out there and just listen—you know, bug the older musicians.

Figure 7: Sonny Red playing with Abe Woodley, vibes, and Alvin Jackson, bass. (Courtesy Charles Boles)

Frank Gant

Sonny and I did a lot of gigs together. He was with Barry Harris's band. He was in there before me. I was playing at Klein's Show Bar with Yusef [Lateef], and Sonny sat in a few times. I remember one time specifically—I got him the gig, 'cause Yusef was out of town. Yusef came to New York to do some recording, and he left me in Detroit, and I filled in with Sonny Red. That was sometime during the late 1950s.

Figure 8: James Kiner. (Courtesy Roberta Marie Leach)

James Kiner

Most of the stuff my brother was doing at this time was at the Blue Bird or Klein's. Klein's was Yusef's permanent job in Detroit. So any time my brother would have played over there, it would have been with Yusef. That was after my brother got out of the sanitarium, sometime around 1956 or 1957. Yusef's band used a lot of written music. I think Yusef required that everybody did some kind of reading, because a lot of the music that Yusef was playing, he wrote. He arranged it. My brother didn't play with Yusef all the time, because Sylvester was a little difficult to get along with. But he played at all the places he could. It was one of those unfortunate things where I didn't get to hear him all the time because once I came into the service, I was working and going to college at night.

Malvin McCray

Red and I played at the Bizerte Bar. That's where they had sessions every Monday night. On the weekends, Friday and Saturday night, we used to play at the West End, after everybody got off their gigs. We would play until daybreak. Yusef had that gig. Red used to come out there all the time and play.

Yusef Lateef

We were all in the same atmosphere there in Detroit, so we rubbed shoulders. Sonny Red worked with me some at Klein's somewhere around 1957. Miles Davis, Red, and I also played some concerts. One of them was in Toledo, Ohio; I remember that. It was a rhythm section and three horns.

By the summer of 1955 Red was diagnosed with tuberculosis, and was admitted to Northville State Hospital in Detroit for a period of 18 months. In September

1955, a benefit concert was given for Red at the Blue Bird Inn. Lung problems would interfere with his playing career for the rest of his life.

Nicole Kyner

When my dad was younger, he caught tuberculosis and was hospitalized for about two years. My dad smoked a lot—they all did—but he did quit smoking 10 years before he got the lung cancer.

Roberta Marie Leach

Being in the sanitarium was hard on Sylvester. He always said that I had given the tuberculosis to him, because I had healed scar tissue in my lungs. But I was never hospitalized, so I don't know where he got it from.

James Kiner

When I got out of the service in 1955, I found out my brother had tuberculosis. I assumed he got it because he was playing around. By then he was playing at some of the local places and they say that he probably got it there. I didn't even know he was ill until I came out of the service.

Curtis Fuller

Yeah, Sonny always had lung problems. He didn't know it, but he had tuberculosis that would later develop into cancer. When I was younger, I had to take a test

Figure 9: Sonny Red with his sister, Roberta Marie Leach (left), and sister-in-law Eddie Mae Kiner (right) at Northville State Hospital, Detroit, July 1955. (Courtesy Roberta Marie Leach)

because of my close association with him. When we were kids we would share Coca-Colas and eat off the same hot dog. They were treating him as an outpatient. That was the beginning of treating people as outpatients. My father, I understand, died with [lung cancer]. I never knew my father; he died when my mother was carrying. So I was sensitive to that.

Elena Knox

Sonny was very young when he got sick, and was still living at his mom's house. He was told after he came out of the sanitarium that he'd never play music again. That was a tough thing to hear, because music was his life.

Sonny's musical style made an impression on those who worked with and heard him. His approach to the saxophone was firmly rooted in the basics: emphasis on the blues, strong rhythmical concepts, lyrical playing, and a command sound on the horn. These strong fundamental beliefs, and his unique way of making the bebop vocabulary his own, gained respect from his peers and mentors.

Sonny Red

I listened to Louis Armstrong, Charlie Parker—all the jazz artists. And the singers, especially—the blues singers. I loved all of them. And Charlie Parker was later in my life, but I listened to the singers first. I'd go to church, and they would sing the spirituals, and I would come home and try to play that on the piano, although it's not my instrument. I would try and get that feeling from it. Some singers bring tears to your eyes—because you feel it, because they are giving you something. That's the only way tears can come to your eyes.

The blues is an institution in itself, which is derivative of the old spirituals, I think. The blues is a way of life; it's the bridge in which jazz crosses. The blues supports it. All the compositions I've written, and I've written quite a few of them, have been blues, or blues-influenced at any rate.

James Kiner

Charlie Parker was my brother's hero. My brother was also close to Sonny Stitt because Stitt played like Charlie Parker. My friends, and probably Sylvester's friends too, we used to try to find Bird's records. We found Jay McShann with Charlie Parker on it. But my brother also understood that he had to *stop* playing like Bird, because nobody can play better than the creator. Many musicians' careers have been hurt by that. I think Sylvester also saw some things in Coltrane; I can hear it in his music, some of his later music.

Louis Hayes

Sonny was a little older than I am. He was a very special person in Detroit, before I became a special person. He was a Charlie Parker person that really loved Charlie Parker, and people loved Sonny in Detroit.

Charles Boles

He was a bebopper, you know? I guess a lot like Sonny Stitt and Charlie Parker, in the style of bebop.

Tommy Flanagan

Sonny was really advanced for his age. Even in high school, he was someone to listen to. He picked up on Bird very early. Sonny was one of the first guys, young alto players, to really have a sound. He sounded like someone different than, you know, Johnny Hodges. Sonny was quite original in his own right. He had his own sound and his own ideas. His way of playing was very personal. I know he loved all kinds of music and was pretty well versed in the classics too.

Curtis Fuller

Out of all the young guys, Red really grasped Charlie Parker. He inherited that. Sonny Stitt and all of them approached jazz like that. But Sonny Red could tell them the inside stuff—you-played-this-note-against-that-chord kind of thing. He could make some of the big boys like Miles Davis stand back with what he knew. I always had a lot of respect for him, because he knew what he was talking about. Red could always tell if a guy didn't know his changes, or tunes. He could tell you while he stood there. Red made you cognizant of everything going on. That made me listen to everybody. He opened that door for me. Sonny had super training, he and Barry Harris. Sonny also played very good piano.

Cedar Walton

Red always used to bolster his ability to play the blues, in a real comical, positive way, but he could play the blues, now! He was bluesy, and was someone who was into developing a style in the jazz idiom. I don't think his sound necessarily got fully developed, because he passed away too soon. He was probably just coming into his own.

Frank Foster

Sonny Red's style was somewhat derivative from Charlie Parker, and yet it had elements of his own creativity in there. I think he practiced runs, licks, and ideas, but I don't think he did too much legit-type exercise practicing. His philosophical attitude toward the music was unique, because he'd say things that made sense, without making sense, you know? He would say things like, "I think I'm playing as much as anybody out there, for what I'm playing"!

Orrin Keepnews

Sonny belonged to a period when the influence of Parker was all-pervasive. To my ear I think that he, like a number of other alto players from his time, suffered from exactly that, you know? He didn't get out from under enough, so I don't really carry any strong feelings of characterizing his playing.

Yusef Lateef

Sonny played his own self, and that's what I admired about him. He didn't emulate anyone else. *Anything* he played was appealing to me. I think he understood that the tradition was to play like yourself and he pursued that path.

Charles McPherson

Red was an interesting player. He was one of the alto players that certainly came from Charlie Parker, but was able to be a little bit different, to take that language and actually have a way of forging a style of your own. That's really the way everybody learns how to play. But he definitely had a little something. So even though he came from Bird like everybody else, he had his own little way of doing things and his sound, which manifested itself on some records. He definitely was underrecorded, and never given his just due, because of this.

Frank Gant

Red loved music, man. He would tell me to don't forget the keyboard. I think that's where he would spend a lot of his time, because he was starting to write. Red put the blues into his playing, and he could swing! He was a swinger!

Malvin McCray

Red was a student of the music. In fact, I owe my latest success to him. Red showed me some key things about the piano and how to approach the saxophone via the piano. I could look at the piano and see what he was doing and how it related to the saxophone. Red also showed me about breathing on the saxophone and how to hold the horn. He told me to grip the mouthpiece further up in order to open up my sound. Red was the kind of guy that could play any horn. Suggestions, you know, it's those small things that make a huge difference. That really opened up the doors for me. Red was such a great guy. He was my main man for me. He's a guy that I truly loved and was a good, dear friend. Nobody who was ever that knowledgeable spent that kind of time with me.

Phil Lasley

Red's concept was just swing and play pretty. He never did get into the technical aspects. He was basically a blues guy. I play *Teef* a lot and am probably one of the few guys around here [Detroit] that still plays his compositions.

Curtis Fuller

Red was a good saxophone player, but he never had the speed. He never got up and went. And that was the scene in those days, like Pepper Adams. They were beasts, you know. I got that background, you know. I was in that crowd, Joe Henderson and all those guys. When I first got with Trane, I remember when I first saw those changes I was running the seventh chords all the time, instead of getting more inventive like Pepper or somebody. I was just spelling that thing, because he's got these chord changes written here. But Sonny was more fluid with adapting a liner line, so I took note. I guess you have to listen to Parker too, because that's where Parker was coming from.

Kiane Zawadi

I liked Sonny's sound and his concept. Sonny sounded like a cross between Bird and Sonny Stitt, if you could say that. He liked Parker, but he might have liked Stitt a little bit better. Sonny sounded more like Sonny Stitt for sound and licks, but he had his own creative approach to soloing too. With some of these other cats, I can't ID them, but with Sonny Red, I can. He had natural, creative ability. He was more self-taught anyway, you know? I remember he'd like to play "Stay as Sweet as You Are" and "Stars Fell on Alabama."

Curtis Fuller

Sonny had a sound! With all the information that he had, he still maintained the lyrical thing. That embedded itself in me. I was out there playing fast licks all the time, and Sonny Red brought me down, he more than anyone, to be more lyrical, and to feel the music. He was a study in lyrical playing. A lyricist. He used to like Nat Cole; he used to like singers. There was one favorite ballad that I used to love to hear him play, "Stay as Sweet as You Are." Through him I learned all those things.

Sheila Kiner

When I was about seven or eight years old, we would go over to my grandma's house on 233 Leicester. We would go in the basement; they made swings in the basement for us on the pipes. But my uncle Sylvester would be in the basement practicing every time I went over there. I didn't understand it, but at that time he was constantly practicing scales, all the time. I asked him, "Why are you playing the same thing over and over again?" He told me to put my hand on his horn while he played, and I did. And he said, "Do you hear that sound?" I said, "Yes." He said, "Well, I'm practicing to do that better."

Elena Knox

Sonny introduced me to Leadbelly. He was also crazy about Charlie Parker. We had a lot of those records in the house. Sonny also really liked Billie Holiday. We used to listen to her records a lot. That was one of the most romantic periods, listening to Billie Holiday records.

James Kiner

My brother's best music was the ballads that he would play. To me, I would have been satisfied if he would've played ballads forever. At one time I probably suggested to him that he should play more ballads. Even the flute things [ballads] that he did were nice.

My brother's first 12-inch demonstration record was made at 138 Duffield, in Detroit, as a matter of fact [*probably during the late 1950s—A.S.*]. He sounds really good, and he was playing more like Bird then, of course, so it's basically a Charlie Parker–type thing. It's a trio date with Herman Wright on bass and Roy Brooks on drums. They play "Cutie," "Jumpin' at the Woodside," "Stairway to the Stars," and "Soleing." It's a hard-type wax-type record. Those were records that they made back then so you could get a job or see if you could make a record.

Elena Knox

Sonny practiced every day. I can't think there was one day that he didn't practice. There would not have been one day that he didn't pick up his horn and play. He practiced lots of scales and riffs too—lots of scales and scale work. He wrote stuff out on the piano.

Jaffiria Leach-Orr

See, I play the piano too, but I played classical music, all written out. Everyone took piano lessons back then; everyone took up some type of instrument when I was growing up in the neighborhood. That was part of childhood. I don't remember uncle Sylvester playing any classical piano, but I remember him sitting down and playing mostly chords. When I was practicing, my uncle would close the music and say, "Come on, now, let's play some music." As soon as he closed the music, I couldn't play.

Charles McPherson

I don't think Sonny Red played with his [top] teeth [on the mouthpiece]. He played with a double cushion [embouchure], like an oboe player. I can tell when a cat plays with a double cushion; it's something about how the articulation happens. There's something about how the tip of the tongue [hits the reed]. It's a slightly softer sound, because instead of teeth on the hard surface of the mouthpiece, you have lips on the hard surface, so the sound is dampened a little bit more. Now, Bird almost sounded like he played with a double embouchure. But I don't think he did, because every time I ask guys that were old enough to know this, they said Bird played with his teeth. But he almost sounds like he played with a double cushion to me. See, Johnny Hodges played with one too. A lot of lead alto players did that. You can bend the note; you have more control when you play with a double cushion.

Phil Lasley

These were the horns that Red played on: he started on one of those old Conn 10Ms [*Lasley probably means either a 6M or a Conn "Chu Berry" alto; the 10M is a tenor saxophone—A.S.*]. That's what he was using when he first went to New York, in the '50s. He played on that with the Jazz Messengers and those early recordings with Curtis Fuller. Red then got the Selmer with the Blue Note recordings, and shortly afterwards he got the [King] Super 20 for those Jazzland records. Like a lot of guys, they really had wished they had kept the first one. The older horns have the sound; they have such beautiful sounds.

Jimmy Heath

Sonny was a great composer who wrote a lot of compositions. One of my favorite songs of his is "Bluesville." Sonny had his own concept. He was a very rhythmical player and he swung hard.

P-R TAPES, incorporated

six ashton place, cambridge thirty-eight, massachusetts
university 4-9137

February 12, 1957

Mr. Sonny Red
233 Leicester
Detroit 2, Michigan

Dear Sonny:

I am enclosing a contract for the exclusive use of your recorded efforts. Doug tells me that you are a "terrible" man on your horn -- that you will "scare" me. Well that's what I want. I need a really exciting man to go with our Louis Smith and Joe Gordon. Louis just made a date for us with Cannonball, Doug, Duke Jordan and Arthur Taylor: they "smoked" all the way.

As you know, Doug is signed with us and has seen no reason to regret it. As he told you, when you formally apply to us to record for other companies, we are quite willing so long as that company puts "by arrangement with Transition Records" on the jacket of the album, in a prominent place. *

Please sign and return the contract along with a picture of yourself and some information on your musical training, who you've played with, etc.

Sincerely yours,

TRANSITION RECORDS

Tom Wilson

TBW/bs

Tom Wilson

* Sonny —
We will allow you to record as leader for any major label (Columbia, R.C.A. Decca, Capitol). TW.

jazz, neo-classical, and folk music

Figure 10: Letter from Tom Wilson of Transition Records offering Red his first record contract. (Courtesy Nicole Kyner)

Figure 11: Sonny Red's first record as leader.

Louis Hayes

I recorded *Teef* twice. It's on my first record date with Yusef [Lateef], Nat Adderley, Sam Jones, and Barry Harris on Vee-Jay. [Louis Hayes Featuring Yusef Lateef & Nat Adderley, *recorded April 26, 1960—A.S.]* Then I recorded it again in the late '90s with David Hazeltine. Now, that's very important that I recorded his tunes two times. That's history.

Central Park: New York, 1957–1979

In early 1957 in Detroit, Red played with Art Blakey and in local concerts with Barry Harris, Elvin Jones, and Yusef Lateef. But like many other musicians from Detroit and other U.S. cities during the late 1950s, Red moved to New York in April 1957, following his childhood friend Curtis Fuller. Fuller and Red took New York by storm the second week of May 1957, making three different records for Prestige in four days. Four months later, a fourth date, featuring Tommy Flanagan, was recorded for Savoy. In August 1957 Red moved back to Detroit, but returned in November to make his first recording as leader: "Two Altos," also on Savoy. "Two Altos" featured Red's Detroit buddies Pepper Adams, Doug Watkins, and Elvin Jones. Red continued to shift between Detroit, New York, and other touring locations, before finally settling in New York in 1960. In late 1959, while playing at the Show Place in New York's Greenwich Village, he gained the attention of Blue Note Records' Alfred Lion.

Sonny Red

I came to New York in 1957. Me and Curtis Fuller made some records together with Red Garland and Paul Chambers. He went to school with me too, Paul Chambers. Paul used to practice all day long. And we see that he's come and gone, but he was a beautiful musician.

New York is the melting pot. It's like Paris was in the 1920s when all of the great artists lived there. Most of the great artists in this country are in New York. But while you're going through the suffering, which is part of it, you acquire the feeling. You also see other artists that give you that stimulation. You see the playwrights, singers, and the dancers. We're all in the same community, a oneness, so to speak. Being in New York, where all the guys are, has its advantages, I think. I know it's got a lot of people, but you must be around all those artists to get that stimulation from them. It's very important.

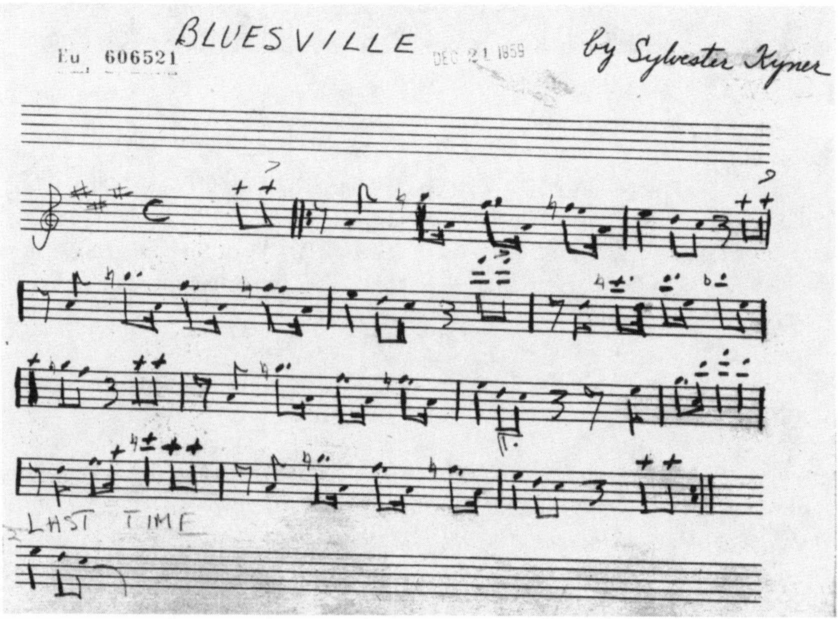

Figure 12: Lead sheet to "Bluesville" as submitted to the Library of Congress.

John Coltrane used to live two streets from me on 58th. We used to all go around to his house and see all the guys around there. And this cat would just sit up there and play two hours on one solo! Well, to be able to do that, you must really have the variations together. He knew enough about the music, not his horn, but the music. Because music is never going to change.

"Bluesville" is a blues of mine that I wrote in 1959. I wrote it on the subway from 103rd Street to 50th Street on the way to the record date. Wynton Kelly, Sam Jones, and Roy Brooks were on that.

James Kiner

Everybody was leaving Detroit at that time: Curtis Fuller, Donald Byrd. Donald and I were in the Air Force at the same time. My brother decided one day that

Figure 13: Lower right photo of Red at an unissued Blue Note session, March 10, 1969. The rest are Red at the *Out of the Blue* session for Blue Note, December 5, 1959. (Photographs by Francis Wolff, copyright Mosaic Images, LLC)

New York was the place to go. It's one of those things. If you're going to make it, you're going to have to make it in New York, as far as music is concerned. Not that everybody went to New York, but there was a big movement of musicians from these cities to New York. That's where the clubs were at the time, and it had always been that way. That's the place where all the musicians wanted to go.

Malvin McCray
Red was dedicated to New York. His mother and sister were here in Detroit. He could have had a place to stay. They would have looked out for him, but he was just the kind of cat who wanted to be on his own in New York—even though it meant living that type of life. He chose that rather than coming back to Detroit.

Curtis Fuller
I came to New York with Yusef Lateef to record, and Sonny Red followed me. Sonny called me from Detroit, and we talked. I told him, "If you want to come to New York, I've got some record dates I could use you on." I had just gotten a new apartment on 101st Street, upstairs over Tommy Flanagan. Sonny spent about a

Figure 14: This 45 r.p.m. single helped establish Red's reputation.

year with Louis Hayes and Doug Watkins in our apartment. We had our own little community there.

Louis Hayes

My main time knowing Sonny Red was here in New York, when we lived together on 101st Street. It was Curtis Fuller, Red Kyner, and myself. Doug Watkins was there also. Tommy Flanagan lived below us. That was his first apartment. We had a room where we had these little beds, and there were about four of them in this one room, which was a very unique situation. It was a very busy apartment.

I remember the first date. It was Curtis Fuller's first recording. We just dealt with the people that were right there. The music, naturally, was marvelous, always. We were just youngsters and I was just beginning to get my life together, to grow to a certain level.

We used to cover every museum in New York, Doug Watkins, myself, and Red. During that time Red wasn't well. He had tuberculosis. I know he had an energy problem, because naturally when you go to a museum you have to walk all over the place, and I remember Red having a problem with the walking. When it was Curtis and Red, I would kind of disappear on them. I would leave Red with Curtis, because I would make it so Curtis had to buy him ice cream and go through that stuff all day. Curtis would take care of him, and I'd disappear, but we'd see each other in the evening. Curtis was the cook, technically.

Barry Harris

Sonny moved to New York in 1957. I moved there in 1955. I knew a *little bit* more than the other guys. Maybe that's why I was considered their teacher or mentor.

Elena Knox

Sonny and Barry, at least in the early 1960s when they were hanging out, were really contemporaries. I don't think there was a mentor-student relationship at all.

Jaffiria Leach-Orr

I remember when I was a kid in the 1950s or 1960s, Uncle Sylvester would come back from New York and they would have jam sessions and rehearsals at the house. I remember Donald Byrd and Barry Harris stopping by. The house was always filled with music and laughter. It was a happy household. We had a parakeet, Jimmy the parakeet, flying around, and the dog barking and howling too.

Cedar Walton

Red and I met somewhere here in New York in the early 1960s, because I got here in 1959, and a year later I was in the army. Sonny was in from Detroit. He was a very likable and very positive cat. At that time, he was hanging out with the Detroit guys like Doug Watkins, Curtis Fuller, and Louis Hayes—people like that.

Charles McPherson

Red went to New York a couple years before I did. I went in 1959 or 1960, and Red had already somewhat established himself. Because when I went to New York, he was already known and had made a couple records with people. Through the years I would see him since both of us were living in New York, occasionally hearing him play.

Frank Gant

Red left Detroit before I did. I came in 1960 with the Yusef Lateef band. So Red was already here and was recommending my name to different guys, like Sonny Rollins. Sonny Rollins was looking for a drummer and Red told him to get me, so Sonny called me up, but it didn't happen.

Charles Boles

New York was tough, man. But you had guys like Tommy Flanagan [pianist] who went there and made it, and Kenny Burrell [guitarist] too. It all depended on what instrument you played and how outgoing you were. There's a difference being an alto player and a piano player. But Sonny was not destitute in New York. I mean, he was there and he did very well.

James Kiner

When Sylvester went to New York, I think one of the first things that he learned is that every young guy out there was trying to play Bird, and a lot of them were doing it better than he was. I'm thinking of the alto player that played at Birdland with Art Blakey, Lou Donaldson. These guys were playing very good Charlie Parker. So there was a different level of competition, if you're going to play Charlie Parker. And it takes an effort *not* to play it. I think in the end, this is what he learned. It's what really sustained him, because if he'd continued to try and play like Bird, he'd just have to leave and drop out.

Charles McPherson

Red was kind of friendly with Lou Donaldson. Him and Lou Donaldson were actually kind of tight. Which is kind of strange, because Lou Donaldson doesn't like anybody, especially saxophone players! [*Laughs.*] He really doesn't have a whole lot to say about any saxophone player, and he's really hard on alto players, in terms of his standards. Lou is a very—especially young Lou Donaldson—good alto player. He doesn't do anything wrong. He's in tune, plays the horn well, he's fluent, and what he does, he does really well. So when people are less than any of that, then you'll have something to say about it. But he liked Red, not only personally, but I think he liked Red's playing. So, I was always kind of amazed that Red would be his friend.

Yusef Lateef

I gave Red my first flute. It was a Lautley. Two-piece flute. This was after we arrived in New York. It was in the 1960s. He was very serious about music and practiced a lot.

Jimmy Heath
I met Sonny Red in New York in the early 1960s. We were good friends; we were very close. At that time we were both learning how to play the flute. We talked about music all the time, not too much about the saxophone. Later on we played together in the Donald Byrd Sextet at Birdland in the summer of 1963. The band was [Albert] Tootie Heath, Herbie Hancock, and Spanky De Brest. Herbie eventually left the band to go play with Miles, and then Barry Harris came into the group. We also did some recording with that band.

Frank Gant
I used to check on Red quite often, when he was here in New York. He was my buddy, you know, my main friend. During that time he didn't work very often.

Figure 15: Red at the Stardust Room in Boston, November 1963, with Oliver Jackson, drums, Red Garland, piano, and Paul Chambers, bass. (Courtesy Nicole Kyner)

Not many guys would give him gigs, as well as he could play. He was a standout! One time I got a gig in Syracuse, New York. It was in the wintertime and it was very cold. I called Red and said, "I've got this gig—it's an organ gig. Do you want to go as the horn player?" I drove up there, and I got the organ player, who was a blind guy, Raymond Jackson, the only organ player that I could find at that time. So we go to Syracuse, and it's 18 below zero and 20 feet of snow up there. We checked into the motel, which was right outside of the city, but the club seemed to have the overtones of a joint for the mob. I think it was a mob joint. So the gig was going along for about three days—we had the engagement for two weeks. So Red on the intermission was doing the John Coltrane thing, practicing on the intermission. So the manager came over to me that night and said, "Frank, now you're all right, the organ player is okay, but that saxophone player, he's got to go." So I had to go into my bag, and I said, "Look, I don't even need to qualify this man, my saxophone player." I said, "The man's got hit records, like that tune 'Stay As Sweet As You Are' on Blue Note records." That was his claim to fame. "And he's also written some other hip tunes. This man is unquestionable. Look, let me do my gig. We got one more week. You won't have any problems out of me because I don't tell you how to run your joint, I don't tell you how to sell your liquor. That's not my problem. The band is with me." So we did it, and I made sure I got the money, paid the band their money, before I got mine. Red didn't know anything about that. I didn't run that down to him. After that, me and Sonny came back to New York.

In the late 1950s Red's first daughter, Nadia, was born in Detroit. She could not be reached for this oral history.

Sonny Red and Elena Knox were married in February 1961. Tommy Flanagan signed the marriage license. On June 4, 1962, their daughter Nicole Kyner was born. Red's publishing company, established in the 1960s, was named Nadianicole, after his two daughters.

James Kiner

I never really met Nadia, I don't think. I know that the mother was Hungarian. I can't recall the mother, although I might have seen her once.

Nicole Kyner

As a child—and an only child at that—I often asked family members what they knew about Nadia. I sensed that it was not always an easy conversation for them to have. There was a sense that she was taken from the family, lost. I've always felt very wistful about Nadia, the big sister that I could never meet. I remember being told that Nadia's mother was Polish and that her name was Lee Novack.

Elena Knox

Sonny and I got married on February 16, 1961. I was 18 years old and kind of immature at the time. Sonny was 10 years older than me. When I met him, he was already "Sonny Red." We met at Birdland on a Monday night. Sonny's band was playing, and he was using Jules Curtis, the drummer, in the band. Jules Curtis was a friend of mine, and I had gone to see him. That's when we were introduced to each other. About a year later, we were married by a Baptist minister at our studio apartment on West 105th Street, between West End Avenue and Riverside Drive. Tommy Flanagan was the witness who signed the marriage certificate. Tommy's (then) wife Anne Flanagan and their son were there; Yusef Lateef was there too. Soon after, we moved from 105th Street to a two-bedroom apartment at 528 Riverside Drive. We were living at 528 for about a year before Nikki was born at Mt. Sinai Hospital. Tommy Flanagan and Anne had moved next door, to 530 Riverside, where they had two more children.

Barry Harris used to come by the house on a pretty regular basis. Sonny had gotten a piano, which was in the living room, so Barry was frequently there. Sonny was also playing with Freddie Hubbard, Blue Mitchell, Horace Parlan, and Lee Morgan during this time. During the day, Sonny would spend a lot of time in that 52nd-and-Broadway area with his friends. That's what they would do every day. That was like his job—he'd go to 52nd Street. They talked about music, where the jobs were, and touched base with each other. It was part of the lifestyle. I think the people who were on Sonny's records would all get together and do stuff, in the daytime and at night. You know, go to each other's gigs, and that kind of stuff.

A year and a half later, Nikki was born. We were married for about two years. After that, we had a separation and I secured an official divorce a couple of years later. One of the main issues why we got divorced was he could be a controlling person. As I got a little older, I wished not to be so controlled and knew that this was not going to work. Oddly enough, he became much more mellow in later years. But at this time, he was probably at his peak of his "opinionated" stage.

Sonny had absolutely no faith in Martin Luther King and that kind of movement. He thought there wasn't a chance that brotherhood was going to win. Sonny didn't have any optimism about brotherhood being workable. We had horrible arguments over this. He was completely cynical about America, because in his life and in the lives of his brothers, sister, his father, and his mother, he had seen and experienced the most horrible kinds of treatment. I remember a story that his brother Rodell told me when he was in the service. It was a story that just horrified me. One of the breaking points for me was a time when I wanted to go on a march and he told me that I couldn't.

Nicole Kyner

My mom and dad met in New York when my dad was playing at Birdland. That was somewhere around 1960. My mom was 10 years younger than my dad, and they got married against her parents' wishes. About two years later, they had me.

My mom left my dad when I was 2. She left him very abruptly. I didn't see him again until I was 13. My mom always used to tell me that "you'll see him when

Figure 16: Elena Knox and Sonny Red, New York, summer 1960. (Courtesy Nicole Kyner)

you're 18 because the circumstances under which I left him were less than favorable." She didn't want to deal with him, because my dad had a terrible temper. I mean, a terrible, horrible temper. Not a lay-your-hands-on-you kind of temper, not like that—he was a small man. I don't think he was going to do anything like that!

Tommy Flanagan

Red lived about two or three doors from me on Riverside Drive. He had a girl, Nicole, that was about the age of my youngest daughter. I used to see her and her mother, Elena.

James Kiner

It was sort of interesting where my brother lived on Riverside Drive. He lived three or four floors up and the windows were open in the summer where you could hear the concert singers practicing at night.

Figure 17: Red with his daughter Nicole Kyner. (Courtesy Roberta Marie Leach)

Louis Hayes

Red and myself used to just hang out in the park in the summertime. He lived on Riverside Drive and we'd go over to the park and sit in the grass and talk. You know, talk about ladies. Music and ladies!

James Kiner

I thought that there was a time when Elena tried to get Sonny to go to school in New York—go to college. She brought back Sylvester an application and stuff like that. College was practically free back in New York. She wanted him to study music. He told her, "If it can't bring me any money, it can't bring me nothing." I guess it was one of his bad days. Elena and Sylvester broke up probably because of his attitude more than anything. He had a very bad disposition with people.

Figure 18: Red playing with four-month-old Nicole. (Courtesy Nicole Kyner)

Like I mentioned the school thing. And I doubt that she would have been doing anything that wasn't in his benefit.

During the 1960s and early 1970s, Red was at his finest as a recording artist and sideman. His work with Jimmy Heath, Donald Byrd, Kenny Dorham, Freddie Hubbard, Howard McGhee, Blue Mitchell, Dizzy Reece, Barry Harris, Bobby Timmons, Milt Jackson, Philly Joe Jones, and many others helped establish him as one of the best saxophonists in New York. Because he remained firmly in the bebop idiom and continued to live in New York, Red's life was financially difficult. Ira Gitler summed up Red's steadfast commitment to the music and the New York scene in his liner notes for Red's Out of the Blue *session (Blue Note BLP 4032): "He returned to New York in June* [1959], *this time more determined than ever to stay. 'Even if I have to eat the bricks' was the way Red put it." Even while enduring these hard times and paying his dues, Red still kept his humor and quick wit.*

James Kiner

My brother would send us his records. I recall the first one with Paul Quinichette. That was his first one. Up to a point, I had all of his stuff. I used to be one of my brother's critics, you know? By this I mean when I was talking to my family, or to his wife, Elena.

Sonny Red

I worked with Donald Byrd for four years during the 1960s. We went to school together. We're from the same neighborhood in Detroit. I worked with Barry Harris, Milt Jackson—the Reverend Milt Jackson, he's from Detroit—and Philly Joe Jones. Freddie Hubbard was with Philly Joe's band in 1961. The great Freddie Hubbard, shall I say. All those cats had one thing in common: they would always practice. All day long.

Figure 19: Red playing with trumpeter Kenny Dorham at Count Basie's club in New York in the mid-1960s. (Courtesy Kiane Zawadi)

Me and Jimmy Heath used to write music together. In fact, I met Jimmy Heath in Donald Byrd's band in 1963. It was Jimmy Heath, Donald Byrd, Herbie Hancock, Eddie Khan, and [Albert] Tootie Heath. That's what the original band was in 1963, so I was around all of these composers and I saw how they put music together. Assembled it, you know? I was just so amazed, and I got a lot from that. I also worked with the late Kenny Dorham, too. He was a brilliant musician and composer. He could really put music together.

Cedar Walton

Yeah, I remember being on the bandstand with Red, Donald [Byrd], and Kenny [Dorham], sure. He was a very positive cat and hard worker. Red was a very proud man and loved his music. He studied considerably and worked hard at his craft, on his own, privately. I could tell that when he played and also how he talked.

James Spaulding

I was a sub for Sonny Red when he was in Donald Byrd's band. That was sometime in the mid-60s, when I lived in Brooklyn. We traveled to Canada to play the gig.

Kiane Zawadi

[Red and I] played in New York at the Village Gate, I remember. He was doing the Monday thing, which was a quartet. But he decided, he said, "Man, I want to use you," and he left out the piano.

Phil Lasley

Years ago when I was a kid, when I first went to New York, Red was like a big brother to me. He got me gigs and introduced me to people. There was a group led by Gloria Coleman. She had a girl named Pola Roberts from Pittsburgh on drums and Leo Wright on saxophone. When Leo Wright was on the road, Sonny would take his place, and when Sonny couldn't make it, I would take his place. Red introduced me to Cannonball [Adderley], and Cannonball called me for a few jobs. And I also took Sonny's place with Philly Joe [Jones], with Elmo Hope and Larry Ridley in the band. Red turned me on to a lot. He was *very* nice to me.

Curtis Fuller

Jimmy Heath would hire Sonny, and we'd do a lot of concerts down to Baltimore or Washington. Thanks to me: I told Jimmy that we should get Sonny Red because he knew all the songs we were trying to play.

Barry Harris

Sonny was very happy with the Jazzland dates. They were great sessions. We just came in and did them.

Figure 20: Red in front of kiosk, October 1964, location unknown. (Courtesy Nicole Kyner)

Orrin Keepnews

There aren't things, or colorful incidences that stand out from the [Red] dates. They were pretty workmanlike, and they were pretty pulled-together dates. They didn't have outrageous things happening. A lot of the Riverside dates will have pretty successful people, or distinguished people playing as sidemen on other people's dates, and very often at their own suggestion rather than mine, but sometimes mine. There was kind of a camaraderie there. We sometimes refer to it as the repertory company, or in the case of one Sam Jones album, the title was *The Soul Society*. And that was the basic idea—that there were a lot of these people that felt at home in our surroundings, and on my dates. It was a pretty good, clean atmosphere, but a cooperative atmosphere. You might've expected there to be funny stories about his [Red's] dates, but there weren't. I mean he was pretty much "take care of business," and people's response to him was that way. I think a lot of people on his dates were conscious of, "I'm here 'cause I like this guy, and I wanna help things go for him, so why screw around?" In general this says to me that the most intriguing thing you can get out of this is, here are these rather unusual lineups and I don't have funny stories to tell about it.

Tommy Flanagan

I remember the session *A Story Tale* that we did with Clifford Jordan. Sonny and Clifford had a nice rapport with each other. They were fond of each other's playing. Both were from the same region, Chicago and Detroit. They had that Chicago-Detroit connection.

Orrin Keepnews

There was a totally aborted session we did, and it didn't work—it didn't click. The tapes weren't even kept on it. Cannonball [Adderley] had the idea of doing a date that he would not be on, but it would be one of the things that he would produce, involving four altos. Sonny Red was one of them, Frank Strozier was one, a legendary guy from Philadelphia, [Clarence] "C" Sharpe, and I don't remember who the other one was, but there were four such people. I'm quite sure of C Sharpe, because it was the only encounter I ever had with him. We're talking probably early '60s. These were four guys on the scene that Cannonball thought deserved more attention then they were getting, and Sonny Red was one of them. I don't even remember exactly the rhythm section, but I know that it had Wynton Kelly and I think that it had A. T. [Arthur Taylor]. So the date didn't work for various reasons. It was not anybody's fault, it's something that will happen sometimes. My point is not anything other than Sonny Red was somebody to that degree at least Cannonball approved of. So that's not a bad thing!

Charles McPherson

I was on a Riverside session with four alto players, maybe sometime around early 1961. Cannonball had something to do with it. I can't remember everybody on the date, but I remember that it had Sonny Red. It was a bunch of alto players and they didn't release it. I remember that the music was a bit tricky and I remember that I didn't feel comfortable. I was very young at the time. I might have been like 19 or 20 years old. That might have been one of the first record dates that I did. I didn't have a clue about the recording part of it or anything. Something just didn't gel right. It was just a bunch of really young guys. I think it was probably a bunch of little things in a pretty stressful situation. This wasn't Cannonball recording, you know, a full-blown, grown guy that's been playing for years. It was a bunch of guys that hadn't been playing that long.

Phil Lasley

There was an all-alto situation with me and C Sharpe, Sonny Red, and Frank Strozier. I think it was Sam Jones, Wynton Kelly, and Jimmy Cobb—that was the rhythm section. You know, there was a lot of funny shit that went down. Originally I was supposed to be taking C Sharpe's place; they couldn't find him. I remember Yusef [Lateef] wrote most of the music, and it was some real different type of music. And a lot of confusion, a lot of confusion! But C Sharpe comes in at the last minute. It was a weird date, man, it was really strange. And I had just been in New York for about two months, so I was shakin' in my boots.

Orrin Keepnews

Sonny's records sold terribly. He was part of that vast body of people who did not establish an audience. They probably sell more when they're reissued now. We didn't sell more than a few thousand copies on any of those things. On the other hand, just about everybody was working for scale. The dates were done with relative efficiency. I did at least one of Sonny's things at Bell Sounds, but basically we worked at Plaza for the most part, and we had an arrangement there where we guaranteed them a certain amount of work. Guaranteed them a dollar figure. And basically we worked in terms of working against that figure. I didn't have to be really worrying about my hours, you know, from a studio standpoint. Usually I ended up paying musicians a little bit more than scale, so that nobody was really going to give me a hard time with the three-hour increments and whatnot. So I worked to take the pressure off of those things. So those were efficient dates. Not expensive dates and they kind of went faster that way.

Charles McPherson

I did a couple of those Charlie Parker memorial tributes with all alto players at the Club Ruby, an event that happened for a couple of years or maybe a little longer. Red was involved as well as C Sharpe. We probably paired or squared off at one time. Then maybe the last set we would all come up and play.

Sonny Red

I love music. I think you have to love it to be able to do it. Because there are a lot of things you go through like economics, which enter into all artists' lives, of all periods. But I think if you really stick by your guns, and you really believe, you can make someone else believe. If you really believe that you have the gift of music, and you love it, well then, keep right at it and don't let nobody turn you away from it. Stick right by your guns and everything will work out all right—that's what I think.

James Kiner

Sylvester was concerned about the music business, from a business viewpoint, like who got jobs and who didn't get jobs. This was controlled fully by the union. They made the decision whether you play or not play, which has an impact on your livelihood. He was aware of this and didn't like it, of course.

Elena Knox

Jack Kerouac called Sonny up on the telephone. They were doing this jazz and poetry thing in San Francisco at the time. This was probably 1961 to 1962, and I answered the phone. Jack wanted Sonny to come out there and play, and Sonny was not that interested. He just wasn't that interested in that beat poetry jazz kind of thing. Sonny had a vision of what he wanted, and it was a pretty rigid, I won't say narrow, it was just very well defined.

Olatunji, the drummer from Africa, had an African jazz thing, and he asked Sonny to come and play with him. But in order to do that, Sonny had to wear a dashiki kind of shirt. Sonny refused. He just said no, which was really weird, because later on, he started wearing them. I remember that very well, because we were so stone cold broke. I was just in shock.

I remember Miles Davis wanted Sonny to play with the group. Miles wanted Sonny to play tenor as a member of his band, but Sonny refused, because he wanted to play alto. I remember that was sometime between 1962 and 1963, because that was the time it was the hardest for us. Nikki had already been born, and it was really hard to keep it all together. I couldn't believe he wouldn't take the business. That was huge.

Nicole Kyner

My dad was incredibly hardcore about playing. I remember my mom once told me that at one point Miles Davis wanted my dad to play in his quintet. He wouldn't play in Miles's group because my dad didn't want to play tenor saxophone. Miles wanted him to play tenor, and my dad wouldn't do it! My mom said that he did this when they had about ten dollars in the bank. She was just beside herself, and I think that's when she noticed that this marriage was not going to work.

James Kiner

One time I went to New York, Sylvester was married then, but he was sick, he had pneumonia. I remember coming home from work (at that time I was working out in Ann Arbor), and my mother was crying. She told me that Sylvester was sick. My mother was threatening to go up herself, so I said, "Look, I'll drive up, and you can go with me." So we rushed off and it was raining. The neat thing about it was that his mother-in-law, Elena's mother, had a doctor there. A Jewish doctor, I think, making a home call. That should have changed his attitude, his thinking [about race], but I doubt if it did. My brother and I stayed up there for a while to make sure he wasn't going to die or anything. We stayed overnight and drove on back to Detroit the next day.

Phil Lasley

Sonny was a nice guy, but sometimes very difficult to talk to. Red used to challenge Joe Henderson [at jam sessions] and Joe never got along with Red because of that. I think it was more or less a musical thing, 'cause Red was a very competitive cat.

Figure 21: Red playing tenor saxophone during the late 1960s or early 1970s. (Courtesy Roberta Marie Leach)

Curtis Fuller

Red just had that look, man, like he wanted to fight everybody. I'll tell you something: if he had calmed down . . . Guys wouldn't give him dates and things—Hank Mobley, none of those guys. He knew that much music that he would challenge everybody, and that turns people off. We would get irritated, because Sonny couldn't help himself, he would challenge everybody—Pepper, anybody. That bothered me about him. He couldn't stand Archie Shepp!

Orrin Keepnews

Sonny was this very pleasant guy, but you got a slight feeling of flakiness about him. He didn't really seem to have both feet on the ground. He did seem to be, you know, a somewhat vague young man, and didn't have an evil bone in his body. He was *very* well liked and very good-hearted.

Talib Kibwe

Sonny was a very upbeat person. He would always say, "What's up?" or "What's going on?" Sonny was always positive.

Frank Foster

I have a funny story about Sonny Red. It involves Rahsaan Roland Kirk. The story goes like this: Sonny Red had a gig in uptown Harlem, probably at the Shalimar, where Grant Green would play. This was in the early 1960s. Rahsaan Roland Kirk came in after finishing his gig downtown, and Sonny said, "Let me invite my friend Rahsaan Roland Kirk to sit in." So Rahsaan came up on tenor, and he did his circular breathing thing. He did something that just wowed the audience. The audience didn't want Rahsaan to stop, and Sonny Red got angry and packed up his horn and went home, and then Rahsaan finished the gig! [*Laughs.*]

Phil Lasley

Frankie Dunlop used to be a comic female impersonator and he used to do impersonations of Sonny Red that cracked everybody up.

Jaffiria Leach-Orr

I was coming back from New York City when I was 14 years old, in the summer of 1965. Elena, Uncle Sylvester, and Nikki were taking me to the airport. So we're going across this walkway, and this guy starts blowing a whistle, to control the traffic flow. He's trying to let everyone know to stop, you know? So he blows his whistle, and my uncle went ballistic. He said, "You're doing this because I'm a black man, and you're picking on me." We're like, "Oh, here he goes again." That kind of thing didn't happen a whole lot, but when it happened, it was a big thing. Because of this little incident we were running late, and I missed my plane back to Detroit.

Malvin McCray

When we met, we weren't even playing music; we were in the poolroom, shooting pool. Red was a comedian. It was always a laugh with him, you know? Especially when you were out with other cats around, it was always a laugh. But Red was a stern cat. He didn't worry nobody for nothing. Red would be in real tough, bad shape, man, but he didn't lean on nobody. He'd tough it out. Red was a true human being. There was nothing he rattled me about. Nothing at all, that I remember, because there were a number of musicians that *did* rattle me. Red and I kicked it around, you know. I remember all of us getting together at Count Basie's when I was living in New York. We'd all sit around, and we just laughed at Sonny's stories.

James Kiner
My brother had a sense of humor, but quite often it was sort of a sharp sense of humor.

Tommy Flanagan
Sonny was very humorous. He could always see humor in other people. I remember he had just bought a brand new topcoat, and it was getting chilly outside. He came into the club, showing it off, and he said, "If you don't have a topcoat on now, you don't have one!" There's another time when a kid approached Sonny on the street and asked him, "Shine, Mister?" And Sonny replied, "Get away from me, boy! I need a new pair of shoes!"

Jimmy Heath
Sonny was a very funny guy. He had a great sense of humor, which you can tell in his playing. You know, Sonny wrote "Mustang" in order to get a car. He had hoped that the tune would bring in enough money so he could buy one.

Figure 22: Detroit, 1969 or 1970. Left to right: Sonny Red, Lottie Lee McAfee-Kiner, Jaffiria Leach-Orr, Rodell Kiner. (Courtesy Roberta Marie Leach)

Cedar Walton

You couldn't help but like Red with his positive outlook. We played at least one if not two gigs with Bags [Milt Jackson] in New York. I remember him moving to New Jersey and working seldom to almost none. So it's not a happy story, that I recall. But I wasn't on his case daily. He wasn't somebody that I'd call everyday, anything like that.

Yusef Lateef

I remember a sad story that happened in the late 1960s. Sonny was supposed to play a gig in upstate New York, but the club owner couldn't honor the contract. Sonny got stood up. He had only bought a one-way ticket to upstate, hoping that the gig would pay for his ride back to New York. Well, Sonny wound up getting a ride back to New York in an animal truck. Sonny paid a lot of dues and he was such a fine musician. Red was a warm human being. In the late 1960s or early 1970s, Sonny moved from New York to Hackensack, New Jersey, where he stayed at the YMCA.

Louis Hayes

Red, he was so funny! He was a very unique, wonderful human being, who wasn't that well. Naturally, I just would have wanted and loved for him to be able to be here longer. He had a special personality. He loved people, and people loved him. He was a hip guy! A personality person. A one-of-a-kind guy.

Donald Byrd

[Red] was a genius. This is what people say today, but I knew this a long time ago. Red was a creative, honest, and thoughtful musician and person. He was very comical and had a fantastic sense of humor. He was a pleasure and very enjoyable to be around. My sister and many of my family knew Red well. They all loved him.

From 1971 through 1977 Sonny Red was very involved with the Jazzmobile program in New York. His teaching methods at Jazzmobile were very similar to the way he approached composition and playing: emphasis on sound, feeling, the blues, and the importance of scales and theory. Red also gave private instruction at the Arts for Living Center at Henry Street Settlement from 1976 through 1979.

Sonny Red

I had a flute class that I was teaching for Jazzmobile for about three years. And I would always stress to the students that the sound comes first. I can't say that enough, because a lot of people forget about it. You're thinking about the music, the chord changes, but music starts before that. And I think it's in the sound first.

Figure 23: Red teaching at Jazzmobile during the 1970s. (Courtesy Roberta Marie Leach)

Jimmy Heath
Sonny and I taught classes together at Jazzmobile. We lectured in the schools and gave workshops on Saturdays. We also played in the streets.

Dave Bailey
Sonny taught flute, saxophone, harmony, and theory and directed the ensembles at Jazzmobile. Sonny was playing tenor saxophone at this time. He never played alto with Jazzmobile; he played mainly tenor.

Malvin McCray
Harold Vick and Sonny befriended one another when they were over in New York. Red didn't have a place to stay, and Harold Vick opened up his house to him. Harold had a small room, and he let Red have that room. He also gave him a saxophone [*a tenor—A.S.*]. They were real good friends. In fact, that's how I met Harold Vick, through Sonny Red.

Frank Gant
I think Harold Vick had something to do with Red playing more tenor. Vick, being the tenor player, told him that maybe he could get more gigs if he was playing the tenor. He might have been instrumental in helping Red get a tenor.

Sheila Kiner
The doctor stopped my uncle from playing the alto, so he went to the tenor. But the alto was his favorite; he really liked the alto, and hated the tenor. He didn't want to switch to the tenor.

Malvin McCray
Bags [Milt Jackson] loved Red. Milt Jackson would always call him for those Jazzmobile gigs. So Sonny and I went together to New York for one gig. When we got there, Red didn't have a place to stay, but he had a car. We would go on the Jersey side across from the George Washington Bridge. Red would park under the overpass, where there wasn't much traffic, and that's where he'd sleep. Safely. And in that time, he made it. He didn't even have a place to stay.

Dave Bailey
Sonny had a practical approach to the saxophone. First he taught his students to learn how to play the blues, then to learn all of their scales. Sonny was a very down-home player. Sonny was an excellent teacher. His students loved him. Sonny was able to establish a great deal of respect from his students.

Talib Kibwe
I was a student at Jazzmobile from 1971 to 1972. Sonny Red was teaching the beginning flute classes. I never saw him with a saxophone. Sonny was the section leader at the big band rehearsals, while Jimmy Heath was the conductor. Sonny would sit off to the side and listen to the saxophone section. He would very casually give pointers to us during the sectionals. Sonny had great ears. He could catch mistakes, even through the fast runs. He'd say, "Hey, you missed the B-flat during that run." He also was very aware of tuning issues. Sonny was a good teacher, and his students always played really well. He always had killer students from his classes.

James Kiner
I have a tape of my brother teaching. He's apparently teaching a group of students, a band or something. The kids were not too hot, you know, but they were learning. Sylvester had a student in Detroit one time, as a matter of fact, a white guy. The guy used to come by for lessons over on Leicester.

I was listening to this one [tape] of Sylvester. He's got this woman who's trying to sing. She was singing "Song Samba," which I had never heard before, and didn't even know there were words to it. Anyway, he's chording [on piano] and one time he hit it so fast, she says, "Look, you're going too fast, I'm gonna fall off the sofa." But she stuck with it, and he lowered the tempo. Now, "Central Park"—there are words to that too.

Kiane Zawadi
I remember getting Red a gig with Dizzy Gillespie's big band on a New Year's Eve date at Buddy Rich's place. I was in the band and this was sometime in the early 1970s.

Elena Knox
Sonny had a strong interest in Afro-Cuban music. He had the beginnings of a suite that he said he was writing, and he wanted very much to go to Cuba. He told

Figure 24: Bassist Herbie Lewis, trumpeter Donald Byrd, and Red in the 1970s. (Courtesy Roberta Marie Leach)

me this a few years before he died. His interest in Afro-Cuban music was a very serious, deep interest. My feeling always was that Sonny just did not live long enough to develop the musical ideas that he would have had, had he lived longer. And then he got sick and that put a premature end to it.

Jimmy Heath

Sonny and I premiered something I wrote called *The Afro-American Suite of Evolution* in Winnipeg, Canada. We also toured Canada together.

Talib Kibwe

I was a test rat for Jimmy Heath's *Afro-American Suite of Evolution*. It was first performed at Town Hall in Winnipeg, Canada. The students performed it in 1976.

Elena Knox

There was this big jazz concert at Carnegie Hall, probably in 1976, that Nikki and I went to. It was a big group where Jimmy Heath was the leader. Both Jimmy and Sonny were playing in the band.

Frank Gant

Howard McGhee hired Sonny a lot, whenever he could, because he had a big band and sometimes he'd get Red in the band to play alto. Me and Red also went to Atlantic City on a gig one time. Red got an organ trio gig, sometime in the 1970s. We played in a place called Grace's Little Belmont, across the street from the Harlem Club, where they have those shows with showgirls and all that. Anyway, we went to Atlantic City and we had Duke Pearson on organ, because you know, he was a pianist. So we get to the gig, and Duke sat down at the organ, and he didn't even know how to turn it on! The waitress had to come over and said, "I think you turn it on like this." But he [Red] would call me whenever he could, and we'd do a gig together. I loved Sonny Red; that was my man!

Elena Knox

I totally and deliberately lost touch with Sonny for a period of time. It had to do with the custody of Nikki and our differences. But when I wanted to find Sonny, so that Nikki could get back in touch with her dad, I'd call Barry Harris. Or I'd go see him at a club. It was just natural that Barry or Tommy [Flanagan] would be the people to get in touch with. We were living in a small little town called Fleischmanns in the Catskills, in upstate New York. At this point, sometime around 1975, Nikki really wanted to meet her dad, and I thought it was okay. So I went down to the city and went to a club where Barry was playing. At the break, I reintroduced myself to Barry. I told him that I really wanted to get in touch with Sonny and I gave him my number. I told Barry that Sonny's daughter wanted to see her dad. So he gave my number to Sonny, and Sonny called me and then we put it all together. Sonny at that point was living on 103rd and Central Park West. About a week or two later, we all got together. I drove Nikki back down to the city so that they could meet. After that, they had a relationship that was independent of me until he died.

There was a time when Sonny moved up to Woodstock, New York [*11 Deming Street—A.S.*]. He wasn't there very long, but he played in a jazz club up there, and I think he was also going to give lessons. I think his moving there had to do with living in the country and being near streams. I remember sitting there in Woodstock with him, near a stream, and that's when he told me he had become a Buddhist. This was just shortly after he and Nikki hooked up again, and Nikki and I were still living up in Fleischmanns, sometime around 1976. He was still opinionated at this time, but not as angry as he had been in the past. His words were, "I've mellowed."

Nicole Kyner

I think my dad could be a confrontational person. When he was younger, my mom found him sort of impossible to deal with. But my mom did meet him again when I was 13. The only reason that happened was because I was just relentless in wanting to meet my father. I didn't want to wait until I was 18. One night I had a terrible nightmare. I woke up crying, and my mom came in and I remember saying something about my dad, like "He's going to die," or something like that. That freaked my mom out. So after that, we went out to find him, which was very easy to do because he was playing around the city. My mom found him, and she took me over there, and he was absolutely gracious. He was very grateful to her. He just said, "Thanks so much for bringing her back." Then we drove to Detroit and met his wonderful family. I felt like the luckiest girl in the world! When I first met my dad, he was living on the West Side, at Central Park West. My mom and I moved to upstate New York, and then he moved up to Woodstock, New York, because he wanted to be closer to me and still be within striking distance to the city. This was sometime between 1973 and 1975. I remember thinking, "This is not a great place for my dad to be living. It's so far from the city where he makes his money." But he was very adamant that he wanted to be near me.

I remember one time my dad and I went to Belle Isle [Ontario]. When we came back from Canada, the police do these random checks of cars—it's totally random—and they selected our car, and my dad hit the roof! He said, "You're doing this because I'm a black man." I had a big Afro at the time, because it was in the mid-'70s, and they wanted to look in my hair. My dad was livid that they wanted to feel my hair. But he threw such a shit-fit that he made it much worse. I was like, "My dad's going to get us thrown in jail!" That was very consistent with who he was. If he thought there was an injustice, he was going to scream about it. He wasn't going to finesse it, he was going to scream at the top of his lungs about it.

Tears: Detroit, 1979–81

Sonny's declining health in the late 1970s brought him back to live with his mother at 233 Leicester in Detroit, though he frequently managed to return to New York for concerts. On December 9, 1979, a benefit concert, organized by Sheila Kiner, Teddy Harris Jr., and Richard Jarrett, was given for Red in Detroit, and the musicians and friends in attendance revealed how many people he had touched as a son, father, brother, musician, and friend. Performers included Marcus Belgrave, Claude Black, Alan Barnes, Roy Brooks, Malvin McCray, Wendell Harrison, Harold McKinney, Sam Sanders, Donald Towns, Harold Vick, Lamonte Hamilton, Phil Lasley, Donald Walden, Hindal Butts, Melvin Jackson, Jimmy Morgan, Ralphe Armstrong, Kasuku Mafia, and Yusef Lateef, with Paul Leonard as master of ceremonies. In 1981, shortly before his death, Red received a $7,500 grant from the National Endowment for the Arts to complete the composition and orchestration of a three-part jazz suite, entitled "Cien Fuegos." One completed part exists from the suite: "Song Samba," written for 17 instruments.

Sonny Red

The music of America, jazz music—that's the only music America has, as an art form. I think it originated in the churches and the street, like the New Orleans street bands. In fact, I'm trying to get a piece together now called "New Orleans Sketches," starting with the street band aspect of it, you know, walking bands with the big bass drum going *boom, boom, boom*.

Figure 25: Page from Sonny Red's sketchbook. (Courtesy Nicole Kyner)

Elena Knox

I had moved to New Jersey and Sonny was living in New York when he found out that he had cancer. I remember him coming to the house to tell me that he was going to go back to Detroit. The doctor had told him that the cancer was very advanced and that it was in his lymph nodes. Sonny told me that they couldn't operate. It was like he knew he was going to die, and he was going home to die. So he went home to his mom's house and that's where he stayed until he went into the hospital.

James Kiner

My brother moved back to Detroit in 1978 [*probably 1979—A.S.*]. At that time I was single and living in an apartment downtown in Lafayette Park off the river. My brother stopped by a couple of times at the apartment. When Sylvester came home, he talked to my mother. I remember that. I think I was there when he came in. She was sad and weeping, trying not to cry, and she said he had cancer. I only saw him a few times, since I wasn't living at home. Usually when I would drop by the house, Sylvester would be in the bedroom laying down. And I'm pretty sure my sister told me that he was still writing music! He was writing a piece for [jazz ensemble] at the time called "Amaneciga" ("Sunrise"). He didn't get the copyright apparently, because I have the copyright form here that was never filled out. My brother said he tried to get somebody to record it. A rock band wanted to record it. [*Laughs.*] But hey, you know, it's better than nothing happening to it.

Malvin McCray

When Red had cancer, he came back to Detroit and stayed here for a while. His mother took care of him in his last days. Red was real close to his mother. When Red came back to Detroit, he wasn't in the union. He was real sick and didn't have any money. I took him down to the union so he could join the union and get the $1,000 insurance policy, so they'd have money to bury him. That was key, because he didn't last long after that.

Kiane Zawadi

In the 1970s Red played with the Howard McGhee and Clifford Jordan big bands. One of the last gigs I remember him doing was at the Tin Palace—the old Tin Palace on the Bowery Inn around 4th street. That was in the mid-1970s. I think he passed soon after that.

Art Zimmerman

I was hanging out with Howard McGhee at his apartment on 69th Street in New York in the early 1980s. I met Sonny during this time, and he was very friendly to me. Sonny was playing tenor saxophone on the library gigs with Howard McGhee. I saw Sonny with Howard at the plaza bandshell in Lincoln Center.

Sonny Redd
c/o Mrs. Kyner
233 Leicester (ct)
Detroit
Michigan 48202

September 16, 1979

Dear Sonny.

I talked to Bags, while he was playing here a few days ago. He told me that you had to return to Michigan for an operation in the lungs.

I am sorry to hear that, and I wish that you have fully recovered by now.

Kepp me posted, Sonny. I'll be in New York (you can reach me at Maggie's pad) on Oct. 7 &8.

Yours sincerely. Take care now

Lars Johansen.

JAZZCRAFT RECORDS
RØDTJØRNEN 28
DK-2791 DRAGØR, DENMARK
PHONE: (01) 53 73 99
BANK: HANDELSBANKEN, DRAGØR
POSTGIRO: 6 32 20 26

TELEX: 16600
CABLE: JAZZCRAFT COPENHAGEN

Figure 26: Letter from Lars Johansen to Sonny Red. (Courtesy Nicole Kyner)

The band was Howard McGhee, Charlie Rouse, Lisle Atkinson, Jules Curtis, and Jim Robertson.

Red's last New York gig as a leader was for Jazzmobile on August 15, 1980. The group included Bill Hardman, Curtis Fuller, Barry Harris, Sam Jones, and Walter Bolden. When Red felt too weak to perform, Harold Vick stepped in to take his place.

Figure 27: One of Red's last gigs in Detroit. (Courtesy Nicole Kyner)

Curtis Fuller

Sonny's last gig was in New York with Jazzmobile. He was in Detroit at that time, and the doctors let him out of the hospital to go to New York to do the gig. Sonny wanted me there for the concert, so I took time off from Basie's band. I went up there to play with him, and he would start the song and get through the melody, but then he'd say, "Take a solo, I can't play anymore." They loved him, yeah, they loved him. I didn't realize the severity of his disease until it happened to me.

Charles Boles

I remember Sonny Red being ill at the very end, sometime around 1980. He had just come back from New York. He and I hung out a little bit. I remember he came by my house, because I was teaching at Oakland University, and he really wanted a position at the university. We tried to hook him up with that, but it never happened.

Frank Foster

I remember my last telephone conversation with Sonny Red, in which he said, "Don't give up on me, I'm coming back out [to New York]." And I said, "I hope so, man!" Shortly after that, he passed away.

Cedar Walton

Red was very sick at the end. I was playing in Detroit, and he was in the hospital. I avoided going. I didn't want to go, but I knew I *had* to go, and I went. And he cheered *me* up! Man, he was in diapers, and it was just a sad sight, just all skin and bones, but man, he cheered me up. That's the kind of guy he was. He was something else!

Figure 28: Lottie Lee McAfee-Kiner's 69th birthday party, 233 Leicester Court, Detroit, 1978. Left to right: Jaffiria Leach-Orr, Eddie Mae Kiner (in back), Sheila Kiner, Ira Kiner, Sonny Red; children unknown. (Courtesy Roberta Marie Leach)

Sheila Kiner

Me and my boyfriend at the time, Melvin Jackson, who was the bassist for Eddie Harris, along with Teddy Harris, helped organize the benefit for my uncle. It was an all-day thing that went late into the night. His mom was there, I was there, my dad Ira, my mother, Roy Brooks, and a host of friends and relatives too.

Appearing

THE ALLAN BARNES BAND

MARCUS BELGRAVE/The New Detroit Jazz Ensemble

CLAUDE BLACK

ROY BROOKS & THE ARTISTIC TRUTH

LAMONTE HAMILTON

HASTING'S STREET EXPERIENCE

MALVIN McCRAY/Creative Element

OCEAN

REBIRTH featuring Wendell Harrison & Harold McKinney

SAM SANDERS/Visions

DONALD TOWNS/The D-Sace Players featuring Naima Shamboiguer

II-V-I ORCHESTRA

Special Guest Performance by HAROLD VICK, New York Tenor Saxophonist
PAUL LEONARD, Master of Ceremonies
— Compositions Written by Sonny Redd will be preformed by various groups —

M.U.S.I.C. STATION
2757 GRAND RIVER (near Perry)
(Located in the H.O.M.E. & Jazz Development Workshop Bldg.)

DONATION: $5.00

Food by: O.S.W.R., Inc.
(Olita Williams, Author of "Nothing Like Home Cooking" and Shirley Reed)

Figure 29: Flyer for the benefit concert. (Courtesy Malvin McCray)

Nicole Kyner

The benefit for my dad in Detroit was very nice. There were a lot of people there. I was 17 when the benefit happened, and at that time, I was trying to deal with the realization that my father was going to die. In 1980, when I was 18 years old, I moved to Berkeley, California. My dad had already been diagnosed with his cancer by this point and he had gone back home to Detroit.

James Kiner

They tried to do a couple of things for my brother. Miss Finnley lived in an apartment next door to our house. She was a nurse. She used to come by and help him out a lot, when he was really getting bad. After that he went up to the University of Michigan hospital, where they did some tests and radiation treatments. I understand he lost a lot of weight. He went into a local rest home and my sister was with him when he died.

Jaffiria Leach-Orr

I can remember the Thanksgiving dinner in 1979 when he still had his appetite. We have a picture of him, and he's just smiling from ear to ear. We had all this food; he was so happy. He was very courageous in his whole fight against cancer. He was in a lot of pain, but he kept fighting. The nursing home was right there on the corner of Leicester and Woodward, so we could easily get to him. I can remember sometimes him wanting to play the saxophone, but he really couldn't, so he'd play the flute.

I can remember taking uncle Sylvester back and forth to the hospital way out there by the airport for his treatments. Now, Miss Finnley, she was a nurse. She lived in the apartment building next door and was very helpful. She was very fond of Uncle Sylvester. She was a very sanctified lady, you know, with the long dresses? Uncle Sylvester told her, "Now, why don't you shorten your dress?" [*Laughs.*] I remember her always sitting on the porch and my uncle would always be teasing her. She truly was a godsend for the family. It was hard for my mom and grandmother, so all of us had to pitch in and help out. My mother ended up giving Miss Finnley the house key so she could come in and help take care of him. She was right there. My uncle really did appreciate her in the end. She was the last one to see him alive.

Sheila Kiner

After my uncle passed, they played his music on the Ed Love Show, 101.9 FM-WDET, a very popular jazz radio show known around the jazz world. I kind of helped arrange the whole funeral. I had his music playing for viewing at the funeral home and at the memorial service at Woodlawn Cemetery, where he was cremated, on Woodward Avenue. I remember Malvin McCray, Roy Brooks, Teddy Harris, and Marcus Belgrave being there.

Jaffiria Leach-Orr

His funeral was a real tribute. All of his friends came from New York. It was very well attended. It was in the largest parlor at the R. T. Wilson Funeral Home on Owen Street, right across from the church we went to: Greater New Mount Moriah Baptist Church. Within three days from the time he died, he was cremated, which was the first cremation in the family, which was kind of hard. But that's what uncle Sylvester wanted, so that's what we did. Uncle Sylvester wanted us to take his ashes back to New York, and uncle Ira went out there and put them in—I think—the Hudson River.

Giving Respect and Honor
To
Sylvester "Sonny Red" Kyner

To the Creator beyond my comprehension I pray and say,

Sonny Red you are a reminder; I will never forget my ancestor, nor my culture. I will always remember my elders and fore-bearers that fought courageously at all times, throughout the all conditions they encountered.
They were, and are responsible for this land we now live in, and for all the riches and pleasures we all enjoy. It is from their sweat, toil/ labor, pain, knowledge and skills that laid the foundation that we then, later, now and in the future will enjoy.
They, very often sustained, endured persevered in spite of denial of life; liberty and justice were unable to pursue freedom, equal economic compensation and happiness for their works. They were not given a chance to entertain, even to desire or aspire to acquire these things, thoughts or ideas. Yet, without reservation they served the needs of others and the needs of self. Yet, in spite of all this punishment "They Kept Moving On Up."

"Sonny Red" or some times we would just say "Red" with all Respect and Honor we, joyously and reverently will not forget you.

All Thanks to the CREATOR

As my father, Rev. E. T. Byrd taught me, and " Red" knew him well "The respect you give to others will reflect in the respect given to you."

"Red" with the greatest respect and highest honor I will remember you. "Sonny" you had a blessed life.

Be of Good Cheer!

Dr. Donaldson T. L. Byrd

Figure 30: Letter from Donald Byrd. (Courtesy Nicole Kyner)

Nicole Kyner

My cousin Jaffiria, who was living in Detroit at the time, would call me and say that he was not doing well and I'd better come back. I remember one time Jaffiria called me and she said that my dad looked like he was in really bad shape and he hadn't been able to move in a week. So I would fly to Detroit to see my dad. One of the times I flew back—I remember this so clearly—when I got off the airplane, my dad was standing there! First of all, he looked like a skeleton. It was so horrifying to see him like that, but the fact that he was standing there was just an amazing thing. I had one of those luggage bags with me, and he insisted on taking it. He was such a proud man. He carried it to the car, and he had this amazing turnaround. He stayed around for another year, and all that time I kept telling him that I'm going to leave school to stay with him, but he wouldn't let me do it. So finally in the end, I got the call that he had died, and then I came out to Detroit for his funeral.

Sonny Red died around 4:00 A.M. on March 20, 1981, at the Ambassador Nursing Home in Detroit. On April 1, 1995, Nicole's first child, Jackson Sylvester Barnett, was born. Her second child, Juliette Marie Ward, was born October 1, 2001.

Figure 31: Nicole Kyner with Jackson Sylvester Barnett and Juliette Marie Ward, Berkeley, California, 2003. (Courtesy Nicole Kyner)

NOTES ON COMPOSITIONS AND SOLO TRANSCRIPTIONS

This section includes every commercially recorded composition by Sonny Red. The record *Curtis Fuller with Red Garland* lists Sonny Red as the composer of "Seeing Red," but a letter from Kiane Zawadi has confirmed that Barry Harris is the true composer of this tune, and so it is not included here.

The lead sheets and solo transcriptions from the records are more or less "performance" lead sheets straight off the recordings. I've added, as accurately as possible, the articulations and nuances that Sonny used, or whichever articulations seemed to suit the overall spirit of the tune. The unpublished compositions have been taken from Sonny Red's sketchbook, which was created in the 1970s. I have not added articulations for the sketchbook tunes, because I wanted to preserve the original format of the lead sheet.

The two solo transcriptions are taken from performances of "Bluesville" and "Mustang," probably Red's best-known blues compositions. I chose these two particular solos because they both came from good, representative periods in his playing. The "Bluesville" solo is from 1959 and shows a strong bebop influence. Red incorporates double-time phrases in a number of strategic spots in this solo, showing the considerable technique and good knack for harmony that most bop players had during this time. "Mustang" was recorded seven years later, in 1966, and Red's playing had changed to some degree. This solo incorporates a very bluesy, down-home sound, revealing more interesting intervallic and rhythmic combinations than the earlier solo. This unique sound would later morph into a mature style that can only be identified as "Sonny Red."

Following the solo transcriptions are two compositions for flute ensemble (most likely written for Red's flute classes at Jazzmobile in the 1970s) and a big band score for "Song Samba," a.k.a. "Amaneciga" (Sunrise). This score constituted the first part of "Cien Fuegos," a three-part suite commissioned by the National Endowment for the Arts. Lead sheets for "Song Samba" and for "Fiesta," the second part of the suite, appear among the other compositions. The third part of the suite, "Puesta del Sol" (Sunset), is missing or was never completed.

Azania

Example 1

Beale Street

Sylvester Kyner
As Recorded on "Blackjack"
Blue Note BLP 4259 (1967)

*** FINE: Fade out on horn intro (mm. 5-6)*

Example 2

Blue Sonny

Sylvester Kyner
As Recorded on "Images" Jazzland JLP 74 (1962)

Example 3

Sylvester Kyner

As Recorded on "Images"
Jazzland JLP 74 (1962)

Blues in the Pocket

Sylvester Kyner

As Recorded on "Out of the Blue"
Blue Note BLP 4032 (1959)

Example 4

Bluesville

Sylvester Kyner
As Recorded on "Out of the Blue"
Blue Note BLP 4032 (1959)

Example 5

Bonita

Sylvester Kyner

From "The Sonny Red Sketchbook"
Previously Unpublished

Example 6

Breezing

Example 7

Brother B.

Sylvester Kyner
As Recorded on "Breezing"
Jazzland JLP 32 (1960)

Example 8

Central Park

FAST SWING

Sylvester Kyner

From "The Sonny Red Sketchbook"
Previously Unpublished

Example 9

The Creeper

Sylvester Kyner

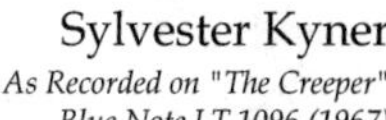

FAST SWING ♩= 195

A B♭7(#11) E♭7 B♭7(#11)

B♭7(#11) A7(#11) A♭7(#11) G7(#11)

F♯7(#11) F7(#11) 1. B♭7(#11) 2. B♭7(#11)

B D7(#11) C♯7(#11)

C7(#11) B7(#11)

A B♭7(#11) E♭7 B♭7(#11)

B♭7(#11) A7(#11) A♭7(#11) G7(#11) F♯7(#11) F7(#11) B♭7(#11)

*** On Last Chorus, Tag Last 4 Measures Two Times*

Example 10

Crystal

Example 11

Defiance

Sylvester Kyner

As Recorded on "A Story Tale"
Jazzland JLP 40 (1961)

MEDIUM UP SWING ♩= 195

Ditty

Sylvester Kyner

As Recorded on "Breezing"
Jazzland JLP 32 (1960)

MEDIUM UP SWING ♩= 170

Continued on the next page

Example 12

"Ditty" continued
Dmi7 G7 CMa7 A7 Dmi G7 CMa7
B
Alto Improvised Bridge
Gmi7 C7 Gmi7 C7 FMa7
Ami7 D7 GMa Ami7 Dmi7 G7
A
F♯ø FMa7 Emi E♭○ Dmi7 G7 CMa7
To Coda
Dmi7 G7 CMa7 A7 Dmi G7 CMa7
CODA - Play after last chorus
Dmi G7 CMa7

Example 13

Dodge City

FAST SWING ♩=220

Sylvester Kyner
As Recorded on "Images"
Jazzland JLP 74 (1962)

Example 14

Fiesta
Sylvester Kyner
LATIN
From "The Sonny Red Sketchbook"
Previously Unpublished
F6
Dmi7
Gmi
C7
F6
Vamp
Piano
2
A
Vamp continues throughout
1.
2.
B
A

Example 15

Hip Pockets

MEDIUM UP SWING ♩= 208

Sylvester Kyner/Clifford Jordan
As Recorded on "A Story Tale"
Jazzland JLP 40 (1961)

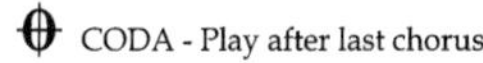

Example 16

Images

MEDIUM UP SWING ♩=205

Sylvester Kyner
As Recorded on "Images"
Jazzland JLP 74 (1962)

Continued on the next page

Example 17

"Images" continued

Example 18

Jelly Roll

Example 19

Ko-Kee
(Blues For KoKee)

Sylvester Kyner

As Recorded on "The Mode"
Jazzland JLP 59 (1961)

MEDIUM BLUES ♩= 140

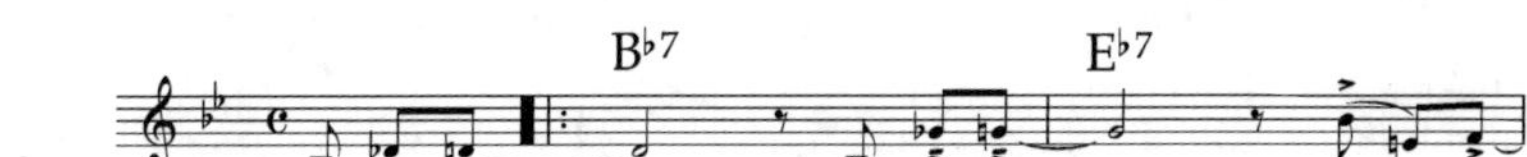

CODA - Play after last chorus

Example 20

Loki

Sylvester Kyner
As Recorded on "Blackjack"
Blue Note BLP 4259 (1967)

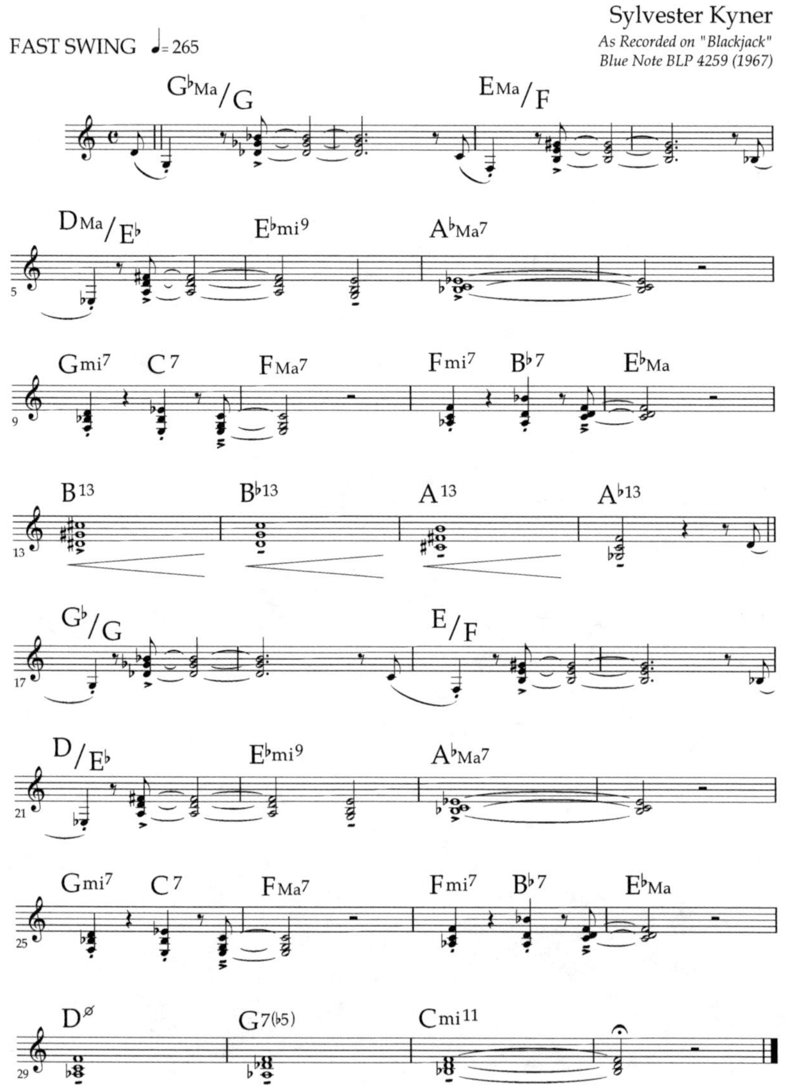

Example 21

The Lope

Sylvester Kyner
As Recorded on "Out of the Blue" Blue Note BLP 4032 (1960)

Example 22

Love Song

Example 23

"*Love Song*" *continued*

Example 24

The Mode

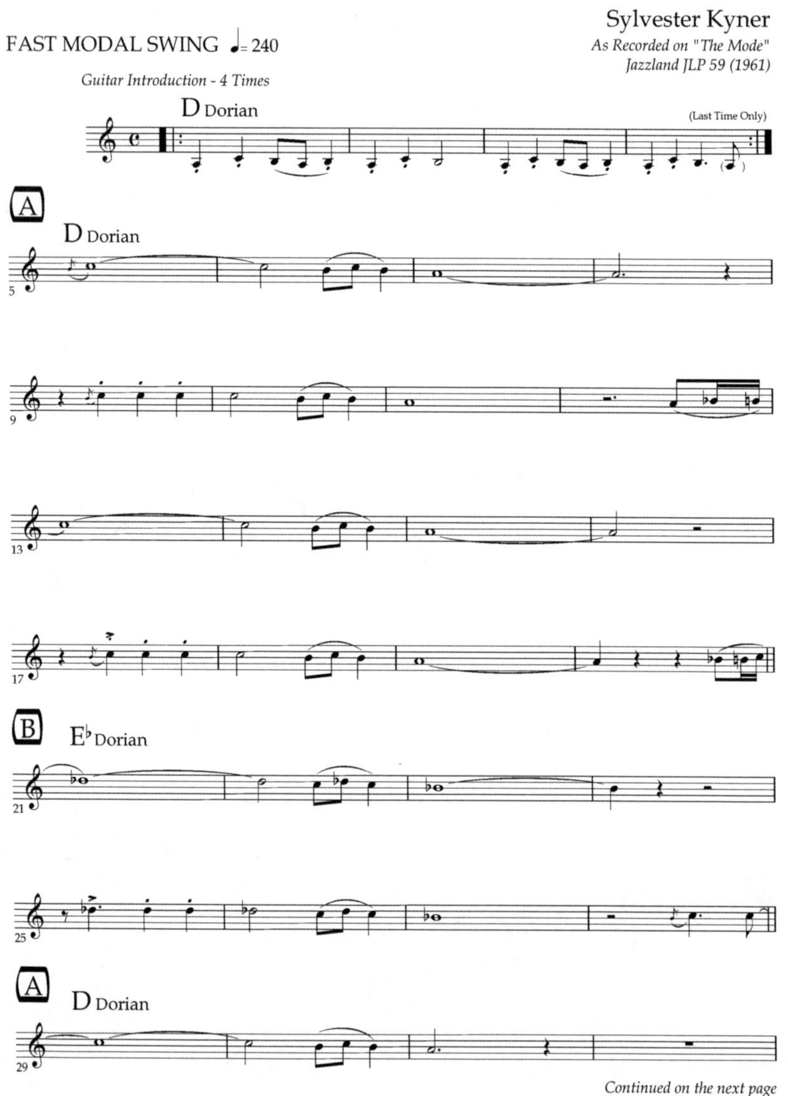

Example 25

"The Mode" continued

Example 26

Mustang

Continued on the next page

Example 27

"Mustang" continued

Tag last 8 Bars on last chorus and fade out

Example 28

Nadia

Sylvester Kyner
As Recorded on "Out of the Blue"
Blue Note BLP 4032 (1959)

MEDIUM BLUES ♩= 145

The New Blues
(Red's Blues)

Sylvester Kyner
As Recorded on "Breezing"
Jazzland JLP 32 (1960)

FAST SWING ♩= 225

Example 29

Nikki

Continued on the next page

Example 30

"*Nikki*" *continued*

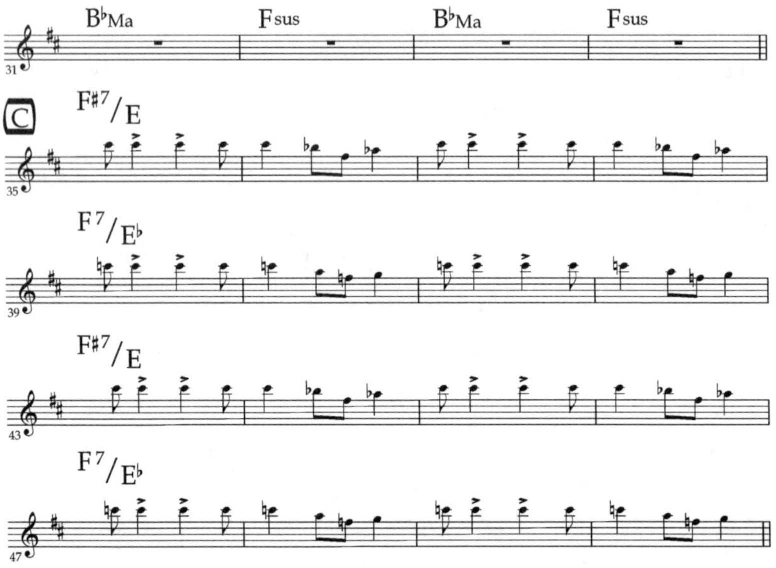

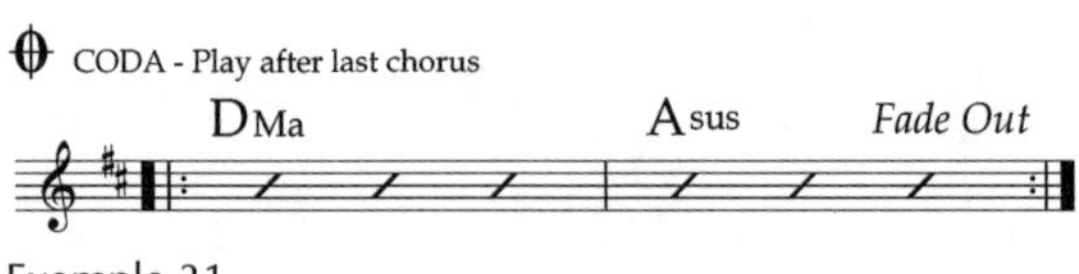

Example 31

Prints

Sylvester Kyner
As Recorded on "A Story Tale"
Jazzland JLP 40 (1961)

Continued on the next page

Example 32

"Prints" continued

Example 33

Redd's Head

Sylvester Kyner

As Recorded on "Two Altos" Regent 6069 (1957)

CODA - Play after last chorus

B♭Ma9

Example 34

The Rhythm Thing

Example 35

Rodan

Sylvester Kyner
As Recorded on "Sonny Red"
Mainstream MRL 324 (1971)

Example 36

Slenderella

Sylvester Kyner

As Recorded on "Curits Fuller with Red Garland"
New Jazz NJLP 8277 (1957)

FAST SWING ♩= 210

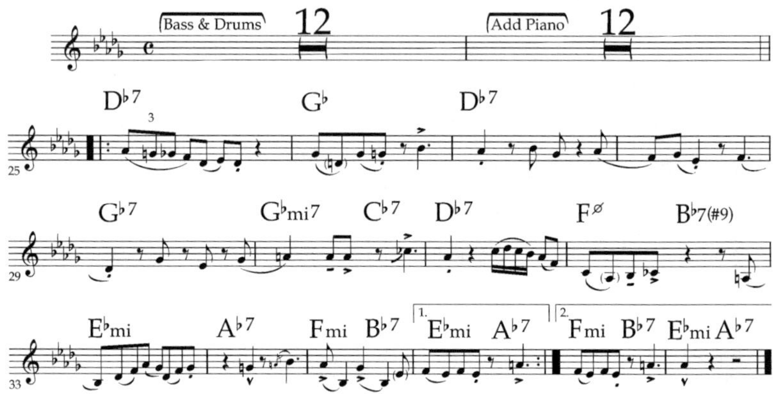

Super 20

Sylvester Kyner

As Recorded on "The Mode"
Jazzland JLP 59 (1961)

MEDIUM UP SWING ♩= 180

CODA - Play after last chorus

Example 37

Song Samba

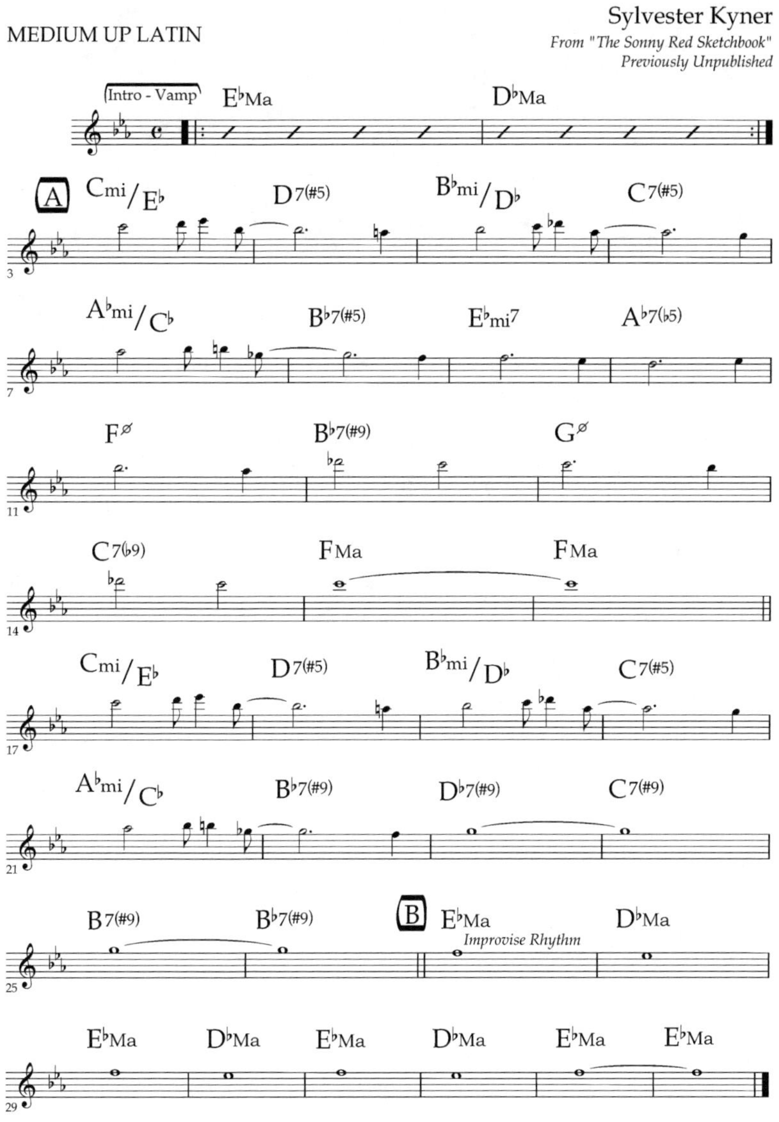

Example 38

Tears

Sylvester Kyner
As Recorded on "Sonny Red"
Mainstream MRL 324 (1971)

Continued on the next page

Example 39

"Tears" continued

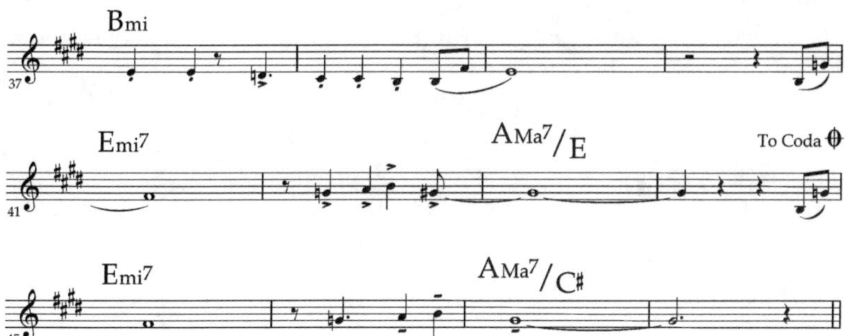

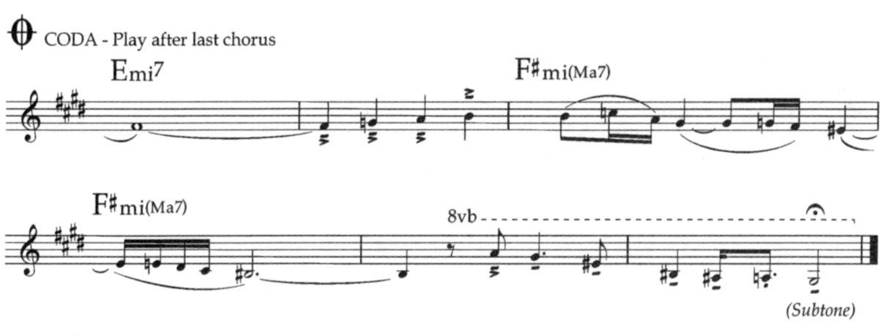

Example 40

Teef

West of The Pecos

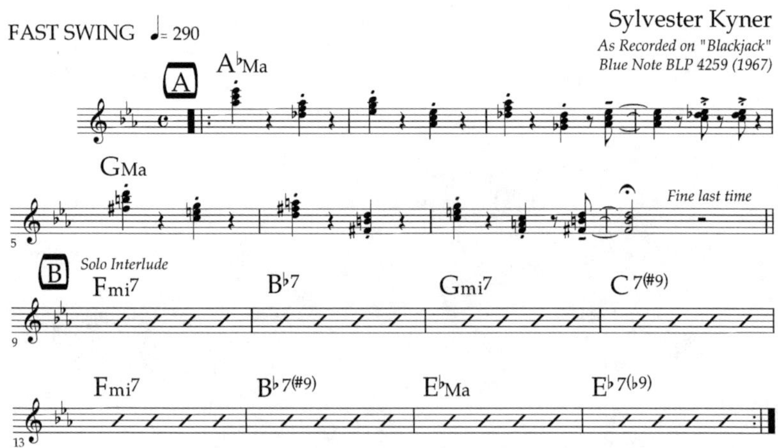

Example 41

Bluesville

Alto Saxophone Solo

Sylvester Kyner

As Recorded on "Out of the Blue"
Blue Note BLP 4032 (1959)

Continued on the next page

Example 42

"Bluesville" solo continued
F7
C7
G7
F7
C7
Fourth Chorus
C7
C7
F7
C7
G7
F7
C7

Example 43

Mustang

Alto Saxophone Solo

Sylvester Kyner

As Recorded on "Mustang"
Blue Note BLP 4238 (1966)

MEDIUM FUNKY BLUES ♩=170

Continued on the next page

* *Palm D - Alto Saxophone fingering*
** *Hold Low C Down and Trill R.H. 4th Finger - Alto Saxophone fingering*

Example 44

** Hold Low C Down and Trill R.H. 4th Finger - Alto Saxophone fingering

Example 45

Colors of Spring

For Flute Quartet

Sylvester Kyner

Previously Unpublished

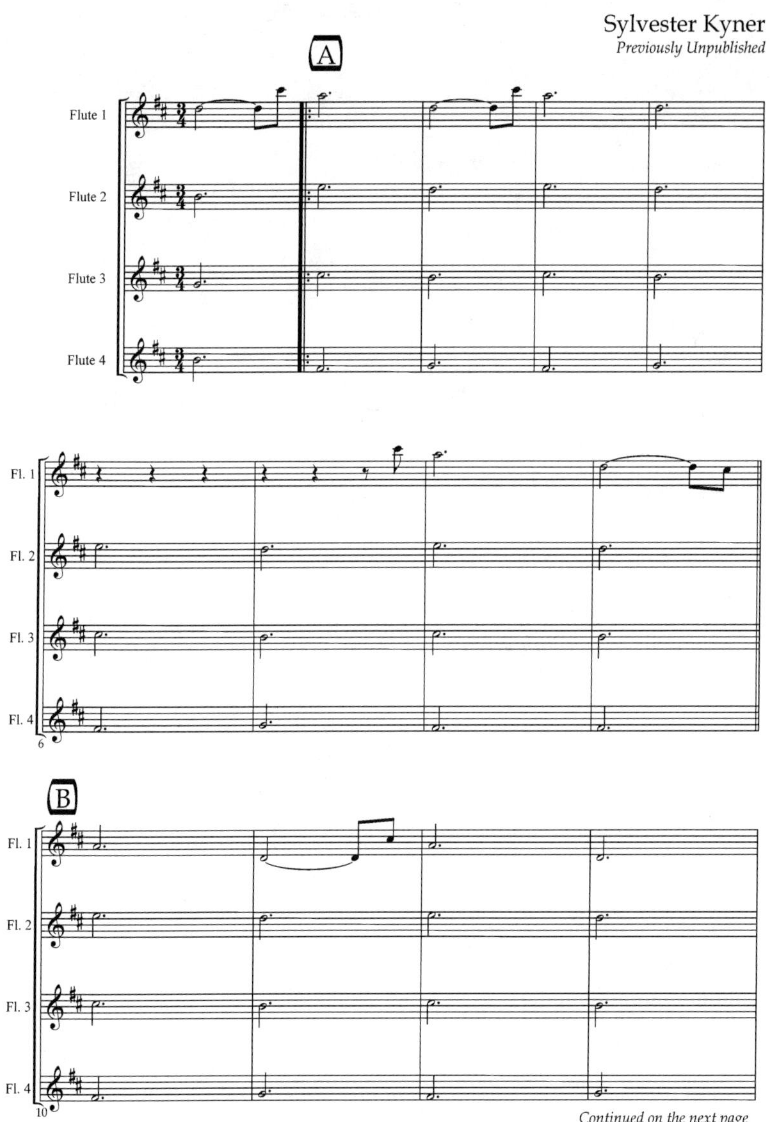

Continued on the next page

Example 46

"Colors of Spring" continued

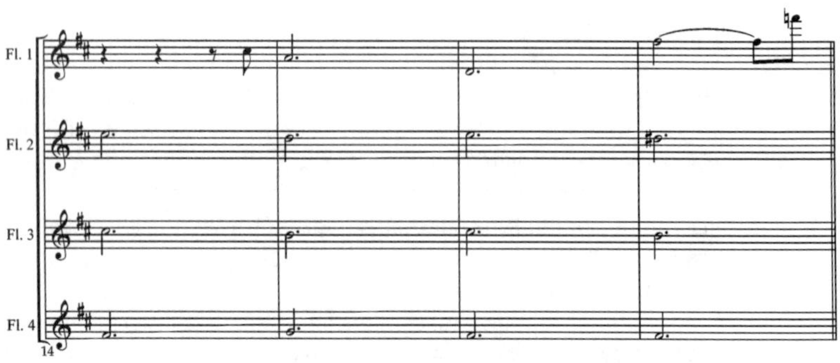

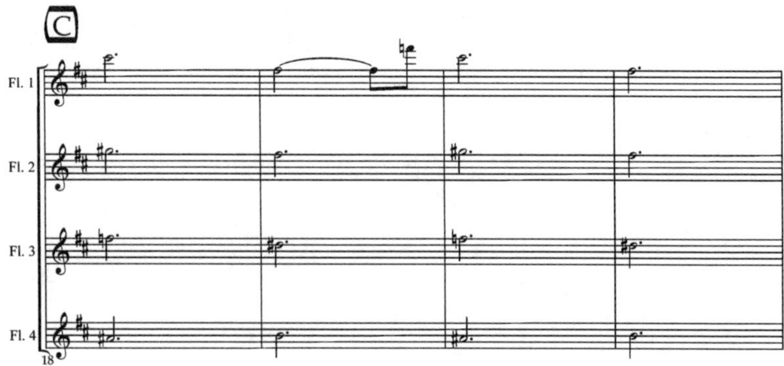

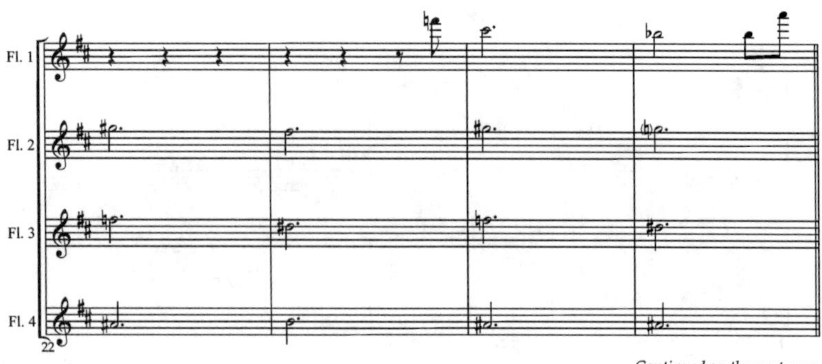

Continued on the next page

Example 47

"Colors of Spring" continued

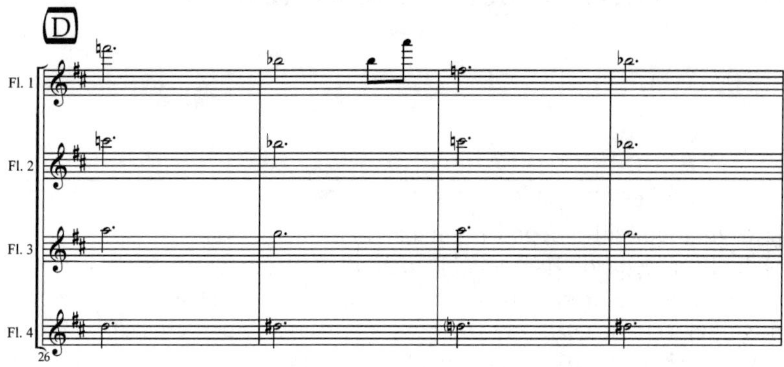

Example 48

Vina's Theme
For Flute Quintet

Sylvester Kyner
Previously Unpublished

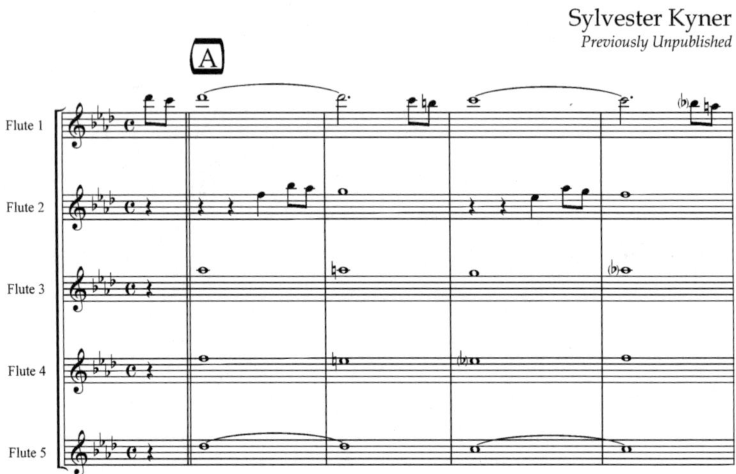

Continued on the next page

Example 49

"Vina's Theme" continued

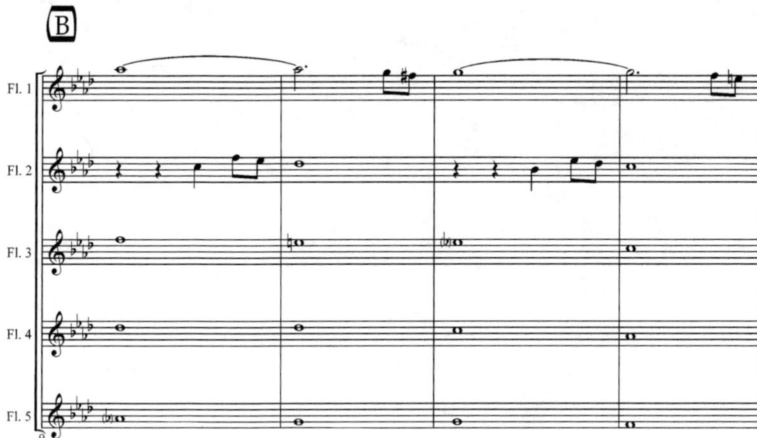

Example 50

TRANSPOSED SCORE
Song Samba
Sylvester Kyner
Previously Unpublished
𝅗𝅥 = 60
Flute
Soprano
Flute
Clarinet
Bass Clarinet
Reed 1
Reed 2
Reed 3
Reed 4
Reed 5
St. Mute
Trumpet 1
Trumpet 2
Trumpet 3
Trumpet 4
Trombone 1
Trombone 2
Euphonium
Bass Trombone
Piano
Arco
Bass
Conga
Timbales

Example 51

Song Samba Big Band Score - 2
Fl.
Sop.
Fl.
Cl.
Bs. Cl.
Tpt. 1
Tpt. 2
Tpt. 3
Tpt. 4
St. Mute
Tbn. 1
St. Mute
Tbn. 2
St. Mute
Euph.
St. Mute
B. Tbn.
Pno.
Bass
Conga
Timb.
7

Example 52

Song Samba Big Band Score - 3
to Alto
to Tenor
to Tenor
to Bari
Fl.
Sop.
Fl.
Cl.
Bs. Cl.
Tpt. 1
Tpt. 2
Tpt. 3
Tpt. 4
Tbn. 1
Tbn. 2
Euph.
B. Tbn.
Pno.
Bass
Conga
Timb.
13

Example 53

Song Samba Big Band Score - 4
17
𝅗𝅥 = 112
Alt.
Sop.
Tnr.
Tnr.
Bari
Tpt. 1
Tpt. 2
Tpt. 3
Tpt. 4
Tbn. 1
Tbn. 2
Euph.
B. Tbn.
to Open
Cmi/E♭
D7(♭9)
B♭mi/D♭
C7(♭9)
Ami/B
B♭7(♭9)
Pno.
Bass
Conga
Timb.
17

Example 54

Song Samba Big Band Score - 5
Alt.
Sop.
Tnr.
Tnr.
Bari
Tpt. 1
Tpt. 2
Tpt. 3
Tpt. 4
Tbn. 1
Tbn. 2
Euph.
B. Tbn.
E♭Ma9(♭5) A♭7(♭9)(♭5) A♭9 F∅ B♭7(♯9) G∅ C7(♭9) FMa7
Pno.
Bass
Conga
Timb.
23

Example 55

Song Samba Big Band Score - 6
31
Open for solos
Alt.
Sop.
Tnr.
Tnr.
Bari
Tpt. 1
Tpt. 2
Tpt. 3
Tpt. 4
Tbn. 1
Tbn. 2
Euph.
B. Tbn.
Cmi/E♭ D7(♭9) B♭mi/D♭ C7(♭9) Ami/B B♭7(♭9) E♭Ma9(♭5)
Pno.
Cmi/E♭ D7(♭9) B♭mi/D♭ C7(♭9) Ami/B B♭7(♭9) E♭Ma9(♭5)
Bass
Conga
Timb.
31

Example 56

Song Samba Big Band Score - 7
Alt.
Sop.
Tnr.
Tnr.
Bari
Tpt. 1
Tpt. 2
Tpt. 3
Tpt. 4
Tbn. 1
Tbn. 2
Euph.
B. Tbn.
Ab7(b9)(b5) Ab9 Fø Bb7(#9) Gø C7(b9) FMa7
Pno.
Ab7(b9)(b5) Ab9 Fø Bb7(#9) Gø C7(b9) FMa7
Bass
Conga
Timb.
38

Example 57

Song Samba Big Band Score - 8
45
Alt.
Sop.
Tnr.
Tnr.
Bari
Tpt. 1
Tpt. 2
Tpt. 3
Tpt. 4
Tbn. 1
Tbn. 2
Euph.
B. Tbn.
Cmi/E♭
D7(♭9)(♯5)
B♭mi/D♭
C7(♭9)(♯5)
Pno.
Bass
Conga
Timb.
2
2
45

Example 58

Song Samba Big Band Score - 9
Alt.
Sop.
Tnr.
Tnr.
Bari
Tpt. 1
Tpt. 2
Tpt. 3
Tpt. 4
Tbn. 1
Tbn. 2
Euph.
B. Tbn.
Ami/B
B♭7(♭9)(♯5)
D♭7(♯9)
C7(♯9)
Pno.
Bass
Conga
Timb.
49

Example 59

Song Samba Big Band Score - 10
55
Alt.
Sop.
Tnr.
Tnr.
Bari
Tpt. 1
Tpt. 2
Tpt. 3
Tpt. 4
Tbn. 1
Tbn. 2
Euph.
B. Tbn.
B7(#9)
B♭13(#9)
E♭Ma9
D♭Ma9
Pno.
Bass
Conga
Timb.
53

Example 60

Song Samba Big Band Score - 11
Alt.
Sop.
Tnr.
Tnr.
Bari
Tpt. 1
Tpt. 2
Tpt. 3
Tpt. 4
Tbn. 1
Tbn. 2
Euph.
B. Tbn.
E♭Ma9
D♭Ma9
E♭Ma9
D♭Ma9
E♭Ma9
Pno.
Bass
Conga
Timb.
57

Example 61

63
Song Samba Big Band Score - 12
Alt.
Sop.
Tnr.
Tnr.
Bari
Tpt. 1
Tpt. 2
Tpt. 3
Tpt. 4
Tbn. 1
Tbn. 2
Euph.
B. Tbn.
E♭Ma9
A♭Ma9
D♭13
G♭13
BMa9
EMa9
Fmi13
B♭11
Pno.
Opt. Ad Lib. Solo
Bass
Conga
Cabaza, Chocallo
Maracas
Timb.
63

Example 62

Song Samba Big Band Score - 13
71
Alt.
Sop.
Tnr.
Tnr.
Bari
Tpt. 1
Tpt. 2
Tpt. 3
Tpt. 4
Tbn. 1
Tbn. 2
Euph.
B. Tbn.
A13(b9) D13(b9) G13(b9) C7(#9) Fmi11 EMa9 EbMa9
Pno.
Bass
Conga
Timb.
71

Example 63

ACKNOWLEDGMENTS

I'd like to give special thanks to everyone who participated in the oral history portion of this book: Curtis Fuller, Barry Harris, Kiane Zawadi, Tommy Flanagan, Yusef Lateef, Malvin McCray, Frank Gant, Charles Boles, James "Beans" Richardson, Orrin Keepnews, Cedar Walton, Frank Foster, Billy Higgins, Jimmy Heath, James Spaulding, Louis Hayes, Charles McPherson, Phil Lasley, Dave Bailey, Johnnie Garry, Talib Kibwe, Art Zimmerman, Donald Byrd, Claude Black, Elena Knox, Jaffiria Leach-Orr, Sheila Kiner, James Kiner, Roberta Marie Leach, and Nicole Kyner for her endless advice, support, and confidence in me.

Additional thanks go to Jonathan Kiner, Lars Bjorn, Jim Gallert, Kim Heron, Michael Cuscuna, David Clements, Don and Maureen Sickler at Second Floor Music, The University of Wisconsin-Madison library system, Mrs. Britain at Northern High School, Sam Perryman at the Library of Congress, Ryan Truesdell for his tireless help with the charts, Mike Fitzgerald for editing the discography, Henry Martin for proofreading the music, Evan Spring and George Bassett for editing the text and charts, Lewis Porter, Ed Berger, my dear wife, Wendy Ward, and my son, Jan-Erik Svanoe.

NOTES

1. Welding, *Down Beat*, vol. 27, no. 25 (December 8, 1960), 46.
2. Tynan, *Down Beat*, vol. 25, no. 15 (July 24, 1958), 36.
3. Gold, *Down Beat*, vol. 25, no. 1 (January 9, 1958), 26.
4. Pekar, *Down Beat*, vol. 35, no. 13 (June 27, 1968), 26.
5. Colin Larkin, ed., *Virgin Encyclopedia of Jazz* (London: Virgin Books, 1999), 503.

DISCOGRAPHY

The session information was taken from the original album liner notes, CD reissue liner notes, interviewees, and a number of different discographies: *Modern Discography* (*Modern Jazz: Bebop/Hard Bop/West Coast*), by Walter Bruyninckx, *The Blue Note Discography,* by Michael Cuscuna and Michel Ruppli, *The Prestige Discography,* by Michel Ruppli, *The Jazz Discography,* by Tom Lord, *The All Music Guide to Jazz*, *The Goldmine Jazz Album Price Guide,* by Tim Neely, *The Penguin Guide to Jazz,* by Richard Cook and Brian Morton, and the *Bielefelder Jazz Katalog*. The number in parentheses before each song title designates where the composition appears on the original LP or CD. Unissued titles are identified with a (-), indicating no placement on the original LP or CD. All issues are LPs unless otherwise noted. An LP that subsequently came out on CD is listed in the Catalog ID—e.g., Original Jazz Classics OJCCD-076-2—or at the bottom of the entry.

[001] May 10, 1957, Hackensack, New Jersey
PAUL QUINICHETTE SEPTET

Recording Location: Van Gelder Studios
Supervision: Bob Weinstock
Recording Engineer: Rudy Van Gelder
Sonny Red: alto saxophone (except 3), John Jenkins: alto saxophone (except 2,5), Paul Quinichette: tenor saxophone (except 5), Curtis Fuller: trombone (except 3), Mal Waldron: piano, Doug Watkins: bass, Ed Thigpen: drums

1250	(2) *Circles* 11:50 (Mal Waldron)	Prestige PRLP7103	
1251	(1) *Blue Dots* 7:54 (Mal Waldron)	—	Prestige 45-106
1252	(3) *On the Sunny Side of the Street* 5:44 (Jimmy McHugh, Dorothy Fields)	—	
1253	(5) *My Funny Valentine* 7:24 (Richard Rodgers, Lorenz Hart)	OJCCD-076-2	
1254	(4) *Cool-Lypso* 19:08 (Mal Waldron)	Prestige PRLP7103	

Session released as ***On the Sunny Side***, Prestige PRLP7103 (Mono), Original Jazz Classics OJC-076 (LP), Original Jazz Classics OJCCD-076-2 (CD), Esquire 32-057 (English), SMJ-6615 (Japanese). *My Funny Valentine* appears on OJCCD-076-2 (CD) only. Prestige 45-106 is a 45 single.

Note: OJCCD-076-2 incorrectly lists John Jenkins and Paul Quinichette as the horn players on *My Funny Valentine*. The correct horn lineup is Sonny Red and Curtis Fuller.

---

[002] May 11, 1957, Hackensack, New Jersey
CURTIS FULLER QUINTET

Recording Location: Van Gelder Studios
Supervision: Ozzie Cadena
Recording Engineer: Rudy Van Gelder
Sonny Red: alto saxophone, Curtis Fuller: trombone, Hank Jones: piano, Doug Watkins: bass, Louis Hayes: drums

1255	(2) *Transportation Blues* 8:18 (Curtis Fuller)	Prestige PRLP7107
1256-1	(1) *Vonce #5 (Young Number Five)* 7:40 (Curtis Fuller)	—
1256-2	(-) *Vonce #5 (Young Number Five)* (Curtis Fuller)	(unissued)
1257-1	(3) *Blue Lawson* 6:51 (Curtis Fuller)	Prestige PRLP7107
1257-2	(-) *Blue Lawson* (Curtis Fuller)	(unissued)
1258	(6) *Alicia* 5:11 (Curtis Fuller)	Status NJST8317, OJCCD-077-2
1259	(5) *What Is This Thing Called Love?* 6:30 (Cole Porter)	Prestige PRLP7107
1260	(4) *Namely You* 9:25 (Johnny Mercer, Gene DePaul)	—

Session released as ***New Trombone***, Prestige PRLP7107 (Mono), Original Jazz Classics OJC-077 (LP), Original Jazz Classics OJCCD-077-2 (CD), Prestige SHJ-6007 (Japanese), VICJ-23748 (Japanese CD). *Alicia* appears on OJCCD-077-2 (CD) only. Status NJST8317 (Mono) issued as ***Donald Byrd, Hank Mobley and Kenny Burrell***.

---

[003] May 14, 1957, Hackensack, New Jersey
CURTIS FULLER QUINTET

Recording Location: Van Gelder Studios
Supervision: Teddy Charles

Recording Engineer: Rudy Van Gelder
Sonny Red: alto saxophone (except 2), Curtis Fuller: trombone (except 5), Red Garland: piano, Paul Chambers: bass, Louis Hayes: drums

1261	(4) *Slenderella* 7:43 (Sylvester Kyner)	New Jazz NJLP8277
1262	(3) *Cashmere* 6:45 (Curtis Fuller)	—
1263	(5) *Moonlight Becomes You* 7:35 (Johnny Burke, Jimmy Van Heusen)	—
1264	(2) *Stormy Weather* 7:17 (Harold Arlen, Ted Koehler)	—
1265	(1) *Seeing Red* 7:00 (Barry Harris)	—
1266	(6) *Roc and Troll* 7:42 (Teddy Charles)	—

Session released as ***Curtis Fuller with Red Garland***, New Jazz NJLP8277 (Mono), Original Jazz Classics OJCCD-1862-2 (CD), Prestige SMJ-6297 (Japanese), VICJ-23749 (Japanese CD).

Note: *Seeing Red* is a Barry Harris composition, as confirmed by Kiane Zawadi.

---

[004] September 5, 1957, Hackensack, New Jersey
CURTIS FULLER/TOMMY FLANAGAN QUINTET

Recording Location: Van Gelder Studios
Supervision: Ozzie Cadena
Recording Engineer: Rudy Van Gelder

Sonny Red: alto saxophone (except 2,4), Curtis Fuller: trombone (except 2,3), Tommy Flanagan: piano, George Tucker: bass, Louis Hayes: drums

70107	(1) *Two Ton* 4:48 (Curtis Fuller)	Regent MG6055
	MEDLEY	
70108	(2) *It's Magic* 4:30 (Jule Styne, Sammy Cahn)	—
70109	(3) *My One and Only Love* 4:32 (Guy Wood, Robert Mellin)	—
70110	(4) *They Didn't Believe Me* 4:37 (Jerome Kern, Anne Caldwell)	—
70111	(5) *Soul Station* 5:42 (Curtis Fuller)	—
70112	(6) *Club Car* 7:15 (Curtis Fuller)	—
70113	(7) *Upper Berth* 8:32 (Frank Foster)	—

Session released as ***Jazz . . . It's Magic***, Regent MG6055 (Mono), Savoy MG12209 (Mono), Savoy SLJ1158, Savoy CY-78807 (Japanese CD), SV0153 (CD), COCY-9025 (Japanese CD).

---

[005] Late 1950s, Detroit, Michigan
SONNY RED TRIO

Recording Location: Special Recordings, 138 Duffield
Sonny Red: alto saxophone, Herman Wright: bass, Roy Brooks: drums

(1) *Cutie*: medium (Sonny Rollins)	Special Recordings
(2) *Cutie*: fast (Sonny Rollins)	—
(3) *Jumpin' at the Woodside* (Count Basie)	—
(4) *Stairway to the Stars* (Frank Signorelli, Matt Malneck, Mitchell Parish)	—
(5) *Soleing* (composer unknown)	—

This session was never released. James Kiner believes it was a demonstration recording.

---

[006] November 12, 1957, Hackensack, New Jersey
SONNY RED QUINTET

Recording Location: Van Gelder Studios
Supervision: Ozzie Cadena
Recording Engineer: Rudy Van Gelder
Sonny Red: alto saxophone, Pepper Adams: baritone saxophone, Wynton Kelly: piano, Doug Watkins: bass, Elvin Jones: drums

(2) *Watkins Products* 9:30 (Doug Watkins)	Regent MG6069	Savoy MG12215
(4) *Redd's Head* 9:09 (Sylvester Kyner)	—	—
(6) *Stop* 8:19 (Fats Navarro)	Savoy MG12123	

Session released as ***Art Pepper/Sonny Redd: Two Altos***, Regent MG6069 (Mono), Savoy MG12215 (Mono), Savoy WL70389 (German), COCY-9825 (Japanese CD), Savoy SV-0161 (Japanese CD). Rest of ***Art Pepper/Sonny Redd: Two Altos*** is by Art Pepper. Savoy MG12123, titled ***Jazz Is Busting Out All Over,*** is by Frank Wess; rest of LP by others.

Note: Pepper Adams is certain this session was done at Van Gelder's in New Jersey, even though it is listed as Chicago in some discographies (Savoy and Jespen).

---

[007] September 25, 1958, Detroit, Michigan
JOE BRAZIL JAM SESSION

Recording Location: Joe Brazil's house (basement)
Donald Towns: trumpet, Joe Brazil: alto saxophone, Sonny Red: alto saxophone, John Coltrane: tenor saxophone (except 2), Joe Henderson: tenor saxophone, Hugh Lawson: piano, Ernie Farrow: bass, Roy Brooks: drums

(-) *Now's the Time* 18:46 (Charlie Parker)	(unissued)
(-) *Woody 'n You* 7:25 (Dizzy Gillespie)	—
(-) *Paul's Pal* 12:20 (Sonny Rollins)	—
(-) *Sweet Georgia Brown* 11:40 (Maceo Pinkard, Kenneth Casey, Ben Bernie)	—

Note: This session is on a private tape that belonged to Joe Henderson.

---

[008] December 5, 1959, Englewood Cliffs, New Jersey
SONNY RED QUARTET

Recording Location: Van Gelder Studios
Producer: Alfred Lion
Recording Engineer: Rudy Van Gelder
Sonny Red: alto saxophone, Wynton Kelly: piano, Sam Jones: bass, Roy Brooks: drums

tk.3	(1) *Bluesville* 5:49 (Sylvester Kyner)	Blue Note BLP4032	Blue Note 45-1761
tk.5	(2) *Stay as Sweet as You Are* 6:12 (Mack Gordon, Harry Revel)	—	—
tk.10	(3) *I've Never Been in Love Before* 5:20 (Frank Loesser)	—	
tk.12	(5) *Blues in the Pocket* 6:29 (Sylvester Kyner)	—	Blue Note 45-1762
tk.13	(6) *Alone Too Long* 2:56 (Arthur Schwartz, Dorothy Fields)	—	
tk.14	*Alone Too Long* 4:08 (Arthur Schwartz, Dorothy Fields)		—

tk.19	(4) *Nadia* 4:04 (Sylvester Kyner)	—
	(-) *All the Things You Are* (Jerome Kern, Oscar Hammerstein II)	(unissued)

Session released as ***Out of the Blue***, Blue Note BLP4032 (Mono), ST84032 (Stereo), Pathe Marconi PM252 (French), King K18P-9243 (Japanese), TOCJ-4032, TOCJ-5941, TOCJ-9093 (Japanese 24-Bit RVG Edition CD), CDP 8-52440-2 (U.S Blue Note Connoisseur Series). Blue Note 45-1761 and 45-1762 are 45 singles. *Stay as Sweet as You Are* and *Bluesville* are sides A and B, respectively, of 45-1761. *Alone Too Long* and *Blues in the Pocket* are sides A and B, respectively, of 45-1762.

Note: Blue Note CDP 8-52440-2 incorrectly lists (3) as *I've Been in Love Before*.

---

[009] January 23, 1960, Englewood Cliffs, New Jersey
SONNY RED QUARTET

Recording Location: Van Gelder Studios
Producer: Alfred Lion
Recording Engineer: Rudy Van Gelder
Sonny Red: alto saxophone, Wynton Kelly: piano, Paul Chambers: bass, Jimmy Cobb: drums

tk.3	(12) *Blues for KoKee* 5:34 (Sylvester Kyner)		Blue Note CDP 8-52440-2
tk.7	(13) *You're Driving Me Crazy* 5:27 (Walter Donaldson)		—
tk.8	(8) *Stairway to the Stars* 6:17 (Frank Signorelli, Matt Malneck, Mitchell Parish)	Blue Note BLP4032	—
tk.10	(9) *Crystal* 5:35 (Sylvester Kyner)		—
tk.13	(7) *The Lope* 5:13 (Sylvester Kyner)	—	—
tk.15	(10) *Lost April* 6:46 (Emil Newman, Herbert Spencer, Edgar DeLange)		—
tk.17	(11) *You're Sensational* 6:28 (Cole Porter)		—

Session released as ***Out of the Blue***, CDP 8-52440-2 (U.S Blue Note Connoisseur Series). *Stairway to the Stars* and *The Lope* found on Blue Note BLP 4032. Tracks 9–13 reflect CD order (CDP 8-52440-2).

---

[010] March 10, 1960, Englewood Cliffs, New Jersey
SONNY RED QUARTET

Recording Location: Van Gelder Studios
Producer: Alfred Lion
Recording Engineer: Rudy Van Gelder
Sonny Red: alto saxophone, Hank Jones: piano, Paul Chambers: bass, Art Taylor: drums

tk.5	(-) *The Lamp Is Low* (Mitchell Parish, Peter DeRose, Maurice Ravel)	(unissued)
tk.10	(-) *How about You?* (Burton Lane, Ralph Freed)	—
tk.12	(-) *Invitation* (Paul Francis Webster, Bronislau Kaper)	—
tk.17	(-) *That Old Black Magic* (Harold Arlen, Johnny Mercer)	—

Unissued Blue Note session.

[011] April 25, 1960, New York City
GRETCH DRUM NIGHT AT BIRDLAND

Recording Location: Birdland, New York City
Producer: Rudy Traylor/Teddy Reig
Sonny Red: alto saxophone (except 5), Charles Greenlee (Harneefan Majeed): trombone (except 5), Tommy Flanagan: piano (except 5), Ron Carter: bass (except 5), Art Blakey: drums (1,2,4,5), Philly Joe Jones: drums (1,2,3), Elvin Jones: drums (3,4,5), Charli Persip: drums (3,4,5)

(1) *Wee Dot* 11:00 (J. J. Johnson, Leo Parker)	Blue Note CDP 8-28641-2	Roulette R52049
(2) *Now's the Time* 6:55 (Charlie Parker)	—	—
(3) *Fours/Drum Solo Exchange (Tune Up)* 20:05 (Miles Davis, Eddie Vinson)	—	Roulette R52067
(4) *El Sino* 15:52 (Charles Greenlee)	—	Roulette R52049
(5) *Drum Ensemble (A Night in Tunisia)* 16:01 (Dizzy Gillespie, Frank Paparelli, Jon Hendricks)	—	Roulette R52067

Session released as ***Gretch Drum Night at Birdland, Vol. 1 and Vol. 2***; Vol. 1, Roulette R52049 (Mono), SR52049 (Stereo), Vol. 2, Roulette R52067 (Mono), SR52067 (Stereo), Bellaphon BJS 40173, Blue Note CDP 8-28641-2. All tracks reflect CD order (Blue Note CDP 8-28641-2).

Note: These are edited performances because of time limitations on the original LPs. The edits were made on the original three-track master, and the unedited performances cannot be found.

---

[012] November 3, 1960, New York City
SONNY RED SEXTET

Recording Location: Plaza Sound Studios
Producer: Orrin Keepnews
Recording Engineer: Ray Fowler
Sonny Red: alto saxophone, Yusef Lateef: tenor saxophone (1,3,5,6), Blue Mitchell: trumpet (1,3,5,6), Barry Harris: piano, Bob Cranshaw: bass, Albert Heath: drums

(1) *Brother B.* 5:02 (Sylvester Kyner)	Jazzland JLP32, Jazzland JLP1001
(2) *All I Do Is Dream of You* 4:03 (Arthur Freed, Nacio Herb Brown)	—
(3) *The New Blues* 5:34 (Sylvester Kyner)	—
(4) *Ditty* 4:36 (Sylvester Kyner)	—
(5) *Teef* 6:26 (Sylvester Kyner)	—
(6) *Breezing* 6:06 (Sylvester Kyner)	—
(7) *A Handful of Stars* 4:42 (Ted Shapiro, Jack Lawrence)	—
(8) *If There Is Someone Lovelier Than You* 2:50 (Howard Dietz, Arthur Schwartz)	—

Session released as ***Breezing***, Jazzland JLP32 (Mono), JLP932 (Stereo), VIJJ-30047 (Japanese). Jazzland JLP1001 (Mono) and JLP 91001 (Stereo), ***Jazzland: The Stars of Jazz, 1961***, is a compilation/sampler LP.

---

[013] February 14, 1961, New York City
SONNY RED AND CLIFFORD JORDAN QUINTET

Recording Location: Bell Sound Studios
Producer: Orrin Keepnews

Recording Engineer: Bill Stoddard
Sonny Red: alto saxophone, Clifford Jordan: tenor saxophone, Tommy Flanagan: piano (3,4,5,6,7), Ronnie Mathews: piano (1,2,8), Art Davis: bass, Elvin Jones: drums

(1) *Cumberland Court* 3:48 (Clifford Jordan)	Jazzland JLP40	
(2) *A Story Tale* 4:48 (Clifford Jordan)	—	
(3) *You're Driving Me Crazy* 5:35 (Walter Donaldson)	—	
(4) *Defiance* 3:23 (Sylvester Kyner)	—	
(5) *Prints* 5:58 (Sylvester Kyner)	—	
(6) *Hip Pockets* 5:00 (Sylvester Kyner, Clifford Jordan)	—	
(7) *They Say It's Wonderful* 5:12 (Irving Berlin)	—	Riverside RM3519
(8) *If I Didn't Care* 5:13 (Jack Lawrence)	—	

Session released as ***A Story Tale***, Jazzland JLP40 (Mono), JLP940 (Stereo), WWLJ-7045 (Japanese), Milestone MCD-47092-2. Riverside RM3519 (Mono) and RS93519 (Stereo) released as ***Great Jazz Artists Play Compositions of Irving Berlin***.

---

[014] May 29, 1961, New York City
SONNY RED QUARTET

Recording Location: Plaza Sound Studios
Producer: Orrin Keepnews
Recording Engineer: Ray Fowler
Sonny Red: alto saxophone, Cedar Walton: piano, George Tucker: bass, Albert Heath: drums

(2) *I Like the Likes of You* 4:19 (Vernon Duke, E. Y. Harburg)	Jazzland JLP59
(4) *Bye, Bye Blues* 4:30 (Fred Hamm, Dave Bennett, Bert Lown, Chauncey Gray)	—
(6) *Never, Never Land* 6:31 (Jule Styne, Betty Comden, Adolph Green)	—
(7) *Ko-Kee* 4:12 (Sylvester Kyner)	—

Session released as ***The Mode***, Jazzland JLP59 (Mono), JLP959 (Stereo), VIJJ-30048 (Japanese), Milestone MCD-47086-2. All tracks reflect LP order (Jazzland JLP59).

---

[015] June 25, 1961, New York City
SONNY RED QUINTET

Recording Location: Plaza Sound Studios
Producer: Orrin Keepnews
Recording Engineer: Ray Fowler
Sonny Red: alto saxophone, Blue Mitchell: trumpet, Barry Harris: piano, George Tucker: bass, Lex Humphries: drums

(1) *Images* 6:25 (Sylvester Kyner)	Jazzland JLP74
(2) *Blues for Donna* 4:44 (Sylvester Kyner)	—
(3) *Dodge City* 5:16 (Sylvester Kyner)	—

Session released as ***Images***, Jazzland JLP74 (Mono), JLP974 (Stereo), Original Jazz Classics OJC-148 (LP), Jazzland 68955 (French), Milestone MCD-47086-2. All tracks reflect LP order (Jazzland JLP74).

---

[016] October 18, 1961, New York City
BILL HARDMAN QUINTET

Recording Location: Medallion Studios
Recording Supervision: Tom Wilson
Recording Engineer: Paul Cady
Recording Production: Herman Lubinsky
Bill Hardman: trumpet, Sonny Red: alto saxophone, Ronnie Mathews: piano, Doug Watkins: bass (2,3,4,5,7), Bob Cunningham: bass (1,6), Jimmy Cobb: drums

SWH1891	(1) *Capers* 7:11 (Tom McIntosh)	Savoy MG12170	Savoy 92879-2
SWH1892	(3) *Jo B* 9:51 (Bill Hardman)	—	—
SWH1893	(5) *Assunta* 6:12 (Cal Massey)	—	
SWH1894	(8) *B-4* (composer unknown)	Savoy SJK 1164	
SWH1895	(-) *Capers* (Tom McIntosh)	(unissued)	
SWH1896	(6) *It Ain't Happened Yet* 5:20 (Bill Hardman)	Savoy MG12170	
SWH1897	(2) *Angel Eyes* 5:57 (Earl Brent, Matt Dennis)	—	—
SWH1898	(7) *With Malice toward None* 3:57 (Tom McIntosh, Jon Hendricks)	Savoy SLJ1164	—
SWH1899	(4) *Buckeye Blues* 10:46 (Bill Hardman)	Savoy MG12170	

Session released as ***Saying Something***, Savoy MG12170, Savoy SJL1164, KIJJ2012 (Japanese), COCB-50607 (Japanese CD), Savoy SJK 1164 (cassette), Savoy 92879-2 (CD). *With Malice toward None* appears on Savoy SLJ1164 (LP) and Savoy SJK 1164 (cassette). *B-4* appears on Savoy SJK 1164 (cassette) only. Savoy 92879-2 (CD) released as Art Blakey and The Jazz Messengers, ***Reflections of Buhania, Featuring Bill Hardman***.

Note: Unknown bass player on composition *B-4*.

---

[017] December 14, 1961, New York City
SONNY RED QUINTET

Recording Location: Plaza Sound Studios
Producer: Orrin Keepnews
Recording Engineer: Ray Fowler
Sonny Red: alto saxophone, Grant Green: guitar (except 6), Barry Harris: piano, George Tucker: bass, Jimmy Cobb: drums

(1) *Moon River* 6:08 (Henry Mancini, Johnny Mercer)	Jazzland JLP 59
(3) *Super 20* 5:32 (Sylvester Kyner)	—
(5) *The Mode* 8:51 (Sylvester Kyner)	—
(4) *Blue Sonny* 8:29 (Sylvester Kyner)	Jazzland JLP 74
(5) *The Rhythm Thing* 5:06 (Sylvester Kyner)	—
(6) *Bewitched, Bothered and Bewildered* 5:41 (Richard Rodgers, Lorenz Hart)	—

Moon River, Super 20, and *The Mode* released on ***The Mode***, Jazzland JLP59 (Mono), JLP959 (Stereo), VIJJ-30048 (Japanese), Milestone MCD-47086-2. All tracks reflect LP order (Jazzland JLP 59). *Blue Sonny, The Rhythm Thing*, and *Bewitched, Bothered and Bewildered* released on ***Images***, Jazzland JLP74 (Mono), JLP974 (Stereo), Original Jazz Classics OJC-148 (LP), Jazzland 68955 (French), Milestone MCD-47086-2. All tracks reflect LP order (Jazzland JLP 74).

---

[018] February 16, 1962, New York City
PONY POINDEXTER NONET

Producer: Teo Macero
Pony Poindexter: soprano saxophone, alto saxophone, Sonny Red: alto saxophone, Eric Dolphy: alto saxophone, Jimmy Heath: tenor saxophone, Clifford Jordan: tenor saxophone, Pepper Adams: baritone saxophone, Gildo Mahones: piano, Ron Carter: bass, Elvin Jones: drums

CO69687	(6) *"B" Frequency* 1:38 (Teo Macero)	Epic LA16035
CO69688-1	(10) *Lanyop* 9:35 (Pony Poindexter)	—
CO69688-2	(?) *Lanyop* 9:03 (Pony Poindexter)	Columbia FC38509
CO69689-1	(1) *Catin' Latin* 4:11 (Pony Poindexter)	Epic LA16035
CO69689-2	(-) *Catin' Latin* (Pony Poindexter)	(unissued)

Session released as ***Pony's Express***, Epic LA16035 (Mono), BA17035 (Stereo), ESCA-5058 (Japanese CD), ECPU-10 (Japanese), Epic EPC65889 (released as ***Super Sax Session***), KOC CD-8591.

Note: Columbia FC38509 released as ***Almost Forgotten: Various Artists; Instrumentalists***, rest of LP by others.

---

[019] April 18, 1962, New York City
PONY POINDEXTER NONET

Producer: Teo Macero
Pony Poindexter: alto saxophone, soprano saxophone (7), Sonny Red: alto saxophone, Phil Woods: alto saxophone, Clifford Jordan: tenor saxophone, Sal Nistico: tenor saxophone, Pepper Adams: baritone saxophone, Tommy Flanagan: piano, Ron Carter: bass, Charli Persip: drums

CO70070	(8) *Basin Street Blues* 3:39 (Spencer Williams)	Epic LA16035
CO70071	(7) *Mickey Mouse March* 3:01 (Jimmy Dodd)	—
CO70072	(3) *Skylark* 3:40 (Hoagy Carmichael, Johnny Mercer)	—
CO70073	(5) *Blue* 5:27 (Gildo Mahones)	—

Session released as ***Pony's Express***, Epic LA16035 (Mono), BA17035 (Stereo), ESCA-5058 (Japanese CD), ECPU-10 (Japanese), Epic EPC65889 (released as ***Super Sax Session***), KOC CD-8591.

---

[020] May 20, 1963, Englewood Cliffs, New Jersey
DONALD BYRD SEXTET

Recording Location: Van Gelder Studios
Producer: Alfred Lion
Recording Engineer: Rudy Van Gelder
Donald Byrd: trumpet, Sonny Red: alto saxophone, Jimmy Heath: tenor saxophone, Herbie Hancock: piano, Eddie Kahn: bass, Albert Heath: drums

tk.5	(7) *All Members* 4:34 (Jimmy Heath)	Blue Note CDP 8-21286-2
	(-) *On the Trail* (Ferde Grofé)	(unissued)

Session released as ***Blackjack***, Blue Note CDP 8-21286-2.

Note: CD lists recording date as May 27, 1963.

---

[021] mid- to late 1960s, Connecticut
BOBBY TIMMONS QUARTET

Recording Location: House Party
Producer: Mickey Bass
Executive Producer: John Rowland
Sonny Red: tenor saxophone, Bobby Timmons: piano, Sam Jones: bass, Mickey Roker: drums

(1) *Here's That Rainy Day* 12:38 (Jimmy Van Heusen, Johnny Burke)	Chiaroscuro CR-2030
(2) *Prelude to a Kiss* 4:45 (Duke Ellington, Irving Gordon, Irving Mills)	—
(3) *Theme* 6:36 (Kenny Dorham)	—
(4) *Now's the Time* 11:45 (Charlie Parker)	—
(5) *Moanin'* 7:08 (Bobby Timmons, Jon Hendricks)	—

Original session released as ***Bobby Timmons Live at the Connecticut Jazz Party, Featuring Sonny Red***, Chiaroscuro CR-2030, Early Bird EBCD-104.

---

[022] February 25, 1966, New York City
KENNY DORHAM QUINTET

Recording Location: WABC-FM Broadcast "Portraits in Jazz" at the Half Note
Engineer: Sid Simon
M.C.: Alan Grant
Kenny Dorham: trumpet (except 3), Sonny Red: alto saxophone (except 4), Cedar Walton: piano, John Ore: bass, Hugh Walker: drums

(1) *Jung-Fu/Introduction* 13:12 (Kenny Dorham)	Raretone FC5022
(2) *Spring Is Here* 8:58 (Richard Rodgers, Lorenz Hart)	—
(3) *Somewhere in the Night* 6:31 (Joseph Myrow, Mack Gordon)	—
(4) *The Shadow of Your Smile* 7:18 (Johnny Mandel, Paul Francis Webster)	—
(5) *Straight Ahead* 8:16 (Kenny Dorham)	—

Session released as ***Last but Not Least, 1966, Vol. 2***, Raretone FC5022 (Italian), and ***Live at the Half Note, 1966***, label unknown, or ***The Shadow of Your Smile***, West Wind 2049 (German CD).

Note: Introduction by Alan Grant.

---

[023] June 24, 1966, Englewood Cliffs, New Jersey
DONALD BYRD SEXTET

Recording Location: Van Gelder Studios
Producer: Alfred Lion
Recording Engineer: Rudy Van Gelder
Donald Byrd: trumpet, Sonny Red: alto saxophone, Hank Mobley: tenor saxophone, McCoy Tyner: piano, Walter Booker: bass, Freddie Waits: drums

1746 (tk.4)	(5) *On the Trail* 7:41 (Ferde Grofé)	Blue Note BLP4238
1747 (tk.9)	(6) *I'm So Excited by You* 5:38 (Donald Byrd)	—

1748 (tk.15)	(1) *Mustang* 8:28 (Sylvester Kyner)	—	CDP 7-89606-2, 8-53233-2 (E), B1-89606
1749 (-)	(-) *Dixie Lee* (Donald Byrd)	(unissued)	
1750 (tk.24)	(3) *I Got It Bad and That Ain't Good* 5:51 (Duke Ellington, Paul Francis Webster)	BLP4238	
1751 (tk.29)	(2) *Fly Little Bird, Fly* 5:23 (Donald Byrd)	—	
1749 (tk.31)	(4) *Dixie Lee* 6:40 (Donald Byrd)	BLP4238, B1-57745, (TOCJ-6100 (J)	

Session released as ***"Mustang!"*** on Blue Note BLP4238 (Mono), BST84238 (Stereo), CDP 8-59963-2, TOCJ-4238 (Japanese).

CDP 7-89606-2 released as ***Donald Byrd—Early Byrd: The Best of the Jazz Soul Years***.

---

[024] January 9, 1967, Englewood Cliffs, New Jersey
DONALD BYRD SEXTET

Recording Location: Van Gelder Studios
Producer: Alfred Lion
Recording Engineer: Rudy Van Gelder
Donald Byrd: trumpet, Sonny Red: alto saxophone, Hank Mobley: tenor saxophone, Cedar Walton: piano, Walter Booker: bass, Billy Higgins: drums

1810 (tk.5)	(3) *Loki* 5:51 (Sylvester Kyner)	Blue Note BLP4259	
1811 (tk.9)	(4) *Eldorado* 7:58 (Mitch Farber)	—	Lib. LN-10200
1812 (tk.10)	(2) *West of the Pecos* 5:17 (Sylvester Kyner)	—	CDP 7-89606-2, B1-89606
1813 (-)	(-) *Blackjack* (Donald Byrd)	(unissued)	
1814 (tk.28)	(5) *Beale Street* 5:24 (Sylvester Kyner)	BLP4259, CDP 7-89907-2, B1-89907, 5-23444-2 (Eu)	
1813 (tk.29)	(1) *Blackjack* 6:14 (Donald Byrd)	BLP4259, B1-89606, B1-35636, Lib. LN-10200, CDP 7-89606-2, B1-7-99106-2, 8-35636-2	
1815 (tk.33)	(6) *Pentatonic* 4:57 (Donald Byrd)	BLP 4259	

Session released as ***Blackjack***, Blue Note BLP4259 (Mono), BST84259 (Stereo), CDP 8-21286-2, TOCJ-4259 (Japanese). Liberty LN-10200 released as ***The Dude***. CDP 7-89606-2 released as ***Donald Byrd—Early Byrd: The Best of the Jazz Soul Years***. B1-7-99106-2 released as ***Blue Break Beats: Vol. 1***. CDP 7-89907-2 released as ***Blue Break Beats: Vol. 2. Beale Street** and **Blackjack** also released as part of **Blue Break Beats, Vol. 1–4** box set Blue Note 23182.* B1-35636 released as ***Blue Note Rare Grooves***.

---

[025] April 10, 1967, Bronx, New York
KENNY DORHAM QUINTET

Recording Location: The Blue Morocco
Producer: Nat White
Recording Engineer: Bernard Drayton

Kenny Dorham: trumpet, Sonny Red: alto saxophone, Cedar Walton: piano, Paul Chambers: bass, Russ Charles: drums, Joe Lee Wilson: vocals (3,4 only)

Title	Issue
(-) *Bags' Groove* 15:09 (Milt Jackson)	(unissued)
(-) *Blue Bossa* 13:31 (Kenny Dorham)	—
(-) *I'll Remember April* 8:34 (Gene DePaul, Don Raye, Patricia Johnston)	—
(-) *What's New?* 6:36 (Bob Haggart, Johnny Burke)	—
(-) *Four* 2:24 (Miles Davis, Eddie Vinson)	—
(-) *The Theme* 8:07 (Kenny Dorham)	—

Note: Edited performances.

---

[026] May 12, 1967, Englewood Cliffs, New Jersey
DONALD BYRD SEXTET

Recording Location: Van Gelder Studios
Producer: Alfred Lion
Recording Engineer: Rudy Van Gelder
Donald Byrd: trumpet, Sonny Red: alto saxophone, Cedar Walton: piano, Walter Booker: bass, Billy Higgins: drums and vocal (1)

Matrix	Title	Issue
1884 (tk.3)	(3) *Book's Bossa* 6:50 (Walter Booker, Cedar Walton)	BST84292, 4-97156-2, B1-89606, CDP 7-89606-2
1885 (tk.15)	(5) *The Loner* 6:14 (Cedar Walton, Ronnie Mathews)	BST84292, CDP 7-89606-2, B1-89606, B1-94708
1886 (tk.18)	(4) *Jelly Roll* 5:19 (Sylvester Kyner)	BST84292, 4-94708-2, 8-56508-2 (C)
1887 (tk.22)	(1) *Slow Drag* 9:44 (Donald Byrd)	BST84292, CDP 7-89606-2, B1-89606, 8-54188 (F), 8-54197-2, TOJC-5733 (J)
1888	(-) No Title	(unissued)
1889 (tk.29)	(6) *My Ideal* 6:21 (Leo Robin, Richard Whiting, Newell Chase)	BST84292
1890 (tk.30)	(2) *Secret Love* 3:56 (Sammy Fain, Paul Francis Webster)	—

Session released as ***Slow Drag***, Blue Note BST84292 (Stereo), 35560-2 (RVG Edition), TOCJ-4292 (Japanese CD). Blue Note 4-97156-2 released as ***Blue Bossa, Volume 2: Cool Cuts from the Tropics***. Blue Note CDP 7-89606-2 released as ***Donald Byrd—Early Byrd: The Best of the Jazz Soul Years***.

---

[027] September 29, 1967, Englewood Cliffs, New Jersey
DONALD BYRD SEXTET

Recording Location: Van Gelder Studios
Producer: Alfred Lion
Recording Engineer: Rudy Van Gelder
Donald Byrd: trumpet, Sonny Red: alto saxophone, Pepper Adams: baritone saxophone, Chick Corea: piano, Miroslav Vitous: bass, Joe Chambers: drums

1957	(-) *The Creeper* (Sylvester Kyner)	(unissued)
1958	(-) *Chico-San* (Chick Corea)	—

[028] October 5, 1967, Englewood Cliffs, New Jersey
DONALD BYRD SEXTET

Recording Location: Van Gelder Studios
Producer: Alfred Lion, Frank Wolff, Duke Pearson
Recording Engineer: Rudy Van Gelder
Donald Byrd: trumpet, Sonny Red: alto saxophone (except 2), Pepper Adams: baritone saxophone (except 2), Chick Corea: piano, Miroslav Vitous: bass, Mickey Roker: drums

1959 (tk.4)	(7) *Blues Well Done* 6:24 (Donald Byrd)	Blue Note LT-1096 (1981)
1960 (tk.6)	(6) *Early Sunday Morning* 6:18 (Donald Byrd)	—
1961 (tk.8)	(2) *I Will Wait for You* 9:05 (Michel Legrand, Jacques Demy, Norman Gimbel)	—
1962 (tk.15)	(5) *Chico-San* 6:43 (Chick Corea)	—
1957 (tk.18)	(4) *The Creeper* 4:38 (Sylvester Kyner)	—
1963 (tk.21)	(1) *Samba Yantra* 9:34 (Chick Corea)	—
1964 (tk.25)	(3) *Blues Medium Rare* 6:06 (Donald Byrd)	—

Session released as ***The Creeper***, Blue Note LT-1096 (Stereo) and ***The Complete Blue Note Donald Byrd/Pepper Adams Studio Sessions***, Mosaic CD MD4-194.

[029] April 23, 1968, New York City
YUSEF LATEEF ORCHESTRA

Recording Location: RCA Studios
Producer: Joel Dorn
Recording Engineer: Ray Hall
Yusef Lateef: tenor saxophone, flute, pneumatic flute, bamboo flute, shenai, tamboura, Taiwan koto, scratcher, arranger (2), Sonny Red: alto saxophone, Blue Mitchell: trumpet, Buddy Lucas: harmonica, Kenny Burrell: guitar, Hugh Lawson: piano, Cecil McBee: bass, Bob Cranshaw: Fender bass, Roy Brooks: drums, James Tyron: violin (2), Selwart Clarke: violin (2), Alfred Brown: viola (2), Kermit Moore: cello (2), William Fischer: conductor (2), The Sweet Inspirations: background vocals (1)

14378	(?) *Chandra* 9:37 (Yusef Lateef)	Atlantic SD1548	Rhino 2-71552
14379	(3) *Othelia* 4:31 (Yusef Lateef)	Atlantic SD 1508	Atlantic 2562
14380	(1) *Juba Juba* 4:20 (Yusef Lateef)	—	Atlantic SD1591
14381	(2) *Like It Is* 7:32 (Yusef Lateef)	—	

Session released as ***The Blue Yusef Lateef***, Atlantic SD1508 (Stereo), 7-82270-2 (Atlantic CD), 7567-82270-2 (German CD), Label M CD: 5724. Atlantic SD1591 released as ***The Best of Yusef Lateef***. Rhino 2-71552 (CD) released as ***The Diverse Yusef Lateef/Suite 16***. Yusef Lateef: flute, tamboura, Hugh Lawson: piano, Cecil McBee: bass, Roy Brooks: drums only.

[030] April 24, 1968, New York City
YUSEF LATEEF ORCHESTRA

Recording Location: RCA Studios
Producer: Joel Dorn
Recording Engineer: Ray Hall

Yusef Lateef: tenor saxophone, flute, pneumatic flute, bamboo flute, shenai, tamboura, Taiwan koto, scratcher, vocal (4), Sonny Red: alto saxophone, Blue Mitchell: trumpet, Buddy Lucas: harmonica, Kenny Burrell: guitar, Hugh Lawson: piano, Cecil McBee: bass, Bob Cranshaw: Fender bass, Roy Brooks: drums, The Sweet Inspirations: background vocals (5)

14382	(7) *Six Miles Next Door* 4:41 (Yusef Lateef)	Atlantic SD1508
14383	(8) *Sun Dog* 3:05 (Yusef Lateef)	—
14384	(5) *Back Home* 4:59 (Yusef Lateef)	—
14385	(6) *Get Over, Get Off and Get On* 3:41 (Hugh Lawson)	—
14386	(4) *Moon Cup* 3:16 (Yusef Lateef)	—

Session released as ***The Blue Yusef Lateef***, Atlantic SD1508 (Stereo), 7-82270-2 (Atlantic CD), 7567-82270-2 (German CD), Label M CD: 5724.

---

[031] 1971, New York City
SONNY RED QUARTET

Recording Location: The Record Plant
Producer: Bob Shad
Recording Engineer: Carmine Rubino
Sonny Red: flute (1,6), alto saxophone (5), tenor saxophone (2,3,4,7), Cedar Walton: piano, Herbie Lewis: bass, viola (2 only), Billy Higgins: drums, conga (1 only)

(1) *Love Song* 5:48 (Sylvester Kyner)	Mainstream MRL324
(2) *Tears* 7:19 (Sylvester Kyner)	—
(3) *Mustang* 5:49 (Sylvester Kyner)	—
(4) *And Then Again* 4:14 (Elvin Jones)	—
(5) *My Romance* 4:44 (Richard Rodgers, Lorenz Hart)	—
(6) *A Time for Love* 5:19 (Johnny Mandel, Paul Francis Webster)	—
(7) *Rodan* 4:35 (Sylvester Kyner)	—

Session released as ***Sonny Red***, Mainstream MRL324 (Stereo). CETA artist application, filed February 9, 1979, lists date of issue as August 15, 1971.

Note: Flute and conga overdubbed on *Love Song*.

---

[032] May 26, 1974, New York City
ROY BROOKS AND THE ARTISTIC TRUTH

Recording Location: Town Hall
Marcus Belgrave: trumpet, Sonny Fortune: alto saxophone, Sonny Red: tenor saxophone, Mickey Tucker: piano, Reggie Workman: bass, Roy Brooks: drums, percussion, musical saw (3 only), Eddie Jefferson: vocals (2,4 only)

(1) *The Last Prophet* 17:16 (Roy Brooks)	Baystate RVJ 6028
(2) *So What* 3:14 (Miles Davis)	—
(3) *Blues for the Carpenter's Saw* 12:33 (Roy Brooks)	—
(4) *Moody's Mood for Love* 4:12 (James Moody, Eddie Jefferson)	—
(5) *Epistrophy* 2:49 (Thelonious Monk, Kenny Clarke)	—

Session released as ***Live at Town Hall***, Baystate RVJ 6028 (Japanese). Roy Haynes was master of ceremonies.

---

[033] October 11, 1978, New York City
HOWARD MCGHEE/BENNY BAILEY SEXTET

Producer: Lars Johansen
Recording Engineer: Michael Ewasko
Mixing Engineer: Ole Christian Hansen
Howard McGhee: trumpet, arranger (1,2,4,5), Benny Bailey: trumpet, Sonny Red: tenor saxophone, Barry Harris: piano, Lisle Atkinson: bass, Bobby Durham: drums, Fritz Pauer: arranger (3,6,7)

(1) *Get It On* 4:22 (Howard McGhee)	Jazzcraft 5
(2) *Nostalgia* 4:18 (Fats Navarro)	—
(3) *Blues for Helene* 4:56 (Benny Bailey)	—
(4) *Jonas* 4:42 (Howard McGhee)	—
(5) *Brownie Speaks* 5:28 (Clifford Brown)	—
(6) *You Never Know* 5:50 (Benny Bailey)	—
(7) *Funky Señor* 7:16 (Benny Bailey)	—

Session released as ***Home Run***, Jazzcraft 5 (Danish), Storyville (Danish) SLP4082 and CD8273.

* * *

The following are Sonny Red compositions recorded by other musicians:

Bluesville

November 17, 1962: Lee Morgan
August 13, 1963: Blue Mitchell
June 13, 1965: Jimmy Heath/Freddie Hubbard
March 28, 1985: Cedar Walton
April 21, 1985: Cedar Walton
July 10, 1986: Joe Van Enkhuizen
August 2, 1994: Jimmy Heath
November 21, 1995: Jimmy Heath/Donald Byrd
August 28 and 29, 1997: Jim Snidero

Images

July 19, 1961: Nat Adderley

Teef

April 26, 1960: Louis Hayes
1970: Shelly Manne
January 1991: Gary Foster
August 27, 1996: Louis Hayes

Mustang

1969: Jimmy Caravan

* * *

The following is a recorded composition written for Sonny Red: *Hey Sonny Redd* (May 21, 1963: Gloria Coleman). *Hey Sonny Redd* honors the alto saxophonist, who worked with Gloria Coleman at *Branker's* at 155th Street and St. Nicholas Avenue in New York City. The Impulse reissue B0001434-02 title is *Hey Sonny Red*.

Jeffrey H. Jackson, *Making Jazz French: Music and Modern Life in Interwar Paris* (Durham and London: Duke University Press, 2003, 266 pp.)

William A. Shack, *Harlem in Montmartre: A Paris Jazz Story between the Great Wars* (Berkeley, Los Angeles, and London: University of California Press, 2001, 191 pp.)

Reviewed by Harry Cooper

Judging from its title, one might expect *Making Jazz French: Music and Modern Life in Interwar Paris* to be at least partly about how French musicians and those working in France deliberately adapted a music from America to give it a French identity. One would be wrong. In the introduction, Jeffrey H. Jackson, an assistant professor of history at Rhodes College in Memphis, Tennessee, is admirably clear: he will take no position on whether jazz in France was different from anywhere else. Why? Because "this book is not about jazz. . . . Rather, it is about France, about what the arrival of a music that was being called jazz meant to people in the turbulent interwar period, and about how they used the concept of jazz to understand and remake their age" (11). In other words, the book is a study of jazz reception tucked inside a larger cultural history. It details the constructions placed upon jazz, the debates that raged around it, and the ways in which it focused and magnified French worries about unemployment and protectionism, Americanization and consumerism, nationalism and cosmopolitanism, pastoralism and urbanization, and modernity itself.

Jackson's overarching thesis is that France after World War I was not nearly as conservative or reactionary as many historians have claimed. To prove it, he shows that jazz sparked a vigorous, freewheeling "culture war" (8). Along the way we learn a great deal about the hopes and fears of France in the period and also about the specific forms that French modernization took, especially in popular culture and its dissemination. Drawing on an impressive range of primary and secondary sources (discussed in a useful bibliographical appendix), Jackson elaborates on such topics as the high taxes on nightclubs, phonographs, and records; the eclipse of cafés and their chansons by music halls and nightclubs; legal restrictions on foreign workers and ways to circumvent them, such as hiring French musicians to stay near the bandstand while Americans played; and the role of Jews and Gypsies as surrogate blacks in the French imagination. Much of the historical detail sounds uncannily contemporary. Who knew that a cultural consumer in 1920s Paris could take a guided tour of "studios of real artists" (64), or go into a Pathé store and push a button to hear any record of his or her choosing while an employee in the basement scurried to retrieve and play the disc (47), or attend a summer institute for artists and musicians (74), or eat an imported Eskimo Pie (59)?

Jackson is also a capable guide when it comes to analyzing the dominant tropes of jazz reception, which is the heart of the book. He is certainly not the first to notice that jazz was greeted as both wildly liberating and soullessly mechanical, but the way he depicts this paradox as "two sides of the same coin" (101) and links it to other dichotomies (jazz was considered both African and American, primitive and modern) is insightful. My only regret here is that he does not treat the jazz writing of Theodor Adorno, which, for all its atrocities, was notable for pinpointing and interpreting similar paradoxes in the German reception early on.[1] Limiting the book to France is understandable but at times regrettable. Shack's interesting comments on the nostalgia sparked by jazz in France might well have been sharpened by comparison with the same phenomenon in the United States.[2] The rest of the world only enters in the last chapter, which treats Charles Delaunay, Hugues Panassié, and the amusingly bureaucratic efforts of the Hot Club to spread jazz around the world. Shack deals with Panassié's jazz writing in some detail, not joining the debate over its quality but rather bringing out its latent pre-modern, aristocratic yearnings.

Missing in all this, however, is any sense of what the music was like. This means that *Making Jazz French* will be most interesting, or least frustrating, to two groups of readers: those who already have an idea of how jazz sounded in France in the 1920s and 1930s (i.e., some jazz historians) and those who, though interested in the broad subject, do not really care how it sounded (i.e., some French historians). But there is a deeper problem with this brand of reception study than its limited audience. By employing a purely nominal definition of jazz ("a music that was being called jazz") and then refusing to flesh it out either intensionally (what were the properties of this jazz?) or even extensionally (what music qualified as jazz?), the author leaves himself little chance of evaluating the truth of French perceptions.

Why would Jackson put himself in such a position? Given that his goal is "a more historically accurate portrait of the true France in the 1920s and 1930s" (201), he is clearly no deconstructionist: he does not believe that an object of historical inquiry like France or jazz is simply the sum of its various representations. Rather, his unspoken assumption is that for the purposes of a study of cultural discourse, the accuracy of those representations just does not matter. He does, however, seem worried enough about this assumption to take comfort in the substantial agreement between proponents and detractors of jazz about what the music was like: "None of the perceived elements of jazz—its supposed primitivism, its noise and rhythm, the emphasis on dancing, the challenge to older moral codes, or the powerful psychological effects of the music—were as much in dispute as what these qualities meant to listeners" (103). He makes the point several times.

In fact, it is far too simple to say that "for jazz's proponents, all these qualities (brutal force, pounding rhythm, hellish sonority) were precisely what constituted the music's great value" (102-03). Ernst-Alexandre Ansermet's appreciation of Sidney Bechet, originally published in a Swiss journal in 1919 but widely read in

France and now a classic of jazz criticism, proves that there were more measured and musically informed responses. Ansermet gets only a nod from Jackson, and then only for his racial attitudes. Darius Milhaud's writing about jazz is treated at greater length, but again more for its racialism than its insights. Piet Mondrian, a keen observer of Parisian popular music and dance of the time, complained that jazz was "treated as barbaric" by the French public; Jackson, who is interested only in broad patterns and dominant responses, would probably take the comment as evidence to support, not contradict, his account.[3]

But even if almost everyone agreed that jazz was, for example, noisy, we cannot conclude that it was. I am not choosing this example at random: the perception of jazz as a noise music was perhaps the most notable feature of its early reception in France and indeed throughout Europe. Wouldn't it be nice to learn how prevalent noisemakers really were in early jazz in Europe and whether instruments bleated and squawked and crashed as much as some journalists and chroniclers reported? Tin pans and car horns were certainly used, but to what extent did the broad perception of jazz as noise reflect a signal-processing failure ("noise" as "nonsense") triggered in European ears by the novelty of the music and some of its instruments, like banjo and saxophone?[4] Jackson admits that at least one critic's description of jazz as "loud" and "exotic" was off the mark, for that description was of jazz in the music halls, a sweeter and more symphonic brand than the jazz played in the clubs (109). If this kind of misperception was in fact widespread, wouldn't that tell us as much about French culture as the debate about noise music itself?[5]

As if to forestall this objection, Jackson violates his own rule against describing the music: "Bands in the early years of the music, in fact, frequently *did little else* but make loud, clashing sounds, as if jazz should express musically some of the chaos of the immediate postwar era" (31, emphasis added). Such a sweeping statement, with its rather simplistic enlistment of social history, does not persuade, even if Jackson does cite several reports of percussion-heavy performances. Of course, firsthand accounts, treated circumspectly, can be helpful in determining what early jazz in France sounded like, but why not listen to some records, too? Jackson ignores them entirely. After mentioning Marcel's Jazz Band des Folies Bergères and the Hot Boys Band, he notes that "an accounting of such early bands is difficult, in part because there were so many musicians playing around the city that to know them all would be nearly impossible" (20). Yet early recordings by these two now-obscure groups and others like them can be heard with just a few clicks on www.redhotjazz.com.

In complaining that Jackson gives short shrift to the music and some of its exceptional early critics, I suppose I am criticizing his book for something it is not. Or to put it another way, I am wishing away the disciplinary boundaries that leave so many cultural histories of jazz skating on the surface of the music. I also wish the book had been better written and edited. It retains the clunky feel of a dissertation, with grammatical goofs ("who" is often used incorrectly instead of "whom"), quotations repeated within the space of a few pages, a token index, and factual mistakes. At one point Jackson quotes Panassié calling Jimmy McPartland and Bix Beiderbecke "the two most renowned white clarinet players of the day" (171); the word is *cornet*, not *clarinette*, in the original.[6] Such a gaffe leaves one feeling uneasy about Jackson's other translations and underscores that, in his account, the music itself doesn't really matter.

* * *

If Jackson's book tells the story of French interwar jazz from the point of view of its consumers, William A. Shack's *Harlem in Montmartre: A Paris Jazz Story between the Great Wars* tells the story from the point of view of the producers, or at least a distinct group of them, the black American musicians, entrepreneurs, and entertainers who for a couple of decades made Montmartre a thriving outpost of Harlem-style life and music. Shack, a black anthropologist at the University of California at Berkeley who died just before finishing the manuscript, was inspired by the stories his father told him about serving in France in World War I and being treated as an equal there but not at home.

Unlike Jackson's book, Shack's has no grand idea and no particular argument. Shack compares his method to an anthropologist's "thick description of social situations" (xv), but in fact the book is really a narrative history of the most traditional and close-grained kind. Like Jackson, he moves more or less chronologically through the period, and he treats several of the same topics: the so-called 10 percent law, which limited the number of foreign performers in France; the development and activities of the Hot Club; and the contrast between elegant, touristed Montmartre and bohemian Montparnasse. Another similarity is that Shack "does not attempt a musicological study of this era" (xv). We get little sense of how the transitions from ragtime to hot jazz to swing manifested themselves in the clubs and streets.[7]

What we do get, in abundance, is a sense of the personalities and venues that made up the changing fabric of "Harlem in Montmartre," or "Black Broadway in Black Paris," or "The Race Colony," as it was variously called. Within the chronological progression of chapters, the book is organized around discrete sketches of people and places. The protagonists, in order of appearance, are Will Marion Cook, James Reese Europe, Eugène Jacques Bullard and his club Le Grand Duc, Arthur Briggs, Florence Embry Jones, Louis Mitchell and his club Chez Florence, Bricktop (Ada Smith du Congé), Josephine Baker and her club Chez Josephine, the Senegalese boxer Battling Siki, The Jockey Club, Alberta Hunter, Henry Crowder and Nancy Cunard, Le Boeuf sur le Toit, Florence Mills, Adelaide Hall, Garland Wilson, Louis Douglas and his Théâtre Nègre, and Django Reinhardt and the Hot Club. Many of these are familiar names, but they have rarely been together in one book, and the cast of supporting characters is even more impressive.[8] Considering that the black community in Montmartre "perhaps never exceeded a few hundred individuals in the mid-1920s" (133), sometimes it seems as if Shack has mentioned them all.

Scholars will love this level of detail, but they will hate the uneven annotation. How do we know that Fernand Léger's suggestion to import a black troupe might have been instrumental in bringing the Rêvue Nègre to Paris (34) or that the Lapin Agile, one of Picasso's early hangouts, engaged jazz bands (56)? We are not told. Perhaps this relaxed approach to sources reflects the fact that Shack derived a lot of information from talking to eyewitnesses like Maurice Cullaz, the jazz critic for Radio Paris, and Jacques Bureaux, one of the five founding members of the Hot Club. Maybe it reflects the fact that the book had to be completed posthumously. In any case, the loose documentation is in keeping with the book's conversational tone. Sometimes the conversation is pointed and refreshing: Baker's "dancing relied more on comedy—crossing her eyes and doing the shimmy—than rhythm" (37). At other times it is overblown or simplistic: French youth "felt the monstrous anger of the guns at Verdun" (26), and Freud's "advice to get rid of inhibitions . . . became a rationale for women to grant their favors to lovers" (50).

Shack is best when he stays close to the ground. He writes about this vanished black community with the confidence of an insider, and indeed it probably takes something of an insider to know, for example, how closely jazz and boxing have been linked in black culture, and how much the great boxing victories of Cyclone Billy Morris, Battling Siki, and Joe Louis meant to black pride. We learn that Eugène Jacques Bullard first came to Paris as a boxer before turning to promotion and percussion (23) and that Panama Al Brown went from boxer to song-and-dance man (39). Like Jackson, Shack is worth reading for his detours.

One puzzle of the Montmartre scene, although Shack does not pose it as such, is how the same small clubs served both as magnet for mostly white "well-to-do tourists" (52) and as "home away from home" (53) for struggling black expatriates. The answer seems to be twofold: the after-hours scene was a world unto itself, more clubhouse than nightclub, while the mixing earlier in the night did not always go smoothly. Another anthropologist might have been interested in the jostlings of class, but for Shack the issue is race. He provides compelling details about ugly scenes caused by white American tourists who could not stand seeing blacks treated as human beings, and the varying responses of the French authorities. While race never becomes the explicit subject of Shack's book (except for an interlude on Jim Crow in 1920s France and England), it is arguably the unifying thread, the emotional center.

But if the treatment of race is one of the strengths of the book, it is also one of its weaknesses. Shack all but ignores the prevalence of white jazz bands, musicians, and styles outside the confines of Montmartre. This context might have offered Shack (and his readers) a measure of perspective, a needed break from immersion in his cherished locale. Without such perspective, it is difficult to get a sense of how important the vibrant but relatively small Montmartre scene was to Parisian life. In a very brief section on Paul Whiteman's 1926 appearance in Paris, Shack acknowledges that the concert came "at a time of lively debate" about jazz but concludes simply that the Whiteman style "never posed a serious threat to black musicians on the Parisian scene" (57). In a similar vein he notes that another white ensemble visiting Paris, Fred Waring and his Pennsylvanians, "played to the curiosity seekers but attracted few true jazz lovers" (57). The real content of such a statement, which is unsupported by any data on the audience for that performance, is simply that Shack does not consider such music jazz. He seems proud of the fact that "Harlem-style jazz was ill suited for the craze that swept Paris in the mid-1920s: dance music," and that there was little room to do much more than wiggle in the mostly tiny Montmartre clubs (51–52).

All this adds up to one thing: Shack is a jazz purist. And while I feel some sympathy for jazz purism as an aesthetic stance, it does not go far as a historical approach, especially in a situation as impure as jazz in France. Even in this "Harlem in Montmartre," jazz must have had its compromises, and of course "Harlem-style jazz," a phrase Shack repeats without ever unpacking, was not so pure to begin with. His purism also marginalizes the often messy nature and role of audiences, and in this way the book is the mirror image of Jackson's, which concentrates on receivers to the virtual exclusion of producers. Indeed, taken together the two books form a kind of parable of academic specialization, a pair of ships passing in the night. But they also raise the hope of a real discussion across disciplines, one in which the music would get the attention it deserves.

NOTES

1. In his 1936 essay "Über Jazz," Adorno attributed the "modern archaic stance of jazz" to similar paradoxes in the structure of commodities, which, he argued, strive to be both reliably unchanging and excitingly new at once. Whether Adorno was really talking about jazz itself or its reception remains a matter of debate.
2. See MacDonald Smith Moore, *Yankee Blues: Musical Culture and American Identity* (Bloomington: Indiana University Press, 1985).
3. The quotation is from Mondrian's 1921 essay "The Manifestation of Neo-Plasticism in Music and the Italian Futurists' Bruiteurs."
4. See also Susan McClary's distinction between "cultural noise" and "real sonic noise" in her afterword to Jacques Attali, *Noise: The Political Economy of Music* (1977), trans. Brian Massumi (Minneapolis: University of Minnesota Press, 1985), 157.
5. Another problem with taking the critical reception of jazz at face value, i.e., treating it as a true and direct reflection of production, is that Jackson does not consider how reception might have influenced production. Truly noisy effects in jazz in Europe must have been partly a response to audience demand. Europeans had a keen interest in noise at this time, judging from the attention given to Luigi Russolo (who presented his noise instruments in Paris in 1921), Edgard Varèse, and others who made music from natural and mechanical sounds. And we know that jazz musicians in Europe were sensitive to the demands and projections of audiences. When Ellington got a lukewarm reception on his 1933 English tour, he decided to substitute fast, raucous numbers for ballads. "I went back and gave a vaudeville show," he recalled.

6. Hugues Pannasié, *Douze Années de Jazz (1927–1938)* (Paris: Editions Corrêa, 1946), 15.
7. The few comments that Shack does allow himself on the music are welcome. On the issue of noise, for example, we learn that Le Jockey and Le Boeuf were probably louder than other clubs (41, 51); that Louis Mitchell's "slam-bang" style of drumming contrasted with the "smooth rhythmic form" of Buddy Gilmore (30); and that "gadgets to make noise" were in the luggage of many visiting black musicians who went to Paris (27).
8. You can be sure that any book that makes three references to my rather obscure namesake, the trumpeter Harry Cooper, has dug deep.

Jeffrey Magee, *The Uncrowned King of Swing: Fletcher Henderson and Big Band Jazz* (New York: Oxford University Press, 2005, 322 pp., $30.00)

Reviewed by Edward Berger

Fletcher Henderson was in many ways an enigmatic figure, both personally and professionally. Often depicted as the symbol of the exploited black artist whose scores propelled Benny Goodman to fame and fortune, Henderson himself was accused of building his reputation on the work of his own stellar sidemen and arrangers. This exemplary study presents a detailed and objective assessment of Henderson's contributions as bandleader and arranger. In his introduction, Magee identifies what he considers the two prevailing views of Henderson's position in jazz history—the "Frustration" and "Inflation" theses:

> The Frustration thesis portrays Henderson as overshadowed by musicians who went on to greater fame after playing in his band, such as Armstrong and Coleman Hawkins. As he shifted his sights from bandleading to arranging, Henderson remained overshadowed by the bandleader who became famous playing Henderson arrangements: Benny Goodman . . .
>
> The Inflation thesis offers a contrasting view. It holds that historical accounts have overcompensated for Henderson's "frustration" by exaggerating his importance at the expense of others. The Inflation theory contends that Henderson receives more credit than equally talented peers, especially in the realm of arranging, where the likes of Don Redman, Benny Carter, Jimmy Mundy, and Henderson's own brother Horace made innovative contributions that Henderson absorbed and got credit for while working with Goodman . . . (2)

The author posits that Henderson's role and legacy transcends the rigid parameters of these two positions (although the book's title might imply his agreement with the Frustration theory) and even defies the compartmentalization suggested by terms such as "bandleader" and "arranger": "To get at what Henderson did, it might be best to describe him as a musical catalyst, facilitator, collaborator, organizer, transmitter, medium, channel, funnel, and 'synergizer,' if such a word existed" (3).

As a musicologist, Magee focuses on the craft of arranging in general and Henderson's contributions in particular. Along the way, he examines the work of the other arrangers for the Henderson band—most notably Don Redman and Benny Carter, but also Fletcher's brother Horace, John Nesbitt, and several contributors from outside the orchestra. He offers fascinating insights into Redman's method of reworking stock arrangements for Henderson. He also adds nuance and depth to our understanding of Louis Armstrong's impact during his relatively brief tenure with the Henderson orchestra, in 1924–25. Without detracting from the trumpeter's contributions, Magee argues that Armstrong's cataclysmic impact was heightened by Redman's orchestral groundwork: "What better place to stand out than in an arranging concept that already stressed surprise, variety, and kaleidoscope changes of color and texture?" (73). He also notes that the band was evolving a jazz identity even before Armstrong's arrival: "Armstrong's powerful presence accelerated a process that had already begun. Each new reed and brass player that Henderson hired since 1923 gave a new jazz voice to the band. . . . These additions had a cumulative effect: by mid-1925 musicians who could play 'hot' dominated the brass and reed sections" (74).

In the early 1930s, with the departure of Redman and Carter, Henderson's role by necessity began to shift from "synergizer" to creator of formal, written arrangements. Magee traces the evolution of the salient features of the Henderson style, culminating in a thorough examination of his work for Goodman. His analysis shows Henderson to be a versatile and far less formulaic arranger than often assumed. Magee demonstrates Henderson's command of a broad range of arranging devices and his effective assimilation of a wide variety of material. Though the book's primary strengths lie in its musical analysis, Magee does not ignore the biographical details and personal aspects of Henderson's life. He discusses Henderson's family background, his education at Howard Normal School and Atlanta University, his move to New York in 1920 and almost accidental entry into the music business as a song plugger for the Pace and Handy Music Company, and his involvement with Black Swan Records as accompanist for blues and pop artists. As Magee points out, Henderson's transition to jazz and blues was quite alien to his upbringing and inclination: "A 'respectable,' middle-class, college-educated young man had absorbed elements of black culture that had existed outside his privileged domains in Cuthbert and Atlanta" (26). The author presents valuable information about the music business in the 1920s, especially the professional hierarchy and interactions among New York's black musical establishment. His understanding of the complex interrelationships between art and commerce is evident in his perceptive and non-judgmental assessment of Henderson's more "commercial" early recordings. Magee also makes valid points about the role of recording in the 1920s and recognizes the disparity between recordings and live performances and the pitfalls of overreliance on discography in reconstructing jazz history.

By the time Magee undertook this study, virtually all of the direct links with Henderson's orchestra had been lost with the exception of Benny Carter. Nevertheless, the author has made excellent use of oral histories, archival collections, and a wide range of previously published works to construct an evocative account of an artist and his era.

While eschewing the amateur psychobabble of some jazz biographers, Magee discusses Henderson's personality insofar as it affected his successes and failures as a bandleader. As Magee notes, Henderson was perceived in different ways ranging from "easygoing" by sidemen who loved playing for him to "phlegmatic" by promoters and supporters such as John Hammond (who brought Henderson together with Goodman), exasperated by Henderson's "lassitude" (Hammond's word) and his band's lack of discipline, particularly in later years. Indeed, in the final analysis, it appears that the "frustration" tag applied more to Hammond's own feelings toward Henderson than to any disappointment the arranger may have had about his own lack of success, commercial or otherwise. After all, it was Hammond who titled the major Columbia Henderson four-LP reissue set released in 1961 *A Study in Frustration*.[1] As Magee writes in the final chapter:

> To conclude that Henderson's story thus forms "a study in frustration" as Hammond did, perhaps too easily casts Henderson as a victim in a familiar ritual of white-guilt expiation. To conclude, as others have, that Henderson's musical goals somehow became fulfilled in Goodman's performances, places the story in another uncomfortably familiar plotline: white agents appropriate African-American music and create a national (and international) phenomenon—which may be *the* story of twentieth-century American vernacular music. Recognizing how Henderson's story links up with such larger historical narratives makes it more than a compelling debate on a continuum between frustration and fulfillment (243).

As most jazz researchers know, Fletcher Henderson was the subject of an earlier and very different work, *Hendersonia*, by Walter C. Allen (self-published, 1973), unfortunately long out of print. Magee acknowledges his debt to Allen's book, which was the prototype of the "bio-discography" and remains unsurpassed as a chronicle of an artist's activities, recordings, and other factual data. Allen wrote in his preface: "Perhaps others will find here the necessary facts for a more interpretive book in times to come" (*Hendersonia*, p. viii). Magee has written that book.

NOTE

1. In a phone conversation on July 29, 2005, Frank Driggs, producer of the Columbia boxed set, verified that Hammond chose the name *A Study in Frustration*. Magee, like many other writers, incorrectly assumes that Hammond produced the set (see his discography, p. 301).

Michelle Mercer, *footprints: The Life and Work of Wayne Shorter* (New York: Jeremy P. Tarcher/Penguin, 2004, 298 + xii pp., $24.95 hardcover)

Reviewed by Patricia Julien

One book cannot be all books. This particular biography—the first—of jazz saxophonist and composer Wayne Shorter is not a scholarly research book, laden with music theory terminology and fully detailed descriptions of events and works (those books will follow). Instead this biography, written with Shorter's full participation, provides a more sweeping overview, occasionally alighting on certain topics in greater detail. The book is infused with the ideas and occasions valued by Shorter; it is the story of Shorter's life as he wanted it told. Readers will likely appreciate the many quotations from original interviews. However, inaccuracies disqualify this book as a reliable resource for career details. In addition, the book contains no substantive discussion of Shorter's music.

Publishers sometimes seem hesitant to publish a biography of a living artist, and so Tarcher/Penguin is to be commended for supporting Mercer's project. It is a delight to reach the final pages aware that the subject is still there—living, creating, spinning the details of a new day.

A brief preface by Shorter himself reveals his concern with "personal stories . . . [that] reveal who we are in the face of obstacles and challenges" (xi). Expressing his appreciation of Mercer's approach, he continues, "She did not attempt to dramatize my life based on professional achievements and fame; instead, she did the kind of research that would be true to the realities we all encounter in life's endeavor (a baseball player's baseball story alone does not sufficiently constitute his *life* story)" (xi-xii). Unfortunately, at the start of the book's introduction, Mercer fails to live up to Shorter's praise. To make Shorter's recent work seem culminating and dramatic, she writes that "after emerging as the leader of the dynamic Wayne Shorter Quartet in 2001, he did finally gain some recognition for his musical gifts" (2). This statement ignores his steady recording contracts and record sales, countless fans worldwide, numerous invitations for sideman work, Grammy awards, *Down Beat* Critics Poll wins in a variety of categories, and unflagging press attention over his lengthy career.

From the outset we see that basic citations are not always provided. On page 2, Mercer's quotation from the *New York Times* includes the year (2003) but no additional information, not even the author's name. No *New York Times* citation is included in the endnotes or among the scant 24 items in the bibliography, which includes the disclaimer "The following is a selection of sources drawn upon for this work. Articles were too numerous to mention" (281). No endnote numbers appear in the main text, so that quotations from sources other than Mercer's original interviews read as though communicated directly to Mercer. For example, Shorter was fiercely praised in a thoughtful profile by Newark friend Le Roi Jones (now known as Amiri Baraka) in the November 1959 issue of *The Jazz Review.* Mercer writes: "Amiri Baraka heard Wayne at many cutting contests. 'Wayne was precocious,' Baraka wrote. 'I heard many pretty astounding things he was doing at seventeen and eighteen. Even then, when he couldn't do anything else, he could still make you gasp at sheer technical infallibility'" (38). "Baraka wrote" is the only clue in the main text that this is not personal correspondence between Mercer and Baraka.

The introduction reviews Shorter's enigmatic and often disarming way of interacting with others. Mercer seems to understand and appreciate Shorter's sense of humor, and she herself employs a playful, informal writing style at times, referring to Shorter as "the cosmic cartoonist" (3), "the Taskmaster of Depth" (6), and a "happy jazz Buddha" (8). A friendship was forged during the writing of this book, and Mercer refers to Shorter by his first name throughout (Mercer follows this common practice of the jazz community for most musicians discussed in the book).

Mercer's writing is easily readable and never dry. She is adept at placing quotations by Shorter in context; his comment that "most time is spent in judgmental, dead-zone talk" (5) illustrates his disinterest in mundane conversation. She also has a poetic way with descriptions, as in this portrait of the neighborhood where Shorter was raised: "It was a thoroughly and starkly composed world of bricks and mortar, sharp angles, and literal iron boundaries" (12). Another example: "When Wayne did emerge from his room and get out among the [Miles Davis] band, his character could be bizarre, and his language tended toward the far side of oblique and the denser part of opaque" (103). About the recording of Joe Zawinul's composition "In a Silent Way," she writes, "In effect, Miles's edit created a grove within the forest of Joe's tune. A grove is naturally silent, well-shaded so that few plants grow, offering no food or shelter for the animals that make noise elsewhere in the forest. On 'In a Silent Way,' Miles cleared out the undergrowth of the tune and got the noisemakers out of the way, so that Wayne's entrance was as quietly dramatic as a deer coming out into the open" (128).

In her introduction, Mercer refers to Shorter's meticulous work habits. Unlike the stereotypical absent-minded composer, with papers strewn about the room, Shorter keeps careful track of his compositions. Mercer mentions the "closet where fifty flat, black music-score boxes were stacked, filled with his life's work as a composer" (3–4). She introduces Shorter's work regime as typically beginning with composition at 6:00 A.M., leading the reader to believe that more information about Shorter's techniques and procedures as a composer and saxophonist will follow. But we get nothing beyond general mentions of his deriving inspiration from movies and books, composing with the television on, composing at the piano, and practicing from cello books. Mercer explains, "We spent hours watching movies, reading passages from his favorite books, and talking. In essence, he was showing me his creative process" (4). Mercer implies that Shorter (like Beethoven) commonly works through multiple rough drafts of a composition, but she provides no information on this editing process. Shorter was apparently not interested in supplying her with such details. Mercer remarks that after reluctantly discussing his music with a different author in a telephone interview he turned to her and asked, "You don't want me to talk to you like that, do you?" (8).

Chapter 1 provides information about Shorter's parents, Louise and Joseph Shorter. Shorter's mother played an essential role in inspiring the imagination of both Wayne and his older brother (and only sibling), Alan. She often brought home materials such as clay or watercolors for the boys and deeply believed that "playtime wasn't just amusement, it was a time for creative industry, and their state of inventive absorption was sacred" (13). Shorter attended services at Mount Zion Baptist Church, and Mercer relates his dislike of the overly serious, self-conscious, and dramatic church music. She also describes his early passion for film music; the Shorter brothers developed an extraordinary ability to recall and re-create extensive portions of sound tracks and movie scenes and dialogue. Young Wayne was an avid reader, collecting all the comic books he could. At age 12 he won a citywide art contest, and his painting talent led him to attend Newark's Arts High School. Not surprisingly, a film "inspired Wayne's first major art project, a thick fifty-four-page comic book of intricate blue pen drawings titled *Other Worlds*" (23). Two pages of this extraordinary work are printed in the book's photograph section.

Chapter 2 begins with Shorter's acknowledgment that bebop, which he first heard on Martin Block's radio program *Make Believe Ballroom*, was the first music to fully capture his attention. He purchased and taught himself the tonette, a recorder-like instrument widely used at the time in grammar school education. Shorter also started listening to classical music and "liked the storytelling role of the clarinet" (28). He knew the clarinet was the horn for him when he saw one in a store window. At age 15 he began his formal musical training.

Mercer retells the well-known story of Shorter regularly skipping school to hear a big band followed by a movie at the nearby Adams Theater. In this setting Shorter heard groups led by Count Basie, Stan Kenton, Woody Herman, Jimmie Lunceford, Illinois Jacquet, Dizzy Gillespie, Charlie Parker, and Lester Young. Upon learning of these numerous absences, Shorter's principal "opted for a constructive punishment, enrolling Wayne in a music theory class as a disciplinary action" (30) midway through the year. Shorter wrote a flawless final exam and realized he was meant to be a musician.

During the summer following Shorter's junior year, he and his brother (who was playing alto saxophone before switching to trumpet) devoted all their time to practicing Lennie Tristano compositions, which they transcribed from Tristano's 1949 *Crosscurrents* album. In his senior year Shorter took harmony, theory, and orchestration, and played clarinet in the school band. With his interest in bebop, Shorter switched to tenor saxophone. He began playing in a local ensemble led by Jackie Bland and was soon the featured player. After the group won a battle of the bands competition against the Nat Phipps Orchestra, Shorter was hired for additional gigs. Mercer relates the story of Shorter's phenomenal guest appearance with Sonny Stitt at the local jazz club Lloyd's Manor. Although Stitt then and there made Shorter an offer to tour with him, Shorter turned it down because of his plans to attend college and study composition.

In 1952 Shorter enrolled at New York University as a music education major and took the required courses in music history, piano proficiency, harmony, and orchestration. He was also required to play in the concert band that represented the school and the department at public functions. Mercer supplies no information regarding why Shorter selected New York University as opposed to, say, Juilliard, or why he chose music education for his major, despite wanting to study composition.[1]

Alan Shorter was attending conservative Howard University but found that his tendency to challenge the status quo was not welcomed and eventually dropped out. Years later he graduated from NYU, but his nonconformity and need to confront authority permeated all aspects of his life, influencing his later move to Europe. Mercer's information about Alan Shorter is particularly useful because it is not found in other sources.

During his time at NYU, Wayne Shorter worked for three years on an opera called *The Singing Lesson* but set it aside after learning that Leonard Bernstein's *West Side Story* addressed similar subject matter. He spent his evenings in New York, listening to jazz musicians, including Charlie Parker and Lester Young, whose jazz hipster language Shorter also admired. Shorter was still living at home and began playing regular weekend gigs around Newark. He joined the Nat Phipps Orchestra to help pay for college, even though it played dance music rather than bebop. This band included such musicians as Grachan Moncur III, Tom McIntosh, and Bobby Thomas. Phipps gladly added more than 20 of Shorter's arrangements to the band's repertoire, along with a Shorter original entitled "No Minors Allowed." Shorter then formed his own quartet, with Eddie White on bass, Jacqueline Rollins alternating with Nat Phipps on piano, and an unnamed drummer (if the "quartet" label is accurate). This group won first prize at an Apollo new-talent contest. Mambos had become an exceedingly popular genre, and on the strength of some mambo originals, Shorter's group opened for Pérez Prado at the Starlight Roof in the Waldorf-Astoria Hotel and was invited to play at the famous Palladium. Max Roach invited the saxophonist to sit in at Café Bohemia at a jam session that included Oscar Pettiford, Art Blakey, Jackie McLean, Percy Heath, and Jimmy Smith. As Shorter became known in the jazz clubs in New York in the 1950s, he acquired the nickname "The Newark Flash."

According to Mercer, Shorter's first professional recording session was on June 8, 1956, not long after his graduation from NYU. The leader was pianist and composer Johnny Eaton, who was signed to Columbia Records. Mercer describes Eaton's first recording, *College Jazz*, and quotes from a *Playboy* review: "*Johnny Eaton and His Princetonians* blast off on a winding, flute-filling journey through a milkyway of originals and standards" (51). Then she begins the next paragraph with "At the session with Wayne" (51), not specifying whether this session is for Eaton's *College Jazz* (issued in the spring of 1956) or perhaps Eaton's second album, *Far Out Near In* (issued in 1957), which she never mentions. My own research shows that Shorter is not included on the personnel listing on either LP. Mercer names some titles from the session with Shorter, none of which is included on *College Jazz* or *Far Out Near In*. Was there perhaps a third Eaton recording? More research is sorely needed here. Given Shorter's rich recording history and the text's incomplete documentation of his recorded work, the absence of a discography (particularly one of "works cited") is a serious oversight.

Shorter was drafted into the Army in 1956 and stationed at Fort Dix, New Jersey, where he was unsurpassed as a sharpshooter. He joined the army band and continued to compose during his free time. In 1958, Shorter was released from the Army a few weeks early to play a few dates with Horace Silver, who advised Shorter about retaining ownership of his compositions. We learn that Shorter sat in with Sonny Rollins at Sugar Hill in Newark, but Mercer provides no details and the reader is left to wonder how this performance came about. At a matinee gig with Silver, Shorter met John Coltrane, and the two spent many hours at Coltrane's house, eating, talking, playing the piano, practicing, and comparing their saxophones. They seemed to share an understanding of each other's musical goals and dreams. Coltrane and Shorter played together one night at Birdland with Freddie Hubbard, Cedar Walton, Tommy Flanagan, George Tucker, and Elvin Jones, opposite Cannonball Adderley's band. Coltrane had written "Giant Steps" by that time, and Shorter, according to his own remark, was able to improvise on the piece's chord changes comfortably. Coltrane was ready to leave Miles Davis's group in 1959 and, apparently without having made his intentions clear to Davis, offered the chair to Shorter, who called the trumpeter but was rebuffed. Around this time Shorter met Joe Zawinul, who recommended that Shorter audition for Maynard Ferguson's big band. He got the gig and had at least one composition ("Nellie Bly") in Ferguson's book, but only five weeks later, on August 1, 1959, joined Art Blakey's Jazz Messengers.

The Messengers were a solid, entertaining, and successful group, and the steady work enabled Shorter to move out of his parents' house and into his own apartment in Harlem. Blakey's well-established record of hiring up-and-coming jazz stars helped Shorter obtain his own record contract with the Vee-Jay label. Shorter had played on Wynton Kelly's Vee-Jay recording *Kelly Great* shortly after joining the Messengers, and Mercer notes that "the record included Wayne's 'Mama G,' a tune he'd written for Maynard Ferguson" (72). She fails to identify this composition as the same one previously referred to as "Nellie Bly," which, as Mercer previously mentioned, was composed during Shorter's undergraduate years at NYU, long before he began playing with Ferguson.

Shorter recorded his first album as leader, *Introducing Wayne Shorter*, for Vee-Jay on November 9 and 10, 1959. Mercer states: "As a leader, Wayne had a chance to test out that reserve tank of tunes he'd written back in the army barracks. Some of them were a little odd: 'Blues a la Carte' had an irregular 21-bar form, with a 13-bar main melody followed by an 8-bar vamp" (72). Mercer does not acknowledge the long-standing confusion about the titles on the Vee-Jay recording and may be confusing "Blues a la Carte" with another piece from the same recording, "Harry's Last Stand." The October 1959 copyright deposit for "Blues a la Carte" (titled "Blues a' la Carte" in the *Short Snorter* collection of pieces submitted by Shorter and Horace Silver to the Library of Congress) presents a 12-bar piece, easily distinguishable as a blues in F. The August 1960 copyright deposit for "Harry's Last Stand" presents a 21-bar piece, matching Mercer's report of a 13-measure melody followed by an 8-measure vamp. Either Mercer relied on the titles provided by Vee-Jay, in which case she did not base her analysis on Shorter's scores; or Shorter's personal score of "Blues a la Carte" differs from the existing copyright deposit under that title. In any case, Mercer missed an opportunity to set the record straight.

Shorter's first recording with Blakey (*Africaine*) featured two Shorter compositions. Four days after this session, the Messengers flew to Paris to begin a month-long European tour. About Bud Powell's December 18, 1959, guest appearance with the Messengers, Mercer writes that Powell "shunned inspiration and played straight" and that "more impressive musicianship actually came from the Messengers' two horn players" (76). No musical details are offered to support her evaluation, and the reader has to guess whether Shorter himself expressed disappointment with Powell's performance. After the show, Shorter returned to his hotel room to drink wine and compose. Around 3:00 A.M., Powell came to Shorter's room and asked him to play something on his horn. Shorter worked through some ideas on Powell's "Dance of the Infidels," which they had played together earlier that evening. Powell thanked him and left saying, "Uh-huh, it's all right" (78). In 1985, on the set of the film *'Round Midnight,* Powell's daughter Celia explained to Shorter that her father's comment 26 years earlier was meant to affirm that "everything was all right . . . for the future of music" (79). At this point readers learn that there is a recording of the December 18, 1959, concert (titled *Paris Jam Session*) and that after speaking to Celia, Shorter uncharacteristically listened to it dozens of times (usually needing to hear something only once or twice to commit it to memory), trying to discern what Powell might have felt or heard in Shorter's playing that long ago Paris night.

Later that month the Jazz Messengers attended a holiday party at Blakey's home in New York City. There Shorter met and spoke at length with Joelle, the French governess of Blakey's young daughter, Sakeena. Joelle reminisced about sitting on a park bench on a winter day in France with Charlie Parker. Parker gave Joelle a package containing a record of a classical alto saxophone concerto (played by Marcel Mule), a violin practice book, and staff paper with a newly composed melody over the chord changes to "Sentimental Over You." Parker instructed Joelle to someday give the package to a deserving person, and she chose

Shorter. Each item reinforced Shorter's sense of affinity with Parker—love of classical music, practicing with classical instrumental technique books, and composing with thoughtful revision. Shorter's sense of musical destiny was profoundly deepened: "These first- and second-hand encounters with Bud and Bird, the bebop elders, made Wayne feel like a chosen one of his generation. They gave him artistic conviction, which he carried quietly within himself: Regardless of the health of his career, he could draw from this reserve of artistic purpose at will" (83).

In Chapter 5, a brief discussion of pieces by Shorter raises two concerns. First, Mercer describes "Sakeena's Vision" as a "catchy variation on *the old 12-bar structure*. . ." (82, emphasis mine), implying the piece is a modified blues. My own analysis reveals this piece to be a 40-measure AABA form, employing an asymmetrical expansion of the standard 32-measure scheme. Mercer's vocabulary seems borrowed from Shorter's remark (in a 1977 *Down Beat* article) that with pieces such as "Sincerely Diana" and "Sakeena's Vision" he was "getting away from the old 12-bar structure."[2] Second, Mercer includes Shorter's observation that "'Sincerely Diana' was about Art's wife" (82). On page 42, Mercer states that "Sincerely Diana," though not titled at the time, was written by Shorter during his undergraduate years at NYU, long before he worked with Blakey.

Chapter 6 begins with descriptions of Shorter's experiences touring with the Jazz Messengers in such countries as France, Algeria, and Finland. The January 1961 tour of Japan was particularly memorable. The Jazz Messengers experienced in Japan what the Beatles would soon experience in the U.S., with thousands of dancing and screaming fans, extensive publicity, and apparel in Japan's department stores modeled after the band. The band members fell in love with the country, its customs, and its people. Shorter married a Chicago-born Japanese-American woman, Irene (who later took the traditional Japanese name Teruko) Nakagami, on July 28, 1961, a few days before their daughter, Miyako, was born. Shorter wrote "Infant Eyes" for his newborn child.

Although many of the Jazz Messengers were strong composers, Blakey designated Shorter as musical director. According to Curtis Fuller, Shorter "would turn out a tune a day" (90), and his challenging chord progressions required extensive practice by the band. Mercer includes no details for the working ensemble between the end of 1961 and the spring of 1964, when Lee Morgan rejoined the band.

In her description of *Night Dreamer*, Shorter's first album as leader for the Blue Note label, recorded April 29, 1964, Mercer explains that his "musical vision had . . . grown to encompass an extensive palette of moods and textures" (93) beyond the hard-bop style of the Jazz Messengers. She includes the well-known quotation from the liner notes, in which Shorter tells Nat Hentoff that he is "playing more emotionally" (93) with "fewer passages of being complicated for the sake of being complicated" (93). Summarizing his Blue Note work, Mercer notes that it spanned "over seven years and eleven albums, a period in which his music would evolve in unexpected ways" (93), and that "Wayne's work as a sideman was a mere sketch of the genius that his Blue Note sessions would present as a complete picture" (93). And yet precious little information about these remarkable recordings is provided. Three of the records—*JuJu, The Soothsayer,* and *Etcetera*—are merely mentioned by name. *Speak No Evil* appears only in a quotation by Freddie Hubbard and in Shorter's brief explanation of the title. *Schizophrenia* is not mentioned at all.

Mercer quotes Shorter remarking that the Blue Note recordings were "like going to the bank for us" (104). Astonishing as it may sound to the many musicians and fans deeply influenced by these sessions, perhaps to Shorter they were just another day job. Shorter may have felt strongly that a few days of rehearsal followed by recording was less organic and profound than recording an actual working group: "These were one-shot things. . . . There was nothing developmental as a band" (104).

Miles Davis began pursuing Shorter for his ensemble in 1961, but Shorter was happy in the Jazz Messengers, where he was able to compose steadily and hear his work on gigs night after night. As Davis assembled what would become known as the "second classic quintet," he and the other members began to feel certain that only Shorter's playing and writing were missing from the group. After Shorter left the Messengers in July 1964, Davis, Jack Whittemore (Davis's agent), Herbie Hancock, and Tony Williams finally convinced him to join the band.

Shorter's first gig with Davis's group was at the Hollywood Bowl in Los Angeles (no date is provided). Mercer quotes Shorter's saying he was well prepared because he "had been listening to the records and playing along at home" (98). In this chapter (7), Mercer includes Shorter's thoughts about Davis as a musician and a man. Quotations from Hancock and Ron Carter also help readers understand just how well Shorter fit in with the group musically (though socially he was a bit of a recluse) and just how vital his playing and writing were to its character and excellence. The quintet had a European tour under its belt before making its first studio recording, *E.S.P.,* on January 20, 1965. Two of Shorter's originals are included: the title track and "Iris." This chapter also recounts Shorter's burgeoning friendship with Hancock, who comments that Shorter's manner of speaking "was much more like poetry, if anything, than how we normally perceive standard conversation" (103–104).

Mercer describes the band's restlessness with playing the old, familiar repertoire when Davis brought the group back together (following his recovery from hip problems) for a series of gigs near the end of 1965. Just before a performance at the Plugged Nickel in Chicago, Tony Williams suggested they all break free of their accustomed musical ideas and techniques. Only upon entering the club did they realize these gigs were to be recorded, but they remained committed to the idea of Williams's "anti-music." Mercer remarks that "the adventurous rhythm section pushed Wayne into some of the most brilliant playing of his career" (110).

In 1966, not long after separating from his wife, Shorter experienced the abrupt and deeply felt loss of his father. Joseph and Louise Shorter had driven to hear the band in Philadelphia, and on the way home their car went off the road and hit a tree. Mercer states that "Wayne's father was killed instantly" (115) but provides not a single remark about the fate of his mother. Readers are left to assume that she survived the crash. Davis had recently experienced similar losses, and he and Shorter shared conversation and alcohol on many long nights. Although he had an iron constitution, excessive alcohol consumption began to compromise Shorter's performance on the bandstand. Mercer offers that "only the most astute ears might have picked up any suspicious slurring in his performances—just as few modern listeners know that the 'Quidlibet' of Bach's Goldberg Variations was based on a German beer-hall song" (117). With this distractingly mismatched comparison Mercer not only forces an opportunity to show off a bit of trivia, but misspells "Quodlibet" in the process.

The band's 1966 recording *Miles Smiles* (which consists entirely of first takes) included Shorter's compositions "Orbits," "Footprints," and "Dolores." In 1967, the composition "Nefertiti" came to Shorter all at once as a complete entity and became the title track for Davis's June 7, 1967, recording. It was Davis's idea for the form of the piece to consist of repetitions of the self-contained melody, allowing Williams to solo over them. Shorter describes Davis's move into pop and electric music as a return to rhythm and blues traits he had grown up with in St. Louis and an attempt to more fully engage an audience.

In 1967, at a Village Gate gig in New York, Shorter met the woman who was to become his second wife, Ana Maria Patricio. As the relationship blossomed, Davis made the transition to electric instrumentation and his personnel changed dramatically. In 1968 Dave Holland replaced Ron Carter, and Chick Corea replaced Herbie Hancock. In early 1969 Jack DeJohnette replaced Tony Williams. A change of personnel was not what was needed for Shorter's position; instead, he switched to soprano saxophone to be heard above the electronic instruments. This was a comfortable and expressive transition for Shorter, likely due to his early experience with the clarinet. At this point Mercer mentions that "John Coltrane had died in 1967, leaving a void as the foremost modern player of the soprano saxophone" (127). Coltrane's death is treated as a technicality, perhaps even a convenience for Shorter's choice to play soprano saxophone. Mercer does not report on what Coltrane's death meant to Shorter personally and musically. This comes as a blow to the reader, particularly after the numerous mentions of Coltrane's influence on Shorter and of the mutual respect and friendship between the two men.

Davis's *In a Silent Way*, recorded in February 1969, comprised an expanded ensemble and featured Shorter on soprano saxophone. In August 1969 Shorter went back into the studio as leader to record *Super Nova*. Later that month Davis recorded *Bitches Brew,* which included Shorter's compositions "Feio" and "Sanctuary." The mention of "Sanctuary" occasions some interesting discussion of Davis's expectation of co-authorship for pieces written by his sidemen. Mercer addresses this subject diplomatically and objectively, noting that Davis himself had had his compositions appropriated as a sideman and felt it was part of the jazz tradition.

Shorter and Ana Maria married and moved to Manhattan's Upper West Side. Shorter had received few visitors while living in Harlem, but with Ana Maria he began to entertain at home (Herbie Hancock and his wife Gigi lived just two blocks away). On September 29, 1969, Ana Maria gave birth to a daughter, Iska. In January, the Shorters took Iska for a tetanus shot, a routine vaccination. Iska suffered a terrible reaction, and seizures deprived her brain of oxygen; her resulting chronic medical condition propelled Shorter into leaving Davis's band. Shorter's last recording with Davis was the March 7, 1970, *Live at the Fillmore East* concert. In August 1970, following a rare and greatly needed break, Shorter recorded *Odyssey of Iska*. This recording focuses on musical textures and timbres, and represents a poetic musical search for an understanding of life and all that comes with it.

Following these recordings, Shorter realized a long-discussed idea to form a band with Joe Zawinul. Miroslav Vitous (who had played on Shorter's *Super Nova* recording) had been imagining putting together a group with Shorter, and the three musicians created Weather Report. Shorter was excited about pioneering a fusion of jazz and rock, and the possibility of playing venues other than clubs with their multiple sets and long, late hours. Weather Report hired a manager and signed a contract with Columbia Records. Along with Alphonse Mouzon and Airto Moreira, they recorded their self-titled debut in May 1971. With personality traits on opposite ends of the spectrum, Zawinul and Shorter nonetheless worked well together in running the band, even with its frequent personnel changes. The 1971 recording *I Sing the Body Electric* garnered strongly favorable reviews in the rock press.

In December 1972 the Shorters moved to Los Angeles to find a climate that might help reduce the severity of Iska's seizures and to join their friends the Hancocks, who had moved there a year earlier. Herbie Hancock had converted to Nichiren Daishonin Buddhism and introduced the practice to Ana Maria, hoping it might ease the stresses of caring for Iska. Although Ana Maria became a dedicated practitioner for whom chanting held deep meaning, Shorter remained skeptical. However, while Weather Report was touring Japan, a Nichiren Japanese drummer invited Shorter to his home and helped him understand Nichiren Buddhist philosophy. Shorter participated in a commitment ceremony on August 7, 1973. Mercer provides excellent context here in explaining the principles of Nichiren Buddhism.

Shorter experienced some disillusionment with music as Weather Report became more commercial. *Sweetnighter*, recorded in 1973, consisted mostly of Zawinul compositions emphasizing groove over mood, and *Mysterious Traveller*, recorded in 1974, marked the full immersion into material defined by groove and funk. Shorter's continued presence, however, helped anchor the Weather Report recordings in the field of jazz.

Later In 1974, Shorter collaborated with Brazilian singer and composer Milton Nascimento on *Native Dancer,* an effective, authentic mix of Brazilian popular music and U.S. jazz. (Mercer identifies the recording year as 1974, but later refers to "Wayne's 1975 *Native Dancer* recording" without clarifying that 1975 was the year of release.) Mercer devotes a surprising number of pages to Nascimento and his music. Shorter and Nascimento continued to make frequent guest appearances at each other's concerts, and Shorter played on several of Nascimento's later recordings.

Meanwhile, Weather Report remained Shorter's primary musical vehicle. Electric bassist Jaco Pastorius made his first live appearance with the band in April 1976, and his presence (in personality and sound) contributed to the band's huge success. *Heavy Weather*, with its hit single "Birdland," by Zawinul, became a gold record, and Weather Report began playing arena venues.

During this period Shorter deepened his commitments to his family and Buddhism. As Zawinul and Pastorius grappled for onstage command of the band, Shorter remained apart from the fray. Explaining Shorter's experimentation with the Lyricon, a breath-controlled synthesizer, Mercer reminds the reader that Shorter "always thought like a composer and orchestrator when he improvised, so he tried to accommodate Jaco's flexible bass personality with an instrument update himself" (179–80). Some critics and fans felt that *Mr. Gone*, Weather Report's 1978 record, symbolized Shorter's decreasing role in contrast to Zawinul's and Pastorius's love of the spotlight

Mercer poignantly discusses Shorter's extensive drinking, his worry for his brain-damaged daughter, and his long first experience with writer's block. "For twenty-five years, he had scribbled out tunes as prolifically and unselfconsciously as a child absorbed in a coloring book. And then nothing came" (185). Shorter struggled to believe it was simply a period of transition from which he would emerge with more profound things to say musically. Even during this period, Shorter's confidence as a player and improviser never waned.

As a film fan living in Los Angeles, Shorter naturally took part in several movies, performing on the sound tracks of *'Round Midnight*, *Glengarry Glen Ross*, *The Fugitive*, and *Losing Isaiah*. Shorter's composition "Call Sheet Blues" was included in *'Round Midnight* and won a 1987 Grammy award in the category Best Instrumental Composition. Mercer misspells the title as "Call Street Blues" (195) and neglects to say this award was shared with co-writers Herbie Hancock, Billy Higgins, and Ron Carter.

Shorter also accepted a few of the many offers to perform with pop musicians. For the title track of Steely Dan's *Aja*, Shorter played only two takes, and instead of Steely Dan's usual procedure of meticulously splicing together several small segments, "they were able to use the beginning of one take and the end of a second" (197). Shorter also recorded on several of Joni Mitchell's albums, including *Don Juan's Reckless Daughter*, *Dog Eat Dog*, *Mingus*, and *Chalk Mark in a Rain Storm*. Shorter and Mitchell shared a love of metaphor, a pictorial approach to interpreting music, and a deep respect for each other's talents. Mercer does not mention that both Shorter and Mitchell are also creative and expressive painters.

In the studio, Mitchell gave Shorter free rein as a soloist and, after multiple takes, selected the moments that moved her. This modus operandi speaks both to Shorter's ability to come up with seemingly endless ideas and Mitchell's ability as a composer to edit materials together to form a coherent, meaningful whole.

Shorter toured Europe and Japan regularly with Weather Report in the late 1970s and early 1980s. His compositional contributions continued to be relatively sparse, and difficulties at home persisted. Iska was often rushed to the emergency room with seizures, and Ana Maria was exhausted and stressed. In October 1983, just after her 14th birthday, Iska suffered a grand mal seizure and died.

Weather Report gave its last live performances in 1984, and in 1985 completed two final recordings. On his own once again, Shorter would soon return to the studio with his compositional ideas flowing. "When Weather Report disbanded, Columbia Records exercised the 'leaving member option' in Wayne's contract, which committed him to recording three albums for the label" (211). *Atlantis*, Shorter's first recording as a leader in 11 years, was released in October 1985. The record was composed programmatically and included electric and acoustic instruments.

Difficulties in Shorter's marriage, due in part to Ana Maria's drinking, resulted in a separation that both seemed to expect would end in divorce. Shorter began to date, but came to the realization that he and Ana Maria had important and happy years together ahead of them. They reconciled, both of them taking active and loving care of their relationship. At about this time Shorter experienced two losses in fairly close succession: his mother died of natural, age-related causes in 1986, and in 1987 Alan Shorter died of a ruptured aorta at the age of 56. In 1988, Ana Maria introduced Shorter to her Brazilian friend Carolina Dos Santos, a dancer and actress who had come to the U.S. to appear in productions by Ana Maria's sister. With help and encouragement from Dos Santos, both Shorters overcame their drinking problems and Wayne took up painting once again.

In the summer of 1988, Shorter joined Carlos Santana for a tour. (Weather Report had opened for Santana's group in 1973, and Shorter had played on Santana's 1980 recording *The Swing of Delight*.) Surprisingly, Mercer describes this period as preparation for Shorter's "eventual comeback" (222). Up to this point the book has emphasized only the unabated success of Shorter's recordings and live performances, so the need for a "comeback" requires some explanation, which Mercer does not provide.

Shorter was selective about his performances in the early- to mid-1990s, which included a "Tribute to Miles" tour with Davis's second classic quintet and Wallace Roney taking Davis's part, and a UNESCO event in Japan. He continued composing steadily and, after receiving a call from Rachel Z, asked her to assist in creating computerized orchestrations of his latest pieces. He and Z worked together for six months, preparing music for the Verve recording *High Life*. Shorter asked Marcus Miller to produce, and members of the Los Angeles Philharmonic recorded the orchestral parts. Percussion was added, followed by Miller's bass parts, electronic drums, Z's keyboards, and Shorter's saxophone solos. The music proved challenging for listeners and difficult for Shorter's musicians to perform live.

In March of 1996, Shorter traveled to Thailand with Ana Maria to join Hancock and his wife, and to instruct young jazz musicians touring with Hancock under the auspices of the Monk Institute. Dos Santos moved into the Shorters' house to look after it while they were away, and at Ana Maria's urging remained after they had returned. Shorter put together a new band and began a summer European tour. Ana Maria and her niece Dalila Lucien planned to meet Shorter in Italy, but their plane (TWA Flight 800) exploded and crashed not long after takeoff. Shorter's tour was canceled and he returned home. His friends and his Nichiren Buddhist practice helped him survive the terrible grief. One month after the accident, Shorter kept to a planned tour of Japan. He knew that Ana Maria, the most ardent supporter of his career, would have wanted him to continue. In 1997, Hancock and Shorter united once again on a duet recording, *1 + 1*, and followed that with a summer tour.

Shorter was commissioned by Jazz at Lincoln Center to compose large-scale works, and the premiere of "Dramatis Personae" (on which Shorter also performed) took place in April 1998. On January 2, 2000, the Detroit Symphony Orchestra premiered Shorter's compositions "Syzygy" and "Capricorn II." Shorter also worked with orchestras in Portugal and at the University of Southern California. Among the jazz musicians engaged for these concerts was John Patitucci on upright bass, and for the September 2000 Monterey Jazz Festival, Shorter added Danilo Perez on piano and Brian Blade on drums. A musical spark was ignited, and Shorter considered an acoustic quartet tour.

Shorter and Dos Santos were married in 1999. In 2001, the Shorters moved to Aventura, Florida, not far from the Florida Nature and Culture Center, a Buddhist retreat where Carolina worked as a translator for international conferences. Shorter began working regularly with his new quartet and revisited earlier compositions, of course newly treated and fully re-arranged. After several shows (including a performance at Carnegie Hall), the Wayne Shorter Quartet seemed to be the group that all the critics and fans were clamoring to see. *Footprints Live!*, recorded at shows in France and Spain and released in May 2002, received glowing reviews, and Shorter won the Thelonious Monk Institute's Founders Award (March 2002), the New School University's Beacon in Jazz Award (March 2002), and European Musician of the Year and Artist of the Year awards. *Alegría*, Shorter's first acoustic studio recording since 1967, was released in March 2003. Mercer writes that "on *Alegría*, Wayne finally achieved an integration of his full musical vision as a composer—the 'Let's make the whole world!' notion he'd had as a kid playing with clay—with the play-your-heart-out feeling of his solos on 1960s tunes such as 'Infant Eyes' and the wry humor of his Messengers masquerades" (265).

Mercer has deftly created a conversational tone in weaving together quotations by Shorter and other musicians. Indeed, perhaps the greatest treasures of this book are the original interviews from sources as diverse as Nat Phipps, Curtis Fuller, Joni Mitchell, Rudy Van Gelder, and Nobu Urushiyama. Mercer explains in the notes, "Unless cited below or attributed to other sources in the text, all quotations in this book are from my original interviews. Between 2003 and 2004, I conducted more than seventy-five interviews with various sources, and had at least that many discussions with Wayne Shorter himself" (273). In the acknowledgments she thanks "all the interviewees, especially those who are not directly quoted in the book but who so richly informed" her perspective (285). By my count, quotations from 34 interviewed sources (not counting Shorter) are included in the book. A listing of names and dates for these interviews would have been helpful and informative.

The index is quite useful, though there are a few missed references, such as the recordings *JuJu* and *Etcetera,* mentioned on pages 93 and 105, respectively. The photographs, most of which came from Shorter's personal collection, are a highlight. They no doubt reflect his choices for inclusion and therefore seem more meaningful than photos selected solely by a biographer. Unfortunately, there are errors in the captions. A photo of three Jazz Messengers in the recording studio incorrectly identifies bassist Jymie Merritt as a pianist. A group photo from the *Jazz at the Opera House* concert identifies Denny Zeitlin as Lew Tabackin and cites "two unidentified men," who on the original record sleeve are correctly identified as Lew Tabackin and Jaco Pastorius.[3]

Too frequently, Mercer makes unfounded generalizations. For example, in demonstrating that Shorter has no patience for ordinary, matter-of-fact conversation, Mercer states that "part of this comes from spending so much time around jazz musicians, who tend not to think or speak in a linear way" (5). What does she mean? She offers no evidence to support this sweeping statement. In another example, Mercer observes that "Wayne's shows are a barometer of the state of jazz, even the health of humanity itself" (258). How do Shorter's performances reflect the "health of humanity"?

In the preface to the notes Mercer states: "My musical analysis is based on study of Wayne's original scores whenever possible" (273). This declaration misleadingly implies that the text contains musical analysis beyond a simple description of compositional form, or general prose referring to, say, Shorter's complex chords. The statement also seems designed to free Mercer from providing citations about particular scores. Though the omission is perhaps a small concern, Mercer nowhere lists her qualifications to undertake musical analysis. The dust jacket simply states that she "is a writer and a music commentator."

Mercer reminds readers that Shorter has served "as one of the principal architects of jazz for more than forty years" (270), in a life of steady work, enduring creative inspiration, and integrity of character. Above all, Shorter has been willing to enjoy his own imagination, creativity, playfulness, and insight without censoring himself to satisfy others' expectations of what it means to be a musician or a human being. This book gives us brief glimpses of that human being, and in those moments Shorter's deep and searching nature comes shining through. His insightful way of understanding the world is revealed through quotations such as "I felt like the best way to show adventure was to just be it myself. . . . But not in a 'Look, Ma, no hands!' way. Your adventure is often not advertised. Results happen to show what is transforming inside you" (215).

Mercer has done much of the work that could be faithfully undertaken only with Shorter's approval and participation—the telling of his story as he saw and experienced it, and as he wants it remembered. However, this book lacks the objective, hard-searching inquiry that a carefully prepared biography would contain. It appears hastily put together and recycles much of its content from earlier articles and interviews. It is not a definitive or authoritative work, and future researchers and journalists will be obliged to do the research that Mercer neglected to do. However, it is a respectful telling of Shorter's story, giving the reader a sense of Shorter's personality, and Mercer's original interviews are frequently revealing, interesting, and informative.

NOTES

1. Curtis Fuller indicated in our 2002 interview that musicians often chose music education because there was no place for jazz studies in academia at that time. (Fuller, Curtis. Interview by Patricia Julien, July 11, 2002, Saratoga Springs, New York. Tape Recording. Skidmore College, Saratoga Springs.)
2. Silvert, Conrad. "Wayne Shorter: Imagination Unlimited." *Down Beat* 44, July 14, 1977, 58.
3. I am grateful to Michael Fitzgerald, who brought this error to my attention through incisive online jazz forum commentary and supplied the correct photo caption information.

Scott Saul, *Freedom Is, Freedom Ain't: Jazz and the Making of the Sixties* (Cambridge, MA: Harvard University Press, 2003, xiv + 394 pp., $29.95 hardcover, $17.95 paperback)

Reviewed by Eric Charry

Jazz in the 1960s has recently enjoyed an explosion of scholarly interest. With an average of one Ph.D. dissertation or university press book published each year since 1999 devoted entirely or in large part to this era, the time has arrived for picking up where Jost and Wilmer left off several decades ago (see references below). While analysis of the music remains elusive and the window for intimate firsthand testimony capturing an era fresh in the mind has shut, a broader cultural studies approach has taken hold, at least in academia. The strengths of such an approach are that it integrates currents circulating at the time (e.g., in literature, visual art, film, politics, and social relations) and puts them in conversation with each other. A good cultural historian can uncover connections that might have been intuitively apparent then, but lost in succeeding generations. The downside is that historians with such breadth of interests may lack in-depth knowledge of the repertory or the expertise necessary to penetrate subtleties of the sophisticated musical language.

Scott Saul's *Freedom Is, Freedom Ain't* is an excellent contribution to scholarship on jazz and American culture in the 1950s and 1960s, reflecting some of the fresher insights that an interdisciplinary approach has to offer. Wide-ranging, well-researched, and relatively jargon-free, the book consists of a framing preface and introduction followed by 10 chapters grouped in pairs to make five parts, all of which address from different angles the relation of jazz to key social currents ("civil rights, the New Left, the counterculture, and Black Power" [xi]). Each chapter is made up of several finely detailed case studies woven together in a fascinating voyage exploring the reach of jazz.

In the preface, Saul indicates that the book serves two ends: "a history of one strand of jazz in the decade between the mid-1950s and the mid-1960s, and a history of its uses" (ix). Although I find the definition and representation of that strand ("hard bop") to be the most problematic aspect of the book, one can easily ignore the label and be thoroughly engaged with the issues the book raises. With just passing mention of the major names associated with the label (e.g., Art Blakey, Lee Morgan, Sonny Rollins, and Horace Silver), a cursory treatment of Miles Davis, and a primary focus on Charles Mingus and post-1950s John Coltrane, the author might have been better served by not investing at all in the idea of hard bop as a unifying thread.

The concluding paragraph in the book indicates a broader purpose, which more accurately reflects the scope: that in order to understand concepts like cool, hip, freedom now, and soul power, "we should turn our ears to the music that gave these ideas expression . . . [and] the ventures, alliances, and debates that the music inspired" (336). Rather than write about hard bop as a genre, Saul has "attempted to write intellectual history with the help of those usually kept on the fringes of such history—black artists and activists" (336).

The introduction, the most valuable and thought-provoking section for me, explores the slippery concept of freedom in American culture and its varied meanings in jazz, using examples from Cold War and civil rights rhetoric. Saul notes that "jazz artists wanted to claim the banner of freedom, but they also wanted to distance themselves from the term's association with individual license and whimsical choice. . . . Freedom for them was rooted in collaborative action" (12, 17). Occasionally during these kinds of discussions throughout the book, the reader may be frustrated by the limited musical scope, which does not extend to the exploratory wing that significantly marked the era. One is left wondering what the author would have to say about artists who directly addressed musical freedom in radically new ways, such as Ornette Coleman (whose LP *Free Jazz* named the era for some), Cecil Taylor, Sun Ra, or any of their associates.

In part 1, the author tracks the rise into the mainstream of the hipster. After a helpful history in chapter 1, Saul settles in chapter 2 on 1957–61, "when the hipster's cultural stance suddenly had political appeal for a wider swath of intellectuals" (63). After contrasting the obligatory "The White Negro" (Norman Mailer) and "Sonny's Blues" (James Baldwin), both from 1957, Saul uses Bob Thompson's extraordinary 1960 painting *Garden of Music* to examine early 1960s black bohemianism in the Village, observing that the painting "not only strikes a balance between Mailer's primitivism and Baldwin's sense of community but also injects a welcome note of absurd humor" (77–78). The chapter ends with a look at Oscar Brown Jr. and Max Roach's *Freedom Now Suite*, which as "a more militant political statement, also created a striking musical alternative to the cool pose" (93–94).

Part 2 looks at white youth culture through the lens of the early Newport Jazz Festival, with careful studies of the 1958 festival documentary *Jazz on a Summer's Day* and the 1960 youth riot (in chapter 3), and the 1960 Newport Rebels festival and Langston Hughes's "Ask Your Mama," a direct response to the riot (in chapter 4). The author effectively probes viewpoints that the riot at this new form of postwar leisure could be seen variously as a sign of "the decadence that threatened jazz if its entrepreneurs pandered to the profit motive" (105), the younger generation's delinquency, "indignation at an abridgement of consumer freedom" (122), and a "foretaste of a late 1960s youth culture" (122).

Part 3 is devoted to Charles Mingus; chapter 5 covers his entrepreneurial efforts, the inner workings of his Jazz Workshop, and *Beneath the Underdog*, and chapter 6 includes four case studies: "Eclipse," "Pithecanthropus Erectus," "The Black Saint and the Sinner Lady," and "Fables of Faubus." Saul's primary thesis throughout is that Mingus's music was rooted in struggle "between an elite modernism built on the heroic strivings of genius and a populist modernism built on the creativity of collaborative revolt" (181). Mingus's Jazz Workshop "worked . . . as a musical battleground, where compositional restraint served paradoxically as a kind of emotional provocation" (159). Although the technical musical analyses may not be compelling (at least to those used to a more sophisticated theoretical vocabulary), other kinds of insights, like his contrast of the mid-1950s onstage managerial styles of Miles Davis and Mingus, are right on target.

Part 4 is devoted to John Coltrane, discussing "Liberia" as a revision of "A Night in Tunisia," jazz criticism of the early 1960s, and several versions of "Afro-Blue" (in chapter 7), and Roy DeCarava's photos of Coltrane, *A Love Supreme*, and Coltrane's similarities with Malcolm X (in chapter 8). Saul hangs much of his argument on Coltrane's "refusal of bebop's ironic pose . . . [his] aesthetics of honesty in extremis . . . [which] pulled jazz away from the ironic hipsterism that infused bebop and much jazz before 1960" (212). Identifying the presence or absence of irony is tricky business (as the author notes). A discussion of the nonoriginals in Coltrane's early 1960s repertory that could attract interpretations of irony (e.g., "My Favorite Things," "Greensleeves," or "Inchworm") may have helped to clarify and bolster the argument. The comparison of Coltrane and Malcolm X, whose "autobiographical conversion narratives" (*A Love Supreme* and *The Autobiography of Malcolm X*) both came out in 1965, is both fruitful and convincing.

Part 5 covers the mid and later 1960s, tracking (in chapter 9) the relationship of jazz to 1960s counterculture, when "rock supplant[ed] jazz as the music of white rebellion and protest" (271), and (in chapter 10) the promise of soul power and the "responses that jazz musicians made . . . [to the crises] in the market for their music and in the communities that they hoped to help rebuild" (304). Noting that "postwar jazz was hip, an insider's music, while rock was participatory, a music meant to please—and generate—a crowd" (271), the author opens up an intriguing line of inquiry, tracing a path from Newport to the 1967 Monterey Pop Festival, via the Monterey Jazz Festival. But there is an important omission here: the folk music revival of the early 1960s, which represented a crucial cultural alternative between 1950s jazz and late 1960s rock for white college youth, especially those who were oriented toward social protest. The Newport Folk Festival (begun in 1959) and the association of folk music with the civil rights movement surely have a role in this story. Perceptive portraits of both playwright-actor Sam Shepard and writer-activist John Sinclair illustrating jazz-to-rock sensibility shifts in their work during the decade finish out the chapter. Chapter 10 contains a comparison of pieces by Betty Carter and Jackie McLean, an analysis of writing from *Liberator* that questioned the growing divide between jazz musicians and black communities, and a discussion of artist-run cooperatives. After a final look at Mingus, Saul concludes with an analysis of "soul power" from the point of view of Cannonball Adderley's 1969 LP *Country Preacher: Live at Operation Breadbasket*.

This is a fertile book, ripe with provocative insights and turns that stimulate new ways of thinking about the relationship of jazz to American culture. Coming out of a university American studies department, it is a healthy sign of the critical potential of an interdisciplinary approach to jazz studies.

REFERENCES

Anderson, Iain D. 2000. "This Is Our Music": Free Jazz, Cultural Hierarchy, and the Sixties. Ph.D. diss., Indiana University.

Bakriges, Christopher G. 2001. African American Musical Avant-Gardism. Ph.D. diss., York University.

Bartlett, Andrew Walsh. 1999. The Free Place: Literary, Visual, and Jazz Creations of Space in the 1960s. Ph.D. diss., University of Washington.

Jost, Ekkehard. 1974/1981. *Free Jazz.* Graz: Universal Edition. Repr. Cambridge, MA: Da Capo.

Monson, Ingrid. Forthcoming. *Freedom Sounds: Jazz, Civil Rights, and Africa, 1950–1967.* Oxford: Oxford University Press.

Porter, Eric. 2002. *What Is This Thing Called Jazz? African American Musicians as Artists, Critics, and Activists.* Berkeley: University of California Press.

Price, Emmett George, III. 2000. Free Jazz and the Black Arts Movement, 1958–1967. Ph.D. diss., University of Pittsburgh.

Schwartz, Jeff. 2004. New Black Music: Amiri Baraka (Leroi Jones) and Jazz, 1959–1965. Ph.D. diss., Bowling Green State University.

Wilmer, Valerie. 1977/1980. *As Serious as Your Life: The Story of the New Jazz.* London: Allison & Busby. 1st U.S. rev. ed., Westport, CT: Lawrence Hill.

JAZZ RESEARCH BIBLIOGRAPHY (2003–2004)

Keith Waters and Jason R. Titus

This bibliography is the third installment in an ongoing bibliography project, compiling scholarly articles on jazz contained in journals not specifically devoted to jazz. This installment lists articles that appeared in print during 2003–2004; volume 11 of the *Annual Review of Jazz Studies* lists articles dating from 1999–2000, and volume 12 lists articles dating from 2001–2002. Special thanks to David Borgo, Walter Everett, Richard Hermann, Fabian Holt, Steve Larson, Henry Martin, Steven Pond, Andrew Scott, Gerald H. Sloan, Alexander Stewart, and others for recommending items for inclusion. Suggestions for academic articles published in nonjazz journals after 2004 may be e-mailed to Keith Waters (Keith.Waters@colorado.edu) or Jason R. Titus (jason@jasontitus.com). Complete citations (date, volume and number, pages) would be appreciated.

Acosta, Leonardo. "The Year 1898 in the Music of the Caribbean: Cuba and Puerto Rico in the Machinations of the U.S. Music Industry." *Centro Journal* 16/1 (2004): 6–16.

Ake, David. "Negotiating National Identity among American Jazz Musicians in Paris 1." *Journal of Musicological Research* 23/2 (2004): 159–186.

Anderson, Gene. "The Origin of Armstrong's Hot Fives and Hot Sevens." *College Music Symposium* 43 (2003): 13–24.

Anderson, Maureen. "The White Reception of Jazz in America." *African American Review* 38/1 (Spring 2004): 135–145.

Appelrouth, Scott. "Constructing the Meaning of Early Jazz, 1917–1930." *Poetics* 31/2 (April 2003): 117–131.

Asai, Susan M. "Cultural Politics: The African American Connection in Asian American Jazz-Based Music." *Asian Music* 36/1 (Winter–Spring 2005): 87–108.

Bell, Kevin. "The Embrace of Entropy: Ralph Ellison and the Freedom Principle of Jazz Invisible." *Boundary 2* 30/2 (Summer 2003): 21–45.

Bernstein, W. "'Tristan und Isolde' from a Jazz-Harmonic Point of View—Reaction to a Recent Article by Altug Unlu." *Musiktheorie* 18/3 (2003): 271–272.

Bethune, Christian. "Jazz as a Second Form of Orality." *L'Homme* 171–172 (July–December 2004): 443–457.

Bleij, Barbara. "On Harmony and Meaning in Clare Fischer's Music." *Tijdschrift voor Muziektheorie* 9/3 (November 2004): 210–216.

Blume, Gernot. "Blurred Affinities: Tracing the Influence of North Indian Classical Music in Keith Jarrett's Solo Piano Improvisations." *Popular Music* 22/2 (May 2003): 117–142.

Borgo, David. "Negotiating Freedom: Values and Practices in Contemporary Improvised Music." *Black Music Research Journal* 22/2 (Fall 2002): 165–188.

Borgo, David. "Between Worlds: The Embodied and Ecstatic Sounds of Jazz." *The Open Space* 5 (Fall 2003): 152–158.

Borgo, David. "The Meaning of Play and the Play of Meaning in Jazz." *Journal of Consciousness Studies* 11/3–4 (2004): 174–190.

Braggs, Rashida K. "Hearing the Rage in *J'irai cracher sur vos tombes*." *Nottingham French Studies* 43/1 (Spring 2004): 100–107.

Brown, Lee B. "Marsalis and Baraka: An Essay in Comparative Cultural Discourse." *Popular Music* 23/3 (October 2004): 241–255.

Buscatto, Marie. "Being a Jazz Singer Is No Longer a Man's Profession: Imperfect Harmony between Voice and Instrument." *Revue Française de Sociologie* 44/1 (January–March 2003): 35–62.

Cabanillas, Francisco. "Entre la Poesía y la Música: Victor Hernández Cruz y el Mapa Musical Nuyorican." *Centro Journal* 16/2 (2004): 14–33.

Chemillier, Marc. "Toward a Formal Study of Jazz Chord Sequences Generated by Steedman's Grammar." *Soft Computing* 8/9 (September 2004): 617–622.

Coggiola, John C. "The Effect of Conceptual Advancement in Jazz Music Selections and Jazz Experience on Musicians' Aesthetic Response." *Journal of Research in Music Education* 52/1 (Spring 2004): 29–42.

Comuzio, Ermanno, and Lino Patruno. "Cinema and Jazz, a 'Hot' Love Affair—An Interview with Lino Patruno." *Cineforum* 44/2 (March 2004): 70–73.

Costa, Adriana. "The Quintet of the Hot Club of France 1934–1948." *Nottingham French Studies* 43/1 (Spring 2004): 53–61.

Cotro, Vincent. "Tribute to . . . Or, Homages in Contemporary French Jazz." *Nottingham French Studies* 43/1 (Spring 2004): 80–88.

Daniels, Douglas Henry. "Los Angeles's Jazz Roots: The Willis H. Young Family." *California History* 82/3 (2004): 48–70, 78–81.

Dutton, Jacqueline. "Jazz Routes or the Roots of Jazz: Music as Meaning in Le Clézio's *Poisson d'or*." *Nottingham French Studies* 43/1 (Spring 2004): 108–116.

Ellison, Mary. "Kalamu Ya Salaam and the Black Blues Subversive Self." *Race & Class* 45/1 (July–September 2003): 79–97.

Everett, Walter. "A Royal Scam: The Abstruse and Ironic Bop-Rock Harmony of Steely Dan." *Music Theory Spectrum* 26/2 (Fall 2004): 201–235.

Fay, Jennifer. "'That's Jazz Made in Germany!': Hallo, Fraulein! and the Limits of Democratic Pedagogy." *Cinema Journal* 44/1 (Fall 2004): 3–24.

Feinstein, Sascha. "Black Pearls: Recovered Memories." *African American Review* 38/2 (Summer 2004): 295–301.

Frederickson, William E., and John C. Coggiola. "A Comparison of Music Majors' and Nonmajors' Perception of Tension for Two Selections of Jazz Music." *Journal of Research in Music Education* 51/3 (Fall 2003): 259–270.

Garcia, Antonio G. "Frank Rosolino and Carl Fontana: Together on 'Rock Bottom.'" *International Trombone Association Journal* 32/3 (July 2004): 36–44.

Gleiser, Pablo M., and Leon Danon. "Community Structure in Jazz." *Advances in Complex Systems* 6/4 (2003): 565–573.

Gordon, Terri J. "A 'Saxophone in Movement': Josephine Baker and the Music of Dance." *Nottingham French Studies* 43/1 (Spring 2004): 39–52.

Grandt, Jürgen E. "Kinds of Blue: Toni Morrison, Hans Janowitz, and the Jazz Aesthetic." *African American Review* 38/2 (Summer 2004): 303–322.

Gumplowicz, Philippe. "Reactionary Musicographers in France during the 1930s." *Mouvement Social* 208 (July–September 2004): 91–124.

Hargreaves, Tracy. "The Power of the Ordinary Subversive in Jackie Kay's Trumpet." *Feminist Review,* no. 74 (2003): 2–16.

Harker, Brian. "Louis Armstrong and the Clarinet." *American Music* 21/2 (Summer 2003): 137–158.

Hasse, John Edward. "'A New Reason for Living': Duke Ellington in France." *Nottingham French Studies* 43/1 (Spring 2004): 5–18.

Hermann, Richard. "Charlie Parker's Solo to 'Ornithology': Facets of Counterpoint, Analysis, and Pedagogy." *Perspectives of New Music* 42/2 (Summer 2004): 222–262.

Hollerbach, Peter. "(Re)Voicing Tradition: Improvising Aesthetics and Identity on Local Jazz Scenes." *Popular Music* 23/2 (May 2004): 155–171.

Holt, Fabian. "Genre Formation in Popular Music." *Musik & Forskning* 28 (2003): 77–96.

Janowitz, Hans. "'Jazz.'" *New England Review—Middlebury Series* 25/1–2 (Winter–Spring 2004): 93–111.

Jeffri, Joan. "Jazz Musicians: The Cost of the Beat." *Journal of Arts Management, Law & Society* 33/1 (2003): 40–51.

Jerving, Ryan. "Jazz Language and Ethnic Novelty." *Modernism/Modernity* 10/2 (2003): 239–268.

Jerving, Ryan. "Early Jazz Literature (and Why You Didn't Know)." *American Literary History* 16/4 (Winter 2004): 648–674.

Joqueviel-Bourjea, Marie. "Jazz et Poésie: Steamin' with Jacques Réda." *Nottingham French Studies* 43/1 (Spring 2004): 126–138.

Jordan, Matthew. "Recorded Jazz and 'la Voix Nègre': The Sound of Race in the Age of Mechanical Reproduction." *Nottingham French Studies* 43/1 (Spring 2004): 89–99.

Joubert, A. "Adorno and Jazz." *Quinzaine Litteraire* 850 (March 16, 2003): 29–30.

Kähäri, Kim, Gunilla Zachau, Leif Sandsjö, Mats Eklöf, and Claes Möller. "Assessment of Hearing and Hearing Disorders in Rock/Jazz Musicians." *International Journal of Audiology* 42/5 (2003): 279–288.

Kleppinger, Stanley V. "On the Influence of Jazz Rhythm in the Music of Aaron Copland." *American Music* 21/1 (Spring 2003): 74–111.

Kodat, Catherine Gunther. "Conversing with Ourselves: Canon, Freedom, Jazz." *American Quarterly* 55/1 (March 2003): 1–28.

Larson, Steve. "What Makes a Good Bridge?" *Tijdschrift voor Muziektheorie* 8/1 (February 2003): 1–15.

Legrand, Anne. "Charles Delaunay: The Beginnings of a Total Commitment to the Recognition of Jazz." *Nottingham French Studies* 43/1 (Spring 2004): 62–71.

Looseley, David. "'*Frères ennemis*'? French Discourses on Jazz, *Chanson* and Pop." *Nottingham French Studies* 43/1 (Spring 2004): 72–79.

Macrae, C. "The Inaudible Music: Jazz." *Yearbook for Traditional Music* 36 (2004): 176–177.

Martin, Henry. "Maria Schneider's *Hang Gliding*: Aspects of Structure." *Tijdschrift voor Muziektheorie* 8/1 (February 2003): 16–24.

Martin, Henry. "From Fountain to Furious: Ellington's Development as Stride Pianist." *Musica Oggi* 23 (2003–2004): 55–68.

Martin, Stephen-Paul. "The Possibility of Music." *Western Humanities Review* 58/1 (2004): 88–98.

May, Lissa F. "Factors and Abilities Influencing Achievement in Instrumental Jazz Improvisation." *Journal of Research in Music Education* 51/3 (Fall 2003): 245–258.

McClendon, John H., III. "Jazz, African American Nationality, and the Myth of the Nation-State." *Socialism & Democracy* 18/2 (July–December 2004): 21–36.

McKay, George. "Just a Closer Walk with Thee: New Orleans–Style Jazz and the Campaign for Nuclear Disarmament in 1950s Britain." *Popular Music* 22/3 (October 2003): 261–282.

McKeage, Kathleen M. "Gender and Participation in High School and College Instrumental Jazz Ensembles." *Journal of Research in Music Education* 52/4 (Winter 2004): 343–356.

McNeilly, Kevin. "Word Jazz 5: Lorna Goodison Leaves Off Miles Davis." *Canadian Literature,* no. 182 (2004): 198–200.

Mongin, O. "Adorno and Jazz: Analysis of an Esthetic Challenge." *Esprit,* no. 3–4 (March–April 2003): 323–324.

Moore, Steven, and Toshiko Akiyoshi. "The Art of Becoming a Jazz Musician: An Interview with Toshiko Akiyoshi." *Michigan Quarterly Review* 43/3 (Summer 2004): 393–403.

Moreno, Jairo. "Bauza, Gillespie, Latin/Jazz: Difference, Modernity, and the Black Caribbean." *South Atlantic Quarterly* 103/1 (Winter 2004): 81–99.

Mouëllic, Gilles. "Boris Vian, from Jazz to Cinema." *Nottingham French Studies* 43/1 (Spring 2004): 149–155.

Murchison, Gayle. "Mary Lou Williams's Hymn *Black Christ of the Andes* (*St. Martin de Porres*): Vatican II, Civil Rights, and Jazz as Sacred Music." *The Musical Quarterly* 86/4 (Winter 2002): 591–629.

Nettelbeck, Colin. "A Cycle of Freedom: Louis Malle's Jazz Films." *Nottingham French Studies* 43/1 (Spring 2004): 156–164.

Parsonage, Catherine. "A Critical Reassessment of the Reception of Early Jazz in Britain." *Popular Music* 22/3 (October 2003): 315–336.

Pautrot, Jean-Louis. "French Jazz in Grand Form: The Contribution of André Hodeir." *Nottingham French Studies* 43/1 (Spring 2004): 19–29.

Perret, Carine. "L'adoption du jazz par Darius Milhaud et Maurice Ravel: L'esprit plus que la lettre." *Revue de musicologie* 89/2 (2003): 311–347.

Phillips, Damon J., and David A. Owens. "Incumbents, Innovation, and Competence: The Emergence of Recorded Jazz, 1920 to 1929." *Poetics* 32, no. 3/4 (June–August 2004): 281–295.

Prieto, Eric. "Ethnography, Improvisation, and the Archimedean Fulcrum: Michel Leiris and Jazz." *International Journal of Francophone Studies* 6/1 (2003): 5–16.

Prieto, Eric. "Alexandre Stellio and the Beginnings of the Biguine." *Nottingham French Studies* 43/1 (Spring 2004): 30–38.

Quinn, Ruth. "The Performative Self: Improvisation for Self and Other." *New Theatre Quarterly* 19/73 (February 2003): 18–22.

Radford, Andrew. "The Invisible Music of Ralph Ellison." *Raritan* 23/1 (2003): 39–62.

Raeburn, Bruce Boyd. "Psychoanalysis and Jazz." *International Journal of Psychoanalysis* 85 (August 2004): 995–997.

Ramanna, N. "Contemporary South African Jazz and the Politics of Place." *Social Dynamics* 30/2 (Winter 2004): 112–127.

Ramshaw, Sara. "'He's My Man!': Lyrics of Innocence and Betrayal in the People v. Billie Holiday." *Canadian Journal of Women & the Law* 16/1 (2004): 86–105.

Rice, Marc. "Break o' Day Blues: The 1923 Recordings of the Bennie Moten Orchestra." *The Musical Quarterly* 86/2 (Summer 2002): 282–306.

Roberts, Brian. "Blackface Minstrelsy and Jewish Identity: Fleshing Out Ragtime as the Central Metaphor in E. L. Doctorow's *Ragtime*." *Critique* 45/3 (2004): 247–259.

Rotella, Carlo. "Jelly Roll Morton's Parole from Hell." *Raritan* 24/1 (2004): 151–165.

Scott, Andrew. "'I See the Fretboard in Diagrams': An Examination of the Improvisatory Style of Herbert Lawrence 'Sonny' Greenwich." *Canadian University Music Review* 24/1 (Summer 2003): 62–78.

Shulman, Peter. "No Room for Squares: Jean-Pierre Melville, Jazz and the French Bachelor." *Nottingham French Studies* 43/1 (Spring 2004): 139–148.

Sloan, Gerald. "Los Huesos: A Closer Look at Latin Trombonists." *International Trombone Association Journal* 31/1 (January 2003): 30–47.

Smyth, Edmund. "Christian Gailly and the Jazz Novel." *Nottingham French Studies* 43/1 (Spring 2004): 117–125.

Solis, Gabriel. "Hearing Monk: History, Memory, and the Making of a 'Jazz Giant.'" *The Musical Quarterly* 86/1 (Spring 2002): 82–116.

Solis, Gabriel. "'A Unique Chunk of Jazz Reality': Authorship, Musical Work Concepts, and Thelonious Monk's Live Recordings from the Five Spot, 1958." *Ethnomusicology* 48/3 (Fall 2004): 315–347.

Stegmann, V. "Hot Music: Jazz and Entertainment Music in the Culture of the Weimar Republic." *German Studies Review* 26/2 (May 2003): 421–423.

Stewart, Alexander. "Contemporary New York City Big Bands: Composition, Arranging and Individuality in Orchestral Jazz." *Ethnomusicology* 48/2 (Spring–Summer 2004): 169–202.

Strunk, Steven. "Wayne Shorter's *Yes and No*: An Analysis." *Tijdschrift voor Muziektheorie* 8/1 (February 2003): 40–56.

Suisman, David. "Co-Workers in the Kingdom of Culture: Black Swan Records and the Political Economy of African American Music." *Journal of American History* 90/4 (March 2004): 1295–1324.

Temperley, David. "Communicative Pressure and the Evolution of Musical Styles." *Music Perception* 21/3 (Spring 2004): 313–337.

Toft, Robert. "Rendering the Sense More Conspicuous: Grammatical and Rhetorical Principles of Vocal Phrasing in Art and Popular/Jazz Music." *Music & Letters* 85/3 (2004): 368–387.

Torres, George. "Sources for Latin Big Band Performance: An Examination of the Latin American Stocks in the Library of Congress." *College Music Symposium* 43 (2003): 25–41.

Tournès, Ludovic. "Introduction—Jazz: A French (and International) Historiographic Work in Progress." *Nottingham French Studies* 43/1 (Spring 2004): 1–4.

Wagner, C. "Sounds from Utopia: The Incident Considered as a Milestone in Jazz History." *Neue Zeitschrift fur Musik* 165/5 (September–October 2004): 52–54.

Warren, Stanley. "Belford C. 'Sinky' Hendricks." *Indiana Magazine of History* 100/2 (2004): 186–196.

Waters, Keith. "Motivic and Formal Improvisation in the Miles Davis Quintet 1965–68." *Tijdschrift voor Muziektheorie* 8/1 (February 2003): 25–39.

Widmer, Ted. "The Invention of a Memory: Congo Square and African Music in Nineteenth-Century New Orleans." *Revue Française d'Etudes Américaines* 98 (December 2003): 69–78.

Wilkinson, Christopher. "Hot and Sweet: Big Band Music in Black West Virginia before the Swing Era." *American Music* 21/2 (Summer 2003): 159–179.

Wills, Geoffrey I. "Forty Lives in the Bebop Business: Mental Health in a Group of Eminent Jazz Musicians." *British Journal of Psychiatry* 183 (September 2003): 255–259.

Zbikowski, Lawrence. "Modelling the Groove: Conceptual Structure and Popular Music." *Journal of the Royal Musical Association* 129/2 (December 2004): 272–297.

BOOKS RECEIVED

Compiled by Vincent Pelote

Following is a list of recently published or republished books added to the archives of the Institute of Jazz Studies.

Ansell, Gwen. *Soweto Blues: Jazz, Popular Music & Politics in South Africa.* Continuum, 2004.

Berrett, Joshua. *Louis Armstrong & Paul Whiteman: Two Kings of Jazz.* Yale University Press, 2004.

Campbell, Robert L., and Christopher Trent. *The Earthly Recordings of Sun Ra*, 2nd ed. Cadence Jazz Books [2000].

Cohodas, Nadine. *Queen: The Life and Music of Dinah Washington.* Pantheon Books, 2004.

Demlinger, Sandor, and John Steiner. *Destination Chicago Jazz.* Arcadia Publishing, 2003.

Dregni, Michael. *Django: The Life and Music of a Gypsy Legend.* Oxford University Press, 2004.

Egan, Bill. *Florence Mills: Harlem Jazz Queen.* Scarecrow Press, 2004.

Eustice, Wayne, and Janis Stockhouse. *Jazzwomen: Conversations with Twenty-One Musicians.* Indiana University Press, 2004.

Friedman, Carol. *Nicky the Jazz Cat.* [A book for children —Ed.] Dominick Books, 2003.

Grazian, David. *Blue Chicago: The Search for Authenticity in Urban Blues Clubs.* University of Chicago Press, 2003.

Haydon, Geoffrey. *Quintet of the Year.* Aurem Press, 2002.

Heffley, Mike. *Northern Sun/Southern Moon: Europe's Reinvention of Jazz.* Yale University Press, 2005.

Hentoff, Nat. *American Music Is.* Da Capo Press, 2004.

Horricks, Raymond. *Gerry Mulligan's Ark.* The Owlet Press, 2003.

Jack, Gordon. *Fifties Jazz Talk: An Oral Retrospective.* Scarecrow Press, 2004.

Jackson, Jeffrey H. *Making Jazz French: Music and Modern Life in Interwar Paris.* Duke University Press, 2003.

Kart, Larry. *Jazz in Search of Itself.* Yale University Press, 2004.

Kenney, William Howland. *Jazz on the River.* University of Chicago Press, 2005.

Kernodle, Tammy L. *Soul on Soul: The Life and Music of Mary Lou Williams.* Northeastern University Press, 2005.

Lajoie, Steve. *Gil Evans & Miles Davis: Historic Collaborations, 1957–1962.* Advance Music, 2003.

Lees, Gene. *Friends along the Way: A Journey through Jazz.* Yale University Press, 2003.

Lees, Gene. *Portrait of Johnny: The Life of John Herndon Mercer.* Pantheon Books, 2004.

Lion, Jean Pierre. *Bix: The Definitive Biography of a Jazz Legend; Leon "Bix" Beiderbecke (1903–1931).* Continuum, 2005.

Looker, Benjamin. *Point from Which Creation Begins: BAG; The Black Artists' Group of St. Louis.* University of Missouri Press, 2004.

Magee, Jeffrey. *The Uncrowned King of Swing: Fletcher Henderson and Big Band Jazz.* Oxford University Press, 2005.

Minor, William. *Jazz Journeys to Japan: The Heart Within.* University of Michigan Press, 2004.

Morgenstern, Dan. *Living with Jazz.* Edited by Sheldon Meyer. Pantheon Books, 2004.

Nimmo, H. Arlo. *The Andrews Sisters: A Biography and Career Record.* McFarland & Company, 2004.

O'Meally, Robert G., Brent Hayes Edwards, and Farah Jasmine Griffin, eds. *Uptown Conversation: The New Jazz Studies.* Columbia University Press, 2004.

Pearson, Barry Lee, and Bill McCulloch. *Robert Johnson: Lost and Found.* University of Illinois Press, 2003.

Robertson, Alan. *Joe Harriott: Fire in His Soul.* Northway Publications, 2003.

Santoro, Gene. *Highway 61 Revisited: The Tangled Roots of American Jazz, Blues, Rock & Country Music.* Oxford University Press, 2004.

Saul, Scott. *Freedom Is, Freedom Ain't: Jazz and the Making of the Sixties.* Harvard University Press, 2003.

Shearing, George, with Alyn Shipton. *Lullaby of Birdland: An Autobiography of George Shearing.* Continuum, 2004.

Stewart, Frank, and others, photographers. *Jazz at Lincoln Center: House of Swing; Frederick P. Rose Hall.* Nazareth Press, 2004.

Talbot, Bruce. *Tom Talbert: His Life and Times; Voices from a Vanished World of Jazz.* Scarecrow Press, 2004.

Travis, Dempsey J. *Jimmie Lunceford: The King of Jazznocracy.* Urban Research Press, 2004.

Vaché, Warren W. *Sittin' In with Chris Griffin: A Reminiscence of Radio and Recording's Golden Years.* Scarecrow Press, 2005.

Van der Tuuk, Alex. *Paramount's Rise and Fall: A History of the Wisconsin Chair Company and Its Recording Activities.* Mainspring Press, 2003.

Vermazen, Bruce. *That Moaning Saxophone: The Six Brown Brothers and the Dawning of a Musical Craze.* Oxford University Press, 2004.

Von Eschen, Penny M. *Satchmo Blows Up the World: Jazz Ambassadors Play the Cold War.* Harvard University Press, 2004.

Wald, Elijah. *Escaping the Delta: Robert Johnson and the Invention of the Blues.* Harper Collins, 2004.

Watson, Ben. *Derek Bailey and the Story of Free Improvisation.* Verso, 2004.

Wein, George, with Nate Chinen. *Myself among Others: A Life in Music.* Da Capo Press, 2003.

White, John. *Artie Shaw: His Life and Music.* Continuum, 2004.

Yanow, Scott. *Jazz on Film: The Complete Story of the Musicians and Music Onscreen.* Backbeat Books, 2004.

ABOUT THE EDITORS

Edward Berger, associate director of the Institute of Jazz Studies, is active as a record producer and photographer. He is coauthor of the recently revised and updated *Benny Carter: A Life in American Music* and author of two other works in the Scarecrow Press Studies in Jazz series.

Henry Martin, professor of music at Rutgers University–Newark, is a composer and music theorist. He is also founder and chair of the Special Interest Group in Jazz Theory of the Society for Music Theory. His *Charlie Parker and Thematic Improvisation* is no. 24 in the Studies in Jazz series. Wadsworth/Schirmer recently issued the second edition of his jazz history text (coauthored with Keith Waters), *Jazz: The First Hundred Years*.

Dan Morgenstern, director of the Institute of Jazz Studies, is a jazz historian and former editor of *Down Beat*. He is the author of *Living with Jazz* and *Jazz People* and has won seven Grammy Awards for album notes. He has taught jazz history at Brooklyn College, New York University, the Peabody Institute, and Rutgers University.

Evan Spring, a freelance writer, holds an M.A. in jazz history and research from Rutgers University and hosts a jazz radio program on WKCR-FM in New York City.

George Bassett studied music theory with James Randall, Milton Babbitt, and Claudio Spies, among others, at Princeton University. For over 25 years he has sung in and arranged for the jazz-, folk-, standards-, and rock-oriented vocal group Cahoots, along with his wife, Nancy Wilson (no, not that one).

ABOUT THE CONTRIBUTORS

ERIC CHARRY is associate professor of music at Wesleyan University. He has published extensively on music in Africa and is currently writing a book on the emergence of an avant-garde in jazz in the 1950s and 1960s.

HARRY COOPER, an alumnus of the jazz department of WHRB-FM, is curator of modern art at the Fogg Art Museum and senior lecturer in art history at Harvard University. His interest in art-music relationships has led to essays on jazz in the work of Stuart Davis, Arthur Dove, and Piet Mondrian. Recent exhibitions include Duo: Oliver Jackson/Marty Ehrlich (in 2002), Mondrian: The Transatlantic Paintings (in 2001), and Frank Stella 1958 (in 2006).

CHARLES O. HARTMAN has published six books of poems, most recently including *Island* (Ahsahta, 2004) and *The Long View* (Wesleyan University Press, 1999), and three books of critical prose: *Free Verse*, *Jazz Text*, and *Virtual Muse*. He has won prizes and grants from the NEA and NEH, Hawthornden, MacDowell, *Poetry* magazine, and *Yale Review* and has been a visiting professor in Moscow and Athens. He plays jazz guitar and writes open source software for literary and linguistic study. He is poet in residence and professor of English at Connecticut College and lives in Mystic, CT.

PATRICIA JULIEN is assistant professor of music at the University of Vermont, where she teaches courses in music theory, jazz improvisation, and jazz composition and arranging. Her dissertation is a study of Wayne Shorter's early compositions, and she has presented her continuing research at the national conference of the Society for Music Theory, the Sorbonne in Paris, and various U.S. universities. She is active as a jazz flutist and composer; her most recently premiered work was "Three Songs at Winter's End" for SATB a cappella voices.

VINCENT PELOTE is the head of technical services/sound archivist at the Institute of Jazz Studies. He has compiled discographies of Billie Holiday, Lionel Hampton, and the Commodore label. He contributed to *The Oxford Companion to Jazz* and has written many LP and CD program notes on jazz guitar, Mary Lou Williams, Benny Carter, Johnny Smith, and others. He has also contributed reviews to the *ARSC Journal* and *Notes: The Journal of the Music Library Association.* He is one of the hosts of the radio program *Jazz from the Archives*, on WBGO-FM in Newark.

ALONA SAGEE is a pianist, composer, and educator holding M.A. and Ph.D. degrees in musicology from Bar-Ilan University, Israel. Her Ph.D. dissertation, "The Influence of Modal Jazz on the Music of John Coltrane and Miles Davis: 1958–1967," was the first in Israel in the field of jazz. She has played alongside Israel's top jazz musicians and teaches historical, theoretical, and performance courses in jazz at the Music Department of Bar-Ilan University. Her father, Professor Zvi Keren, is a major figure in the development of Israel's jazz and contemporary music.

MATTHEW SANTA is associate professor of music theory at Texas Tech University. He has taught music theory at Queens College and Hunter College and holds degrees from Louisiana State University and the City University of New York. His articles have been published in *Theory and Practice*, *Music Theory Spectrum*, and *Music Analysis*, and his book *Flute/Theory Workout*, cowritten with Dr. Lisa Garner Santa and Dr. Thomas Hughes, is forthcoming from Mel Bay Publications. His works as a composer are published by Conners Publications, and his song cycle, *From Noon to Starry Night*, was recently recorded by Texas Tech University faculty members Lisa Garner Santa and Lora Deahl.

ANDERS SVANOE teaches saxophone and directs the saxophone ensemble at Beloit College. In addition to his duties at Beloit, he also teaches saxophone at the Eastwood School of Music and directs the jazz combo at Memorial High School in Madison, Wisconsin. In 2004 he was selected to be a member of the Transatlantic Art Ensemble to perform and record Roscoe Mitchell's *Composition/Improvisation No. 1, 2, & 3* (ECM Records 1872) in Munich, Germany. He has also been a guest artist with Mitchell's Note Factory on *Song for My Sister* (PI Recordings P103) and has made over a dozen local recordings as a leader and sideman. His own *Lines and Spaces* (Solitaire Records SR005) was recorded in 2002. He received his B.A. from Luther College in 1991 and his M.M. from the University of Wisconsin–Madison in 1994.

JASON R. TITUS holds degrees in music from the Eastman School of Music, Indiana University of Pennsylvania, and Louisiana State University. He is currently a Ph.D. student in music theory at Eastman. His research interests include the chord voicings of Thelonious Monk and the modal jazz of Miles Davis.

KEITH WATERS is associate professor of music and chair of the Department of Music Theory and Composition at the University of Colorado at Boulder. He has published articles pertaining to jazz improvisation and analysis, and his book *Jazz: The First Hundred Years*, coauthored with Henry Martin, is published by Wadsworth/Schirmer. As a jazz pianist, he has performed throughout the United States and Europe and in Russia and has appeared in concert with James Moody, Bobby Hutcherson, Eddie Harris, Chris Connor, Sheila Jordan, Buck Hill, and others. His playing has been featured in *Jazz Player* magazine. His most recent recording is a Chet Baker tribute CD with former Baker sideman Phil Urso and trumpeter Carl Saunders.

ABOUT THE INSTITUTE OF JAZZ STUDIES

The Institute of Jazz Studies of Rutgers—The State University of New Jersey is a unique research facility and archival collection, the foremost of its kind. IJS was founded in 1952 by Marshall Stearns (1908–1966), a pioneer jazz scholar, professor of medieval English literature at Hunter College, and author of two essential jazz books: *The Story of Jazz* and *Jazz Dance*. In 1966, Rutgers was chosen as the collection's permanent home. IJS is located on the Newark campus of Rutgers and is part of the John Cotton Dana Library of the Rutgers University Libraries.

IJS carries on a comprehensive program to preserve and further jazz in all its facets. The archival collection, which has more than quintupled its holdings since coming to Rutgers, consists of more than 100,000 sound recordings in all formats, from phonograph cylinders and piano rolls to CDs and DVDs; more than 6,000 books on jazz and related subjects, including discographies, bibliographies, and dissertations; and comprehensive holdings in jazz periodicals from all over the world. In addition, there are extensive vertical files on individuals and selected topics, a large collection of photographs, sheet music, scores, arrangements, realia, and memorabilia.

IJS serves a broad range of users, from students, teachers, researchers, and authors to musicians, the media, record companies and producers, libraries and archives, arts agencies, and jazz organizations. The facilities are open to the public on weekdays by appointment, at (973) 353-5595.

For further information on IJS and its programs and activities, write to:

The Institute of Jazz Studies
Dana Library, Rutgers—The State University
185 University Avenue
Newark, NJ 07102

or visit the IJS website at http://newarkwww.rutgers.edu/IJS/. The website features digital exhibits, an online tour of the facilities, and a schedule of the Jazz Research Round Table, a monthly IJS forum for presentations by jazz scholars.